Rob 1

The
New
Arabians

The New Arabians

By Peter Mansfield

Published by J. G. Ferguson Publishing Company, Chicago.
Distributed to the trade by Doubleday and Company, New York.
1981

Acknowledgments

The idea for this book was suggested by Bechtel Power Corporation, the company which has played a key role in the extraordinary economic development of modern Arabia, and it was Bechtel which made it possible for me to write it. Beyond this the company has no responsibility for its contents. The same applies to the Ministries of Information of the Arab Gulf states—especially that of the Government of Qatar—which assisted me greatly in my research. I would also like to express my gratitude to the Economist Intelligence Unit for its generous help with analysis and statistics. Finally my thanks go to the people of Arabia who have answered so many of my questions with such courtesy.

Contents

Introduction

Few people can be unaware of the importance of the Arabian Gulf today. The stretch of water between Iran and the Arabian Peninsula is one of the world's vital organs. More than half the world's proved oil reserves lie near its shores or under its waters. In normal times two-thirds of the West and Japan's fuel supplies pass through its narrow eastern exit—the Straits of Hormuz. Any move by the Soviet Union to secure control of the Gulf would be regarded as a *casus belli* by the West. The conflict between two leading Gulf states—Iraq and Iran—affects the economies of all nations.

If the region is critically important, it is also the scene of one of the most remarkable examples of social change in any human community. In the Arabian Peninsula an impoverished semi-nomadic society is being transformed in a single generation into one that can deal with the advanced industrial nations of the world on an equal footing. Moreover, the attempt is being made to carry out this monumentally difficult task without the loss of the people's identity or the essential values of their ancient society.

The past of the New Arabians is important to them because of their lively awareness of their place in the mingled strands of Arab and Islamic history. But it is their future which requires urgent attention. The dazzling statistics of their current wealth conceal the fact that this is based on a wasting asset. Everything that is being done in Arabia today needs to be seen in the light of its results over the next fifty years—that is "before the oil runs out."

Some may feel that this account is too optimistic. But the achievements of the Arabian "conservative revolution"—that is one which aims to achieve rapid change without destroying anything essential—have not been given their due. No doubt this is partly because the people of the region are not yet sufficiently relaxed to tolerate attempts at objective analysis of their society. Most of the writing about the area is too dismissive or too blandly complimentary. It remains true that the story of the New Arabians must be counted a success when measured against the goal they have set themselves. That errors have been committed—sometimes on a grand scale—is undeniable but it is well to remember the catastrophes which might have occurred and were predicted but have not taken place.

One example of the accomplishment has been the handling of the unavoidable use of foreign labor and expertise on a massive scale. The dangers and difficulties involved are obvious and have often been underlined by outsiders. What is less often mentioned is the extent to which the huge expatriate labor force has contributed to the development of modern Arabia without political or social disaster.

The New Arabians have proved to be apt pupils of experience. This has enabled them to carry out revolutionary changes in their society without the destructive upheavals which so often nullify the benefits of such experiments. One can only hope that their success will continue.

Foreword

For the economy of the world, and perhaps its politics as well, no other landlocked body of water rivals in importance the gulf lying between Iran to the north and Arab states on the other sides. Oil extracted from the Iranian and Arabian mainlands and from the seabed of the gulf itself and exported in immense quantities is vital to the well-being of Western Europe and Japan and only to a somewhat smaller degree to the well-being of the United States. A relatively small amount of the exports flows through pipelines to the Mediterranean, while the bulk, including all the oil bound for the Far East, is carried by tankers passing through the gulf's narrow exit or chokepoint, the Strait of Hormuz. Looming not far from the gulf are the Soviet military forces in Afghanistan, which could, presumably, roll southward with comparative ease to close the strait or even to seize some of the rich oilfields. The United States has responded to the possible Soviet threat with the Carter Doctrine and the building up of a Rapid Deployment Force in the Indian Ocean outside the gulf. Whether this response will be effective remains to be seen. In any event, the economic significance of the gulf and the possibility of a confrontation of the superpowers behoove the people of the West and Japan to acquaint themselves as fully as they can with the realities of the situation there and to dispel quite current misconceptions. This book is particularly welcome as a corrective to many of these misconceptions and as a valuable contribution to accurate knowledge and better understanding of the gulf region and the people who live there. For years Peter Mansfield has known the region at first hand, he is familiar with the people of high and low estate, and he writes about their aspirations and problems with genuine sympathy. His book deserves to be widely read and pondered upon.

The gulf has long been known to the Western world and also to many Arabs as the Persian Gulf, a name derived from the former name of Iran. In recent years Arabs have taken to describing the reach of their world as "from the Ocean [the Atlantic] to the [Arabian] Gulf." As the author concentrates his survey on the countries and people across the way from Iran, he is justified in using Arabian for the name of the gulf.

Another distinction in nomenclature should be pointed out. As indicated, the Arab world stretches from the Atlantic to the gulf, or indeed to the Arabian Sea, the arm of the Indian Ocean outside the Strait of Hormuz. The people of North Africa (aside from the Berbers) and the Egyptians (the Arab Republic of Egypt) are accepted as Arabs, as are also the Somalis (Somalia is now a member of the League of Arab States), even though for most Somalis Arabic is a foreign language or at best a language for Islamic ritual.

The ''Arabs'' of the outer lands may be considered, to some extent, distinct from the ''Arabians,'' the inhabitants of the peninsula, the original home of the Arabs.

Mansfield's ''New Arabians'' are the indigenous folk living today in five peninsular states with coasts on the gulf: Kuwait, Saudi Arabia, Bahrain, Qatar, and the United Arab Emirates. Iraq at the head of the gulf, not being peninsular, is excluded, as is Oman on the eastern periphery of the peninsula. Mingled with these indigenous folk are many of those Mansfield calls the ''Northern Arabs'' (Syrians, Lebanese, Palestinians, Egyptians, and even Sudanese). These immigrants contribute much to industry, education, and even to government, but they are not the real molders of opinion or arbiters of change in the structure of society. The chapter on guest workers provides a good picture of the role they play, along with that of a variety of other expatriates, and the problems that the presence of all of them may pose.

Essential to an understanding of modern Arabia is some grasp of the geography and early history of the peninsula, which are dealt with in the opening chapters. The religion of Islam, basic then and now to what goes on in Arabia, is portrayed sympathetically, and distortions regarding its beliefs and practices that are often prevalent in non-Muslim circles are set aright. Emphasis is placed on the fact that Islam is a total way of life, making, unlike Christianity, no distinction between the religious and the secular. Islam has its theological scholars, doctors of the Sacred Law (the *ulama*), but they are not clergy in the Western sense of the word. They wield considerable and sometimes great influence, but as the author shows, they have more than once been put in their place by the ruler of the day, such as Ibn Saud or his son Faisal.

Of the five peninsular states reviewed, Saudi Arabia stands

in the front rank by virtue of its size and wealth. It is the only one of the five whose territory crosses the peninsula from the Arabian Gulf to the Red Sea. With the overthrow of the Shah in Iran and the subsequent turmoil there Saudi Arabia has acquired greatly enlarged responsibility as a power in the gulf.

Contrary to a commonly held belief, Saudi Arabia is not a new state. Its existence as a sovereign political entity dates back to 1744, thirty-two years before the British colonies in America declared their independence. In that year the head of the House of Saud, the present ruling family, formed an alliance with Muhammad ibn Abd al-Wahhab, founder of an Islamic reform movement that came to be called by the inaccurate name of Wahhabism. Together the House of Saud and the reformer and his descendants constructed a state that was the true forerunner of the Kingdom of Saudi Arabia. The alliance has held good until this day. The doctrines preached by the reformer—essentially a return to the original principles of Islam as revealed in the Koran and supplemented by the conduct of the Prophet Muhammad and his pious Companions—have remained the official version of the state staunchly adhered to by the vast majority of its citizens.

During the nineteenth century the new state had its ups and downs, and toward the end of the century it was at its deepest down. In 1902 Abd al-Aziz, a strong and gifted scion of the House of Saud popularly known as Ibn Saud, began restoring the fortunes of the family by installing himself in the ancestral capital Riyadh. The passages here dealing with the career of Ibn Saud give a clear picture of the character of the man and his accomplishments. After occupying the Hejaz, the Holy Land of Islam, Ibn Saud in 1926 became the first of his family to receive the title of King (without the usual accouterments of a crown and throne), and six years later the Kingdom assumed the name of Saudi Arabia. Ibn Saud expanded the territory of the Kingdom to roughly its present limits, while at home he favored changes not in conflict with the principles of Islam, particularly the adoption of modern technological devices such as automobiles, airplanes, the telegraph, and the telephone. His struggle to overcome the opposition of his more fanatical followers is here depicted.

The contrast between the reigns of Ibn Saud's two immediate successors could hardly have been sharper. The first, Saud, Ibn Saud's oldest surviving son, got the Kingdom into serious trouble with his misguided behavior. Faisal, the next son, who took Saud's place, got the Kingdom out of trouble with his talent for leadership and wise policies. The only son of Ibn Saud descended on the distaff side from the reformer of the eighteenth century, Faisal reinforced the alliance of 1744. The smooth transfer of power after the assassination of Faisal demonstrated the unity of the members of the House of Saud and the scope of their control of the government. Several descendants of the reformer have joined them in heading ministries. Under King Khalid, Faisal's commendable policies are being continued.

Turning from Saudi Arabia, the author takes up four smaller peninsular states: Kuwait, Bahrain, Qatar, and the United Arab Emirates. The first three are strongly influenced by their big neighbor; the UAE perhaps not so much so. Each, however, has its own individuality. Tending to be less conservative, they have in some respects moved ahead of Saudi Arabia; they can, as the author says, be "more daring and experimental."

Mansfield ably treats the much misunderstood subject of oil prices. The reiterated accusation that the Arabs are primarily responsible for soaring prices is false. A number of the members of the Organization of Petroleum Exporting Countries are not Arab, and non-Arab Iran under the Shah and others plumped for higher prices while Saudi Arabia advocated moderation. Inflation and financial instability in the West may have done more harm to the world economy than higher oil prices.

Looking toward the future, the author discerns signs for optimism. The New Arabians have made mistakes, but they have shown that they can learn from them. In the Arabian Gulf they are moving toward ever closer cooperation with each other. They have the will and spirit that should carry them through.

GEORGE RENTZ

Arlington, Virginia
June 1981

xiv

1
A Riverless Giant

On the globe the Arabian Peninsula looks similar in size and shape to the Indian subcontinent which lies to the east across the Arabian Sea. But whereas the subcontinent is teeming with 850 million people, there are no more than 20 million in the whole of Arabia.

The reason is easy to see. Although surrounded on three sides by sea, the Peninsula is the most arid part of the earth. The Kingdom of Saudi Arabia, which forms some 75 percent of the Peninsula, is the largest country in the world with no rivers and few streams.

The whole region is a vast detached fragment of a larger continental mass that included Africa. As it split off, with the opening of the Red Sea and the Gulf of Aden, the Arabian Peninsula tilted so that the western edge forms the highlands which stretch along the southwestern half of Arabia from the Hejaz to Aden. This uplift in the west was accompanied by widespread fracturing and faulting which gave rise to the steep scarp overlooking the Red Sea and the extensive and geologically recent lava fields, known as *harrahs*, in the western region. The southwestern mountain chain rises to peaks of over 8,000 feet in what is now the Kingdom of Saudi Arabia and over 12,000 feet in the Yemen Arab Republic.

The great Arabian platform tilts gradually eastwards from the Red Sea to the Arabian Gulf. Here a succession of younger sedimentary rocks have been eroded to give a series of scarps or ridges of the harder rocks, interspersed with valleys where the

1

strata were less resistant. But in the Pleistocene Ice Age—that is, between one and two million years ago, the relatively recent past in geological terms—central and northern Arabia were covered by a vast lake system which stretched into southern Mesopotamia or Iraq. As these dried they left great chasms of wadis or riverbeds which generally run from the southeast to the northwest, cutting through the series of scarps. Today these wadis are flooded on rare occasions after winter thunderstorms. Only a chain of ancient wells remains to mark the course of the rivers, but fossils of mollusks and starfish can easily be found among the broken rocks that cover the valley walls.

This central area of the Arabian platform—still some two thousand feet above sea level—is the Najd, homeland of the Al Saud or clan of Saud which now rules most of the Peninsula. Much is covered with sand. To the north lies the Great Nafud in which eroded sandstone alternates with sand desert basins. Here there are some oases with settled agriculture and even occasional rainfall, providing a living for pastoral nomads. Tamarisk and other bushes that grow with very little water provide firewood and graz- ing crops for the beduin's flocks of goats and sheep and camels. The leaves of the varieties of saltbush give the animals the salt they need. The *rak* tree supplies the local version of the tooth- brush. Occasionally the beduin can plant a fleeting crop of grain in a damp wadi bed after a rainstorm. Sometimes the name of an oasis may apply to a whole group of settlements, covering several scores of square miles. Each town or village will have its own belt of date palms. This is the case of the Hasa oasis in the east of the Peninsula which today includes the two substantial towns of Hufuf and Mubarraz.

Rain does not reach south of the Najd, and here lies the Rub al Khali or Empty Quarter—some 400,000 square miles of fearful shifting desert sands where even the nomads and their marvelously adapted camels have a hard time surviving. The Sahara Desert is benign and less of a barrier to human movement in comparison. It is now known that the Empty Quarter went through a less arid phase some 2,500–3,000 years ago. The bones of animals that have been discovered show that there was relatively abundant wildlife—antelope, leopards, lions, and ostrich—especially on the fringes of the Empty Quarter. Now there are only a few small Arabian hares and jerboas or kangaroo rats and suchlike. But even in the heart of the Empty Quarter there are a few wells known to the occasional beduins who dare to cross it.

It is only on the southern and southwestern fringes of Arabia reached by the Indian monsoon, which blows steadily from the northeast from November to March and is strongest in January, that there is enough precipitation for rainfed agriculture assisted by irrigation. In the Asir region of southwestern Saudi Arabia and on the steaming Tihamah coastal plain on the Red Sea, in Yemen (Sana), in Dhofar, and the Jabal Akhdar or Green Mountain of Oman, fruit, vegetables, cotton, coffee, and other crops can be grown on a large scale. It was these areas, with their settled and prosperous farming populations, that caused the Romans to speak of Arabia Felix or Fortunate Arabia. Here there are perennial streams, although none reaches the sea, and Arabia's only forests of juniper, wild olive, and some larger trees. It was here at the sole of boot-shaped Arabia that, according to Genesis, Jehovah set the limit of the known world. This is the only part of the Peninsula that can have been the source of inspiration of the poet Walter de la Mare:

> Far are the shades of Arabia
> Where the Princes ride at noon
> 'Mid the verdurous vales and thickets
> Under the ghost of the moon.

Today Arabia's good fortune would be associated with a different part of the Peninsula. It is in the eastern region where, in sandstones and limestones laid down in shallow water, organic material has been transformed into petroleum and natural gas hydrocarbons. They are found at relatively great depth in the Arabian Gulf itself and also in shallower strata lying inland as far as the Empty Quarter.

The eastern coast of Arabia on the Gulf is in sharp contrast to the western coast on the Red Sea. It has lagoons, mangrove swamps, sandbars, coral reefs, and islands with stretches of saline mudflats or *sabkhahs*.

Because it is so arid and relatively cloudless, Arabia suffers great extremes of temperature. The summers are overwhelmingly hot with sauna-like temperatures of up to 125°F when the dark rocks hold the heat. But in winter, in the mountains of the south and southwest there is severe frost and occasional snowstorms. Even at the relatively low altitudes of the Najd, the winter nights are sharp and cool. The wide alternations of temperature give rise to sudden and violent winds, especially in the spring. On the Red Sea and Arabian Gulf coasts, on the other hand, humidity is high and the summer heat is oppressive. But the Gulf coast in particular has a fine winter climate. International tourists of the late twentieth century are just beginning to discover that the weather in this region is ideal from November to April.

The racial origins of the inhabitants of Arabia are obscure. The Arabs themselves have inherited a tradition that they come from two stocks. The first originated in the rainfed highlands of the southwest and are descended from the patriarch Qahtan. The second come from the north and center of the Peninsula and are descended from the patriarch Adnan. Almost every Arab tribe claims descent from Qahtan or Adnan.

Of the two, it is the southerners or Yemenis who are called the "true Arabs" and the sons of Adnan who are *Mustarib* or "Arabized Arabs." Today this Qahtan-Adnan division does not correspond to any recognizable racial difference. Yet it is possible to distinguish two racial types among the inhabitants of Arabia: the tall bearded men with clean-cut, hawk-like features who come mainly from the north and the smaller, darker people of southern Arabia with softer features. By origin the latter are probably related to the Abyssinians. Yet it is they who can claim to correspond to the "true Arabs," although it is the northerners who provide the popular image of what an Arab should be. Moreover it was the language of the northerners and not that of the southerners that developed into classical Arabic, the common tongue of the 120 million Arabized people who today are known as Arabs. Until very recent times it could be said that the population of central Arabia was among the most racially homogenous in the world. It was on the fringes of the Peninsula where the people had strong overseas trading connections that there was an admixture of other racial strains—Baluchi in Oman, Indian and Persian in the Arabian Gulf, and Malay in the Hadhramaut. The other important exceptions are the descendants of black African slaves who are found in all parts of the Peninsula. It is only in the past two decades that a great mingling of races has begun to take place in all the main population centers of Arabia affected by the oil rush. Even Riyadh, which for more than a century was virtually a forbidden city to outsiders, is on its way to becoming as cosmopolitan as Alexandria or Beirut.

2

Southern Dawn

*T*he early civilizations of southern Arabia disappeared and are only now being rediscovered with the help of a rich variety of inscriptions in their lost languages. They show the existence of complex and wealthy settled communities with a history spanning several centuries before and after Christ. (The chronology has still not been fixed with a high degree of certainty.) These communities were monarchies with sophisticated governmental and legal institutions. Their societies seem to have been monogamous, and they prospered on the export of spices such as frankincense, laudanum, myrrh, and precious woods. They worshipped a pantheon of local gods supervised by a priesthood.

One of the first of these kingdoms was that of Saba which probably dates to a thousand years before Christ and may be identical with the biblical Sheba whose queen paid the famous visit to King Solomon. One of the Sabaean kings built the great Marib Dam in about 750 B.C. which lasted some 1200 years until the sixth century A.D., when its collapse undermined the irrigation system on which the agriculture of the region was based. The ruins of the dam survive in the Yemen Arab Republic. The Sabaeans colonized parts of eastern Africa and are thought to have founded the Kingdom of Abyssinia whose name is derived from a southwest Arabian people, the Habashat.

Arabia forms the natural transit area between the Mediterranean and the Far East, and it was this that determined the Penin-

7

sula's history in ancient times. There were three main routes along the length of Arabia. The first and the most important ran from the northern Red Sea ports along the inside of the coastal range via Mecca and Medina to Yemen. The second, the Wadi Sirhan, linked central Arabia with Damascus via the Jawf oases. The third was the Wadi Dawasir running from the extreme northeast of Yemen to central Arabia and then via the Wadi Rumah to southern Mesopotamia. This was the main link between southern Arabia and the ancient civilizations of Assyria and Babylon.

The two long, narrow inlets on either side of the Arabian Peninsula also provided access to India and the Far East. The Red Sea takes the name from the Greek *erythra* which means "red." There are various explanations for this name, which seems as inappropriate to present-day travelers as that of the "Blue" Danube. One is that the term was applied to Phoenicians who voyaged around the Arabian Gulf and who were considered red or sunburned. Another is that it commemorates Erythras, a Persian king, or Himyar the Red, a ruler of ancient Arabia. Finally it may derive from a floating bluegreen seaweed that occasionally has a red accessory pigment.

Whatever the origins of its name, mariners have always disliked the Red Sea since ancient times. Apart from its atrocious heat throughout most of the year, its shoals, reefs, irregular currents, and sudden storms make navigation highly dangerous. Nevertheless, from at least 3500 B.C. the ancient Egyptians sailed the Red Sea and even passed the Bab al Mandab Straits into the Indian Ocean. In about 1500 B.C. Egyptian Queen Hatshepsut—known as "the first great woman in history"—sent an expedition to the land of Punt, which may have been Somalia on the Horn of Africa.

On the other side of Arabia, the shallow Arabian Gulf, although subject to sudden storms, was easier to navigate. The Sumerians who flourished between 3000 and 2000 B.C. sailed from their city of Eridu whose site is now in the desert of southern Iraq but at that time stood on the sea. They maintained a flow of trade with the rival civilization of the Indus Valley. Dilmun, or the island of Bahrain, flourished as a great commercial empire halfway between them. Their Babylonian successors were trading with India before 700 B.C., and the Phoenicians in their amazing voyages throughout the ancient world reached Ophir, still unidentified but somewhere on the coast of southern Arabia, and came to dominate the commerce of the Gulf in the following century. Indian and Persian vessels also plied these busy waters while the people of Arabia themselves made coastal voyages to East Africa, southern Asia, and the Indian coasts.

The Greeks did not arrive on the scene until the sixth century B.C. when a Carian named Scylax explored the estuary of the Indus and, coasting westward before the monsoon, reached Arsinoe near the modern Suez. His account of his voyage was probably the source for the Greek historian Herodotus's colorful but inaccurate account of the South Arabian spice industry. He wrote that the trees bearing frankincense were guarded by small multicolored, winged serpents. Cinnamon was found in the nests of birds in high, inaccessible cliffs. The cinnamon producers had to tempt them with chunks of meat which caused their nests to collapse under the weight. According to Strabo, a later Greek geographer, the production of spices was so successful that the South Arabians used sticks of cinnamon and cassia for firewood.

Two centuries after Scylax, Alexander the Great, having defeated the Persian Empire, set out to conquer India. But having crossed the Indus, he was forced to turn back by his own weary troops. However, he sent his admiral Nearchus to travel westward from the Indus estuary and explore the Gulf up to the Euphrates. His voyage in 326–325 B.C. has been described as "the first great event of historical importance to mankind in the history of navigation." It opened up a direct communication between Europe and the most distant countries of Asia. Along the Gulf coast he observed shoals, reefs, headlands, frankincense trees, the pearling industry, and "sea hedgehogs" which may have been turtles.

Alexander the Great died two years later, but those who followed him gradually drew the veils away from Arabia.

The Ptolemies of Egypt sent ships to explore southern Arabia and established a regular trade with Yemen. Their successors in the Near East maintained their interest. As the power of Rome spread in the first century B.C., its dominion extended to Egypt and the Red Sea. Roman money flowed into Arabia and India to finance the trade in spices, pearls, ivory, gums, perfumes, and precious stones.

What was happening in the interior of Arabia through these centuries? Kingdoms rose and fell in the relatively fertile lands of South Arabia, as we have seen, but the land could support only a limited population, and successive waves of population were forced out into the wilderness. In order to live they adopted the nomadic way of life, raising flocks of sheep and goats and herds of camels. The general trend of the movement was northeastward across the Peninsula to Mesopotamia—hence the ancient Arab saying that "Yemen is the cradle of the Arab, and Iraq is his grave."

Some of the Arabs settled down around the oases where a sedentary civilization was possible. One of these was Yathrib in western Arabia, which became Medina after the time of the Prophet Muhammad; another was Petra, the valley hidden among the bare mountains of what is now southern Jordan and which in the second century B.C. became the center of the powerful Hellenized Arab kingdom of the Nabataeans.

The Sabaeans of South Arabia controlled the immensely valuable trade in spices, gold, and precious stones to the Roman Empire. In the first century B.C. the Emperor Augustus decided to make their land into a dependency of Egypt and, through his control of the Red Sea shore of Arabia, to establish a direct trade link by sea to India, cutting out the expensive land caravan route and the role of the Sabaeans as middlemen. He had the enthusiastic support of the Nabataeans who wanted the control of the spice trade for themselves. In 24 B.C. Aelius Gallus, commanding some 12,000 men (one third of the garrison of Egypt and 1,000 Nabataeans), built a fleet of transport vessels near Suez, crossed to the North Arabian coast, and marched 900 miles towards the Sabaean capital of Mariaba (Marib). He reached Yemen after six months but was forced to turn back without capturing Mariaba because of lack of water and fierce opposition from the local tribes. Nevertheless, Gallus's feat was extraordinary. He spanned most of the length of Arabia and returned with a still disciplined and organized force. But it was the only Roman attempt to colonize Arabia.

The caravan trade continued but the South Arabians seem to have recognized a vague Roman overlordship. The direct sea trade between Egypt and India and the Horn of Africa expanded. Through men like Gallus and these traders, contemporary geographers began to give more accurate accounts of Arabia than those of Herodotus four centuries earlier. The Greek Strabo described the dimensions of the Peninsula and its sparse supplies of water and vegetation. He wrote of the people of Gerrha, the important trading center on the Arabian Gulf which may be identified with the Saudi port of Uqayr, with their houses made of salt which they sprinkled with water to prevent them from flaking in the fierce sun. He described the Red Sea coast where trees resembling the laurel and olive grew at the water's edge and were sometimes covered at the high tide. "This is the more singular as the coast inland has no trees," he added.

Strabo also described the fertile and prosperous land of the Sabaeans where the air was heavy with the oriental perfumes the people exported to Syria and Mesopotamia. "When the carriers become drowsy with the odor of aromatics, the drowsiness is removed by the fumes of asphalt and goat's beard," he said. The king and his entourage "pass their lives in effeminate voluptuousness" while, because of the abundance of the soil, "the people are lazy and indolent in their mode of life. The lower classes live on roots and sleep in the trees." Arabia Felix indeed.

It is hardly surprising that this self-indulgent civilization went into a long decline. In the 6th century A.D. the great Marib Dam fell into disrepair, and the irrigation system on which it was based collapsed. One of the last great Arab rulers of South Arabia was the handsome Dhu Nawas, the man with the hanging locks, who, according to Arab tradition, came to power by eluding the homosexual advances of his predecessor and so releasing the youths of Yemen from erotic servitude to their monarch. In about A.D. 510. Dhu Nawas was converted to Judaism and at once set about persecuting the settlers in South Arabia from Christian Ethiopia in reprisal for Byzantine persecution of the Jews. This provoked a long war in which an Ethiopian invasion was ultimately successful with local Christian support, and the Sabaean kingdom was brought to an end. However, Christian rule in South Arabia was soon terminated by a Persian invasion in A.D. 575 which reduced South Arabia to a Persian dependency with little difficulty.

3

The End of Ignorance

*B*y the beginning of the sixth century of the Christian era the whole of Arabia was a conglomeration of petty autonomous states. Although quite a high proportion of the population adopted a sedentary way of life around the oases of the center and north as well as in the fertile south and southwest, it was the nomads who held the military advantage. They remained convinced of the superiority of their own style of living, and the settled peoples accepted this by adopting nomadic values. Some of them abandoned their settlements for the freedom of the desert.

The vast horizons of the desert provided a sense of liberty, but the harshness of the environment created its own iron laws which molded the structure of tribal life. Since survival depended on the solidarity and self-protection of the tribe, the system whereby the whole family, clan, or tribe was held responsible for the act of any one of them helped to create such security as there was. Individual crimes were restrained by the fear of lasting vengeance, and there was no written code of laws. No such restraints however applied to communal acts of violence. Intertribal disputes might be settled by an arbiter, some wise authority on tribal customs, but meanwhile they were the excuse for a *ghazu*, or raid, aimed chiefly at seizing and driving off their opponent's camels, which for many centuries would be regarded as the natural pastime of the Arabs.

13

Desert life was exceedingly harsh. The nomads lived off their camels, consuming their milk and very occasionally eating their meat. The other staple food was the date, "the mother and the aunt of the Arabs," as it was known. After one of the rare rainstorms, causing flash floods in the wadis, there would be brief periods of relative ease after which life would once again be centered on the waterholes where a few shrubs survived.

The nomads of Arabia in the first centuries after Christ worshiped trees, rocks, or springs. Over the years this developed into a polytheism—a belief in a variety of spirits who could be of either sex and were often based on a particular rock or tree shrine. The most famous of these was the shrine of the Kaabah at Mecca, where the great Black Stone (probably a meteorite) was a place of pilgrimage for centuries before it became central to the religion of Islam. According to popular legend, the Black Stone was given to Adam on his fall from Paradise. Friendly and helpful spirits were the *jinn* (or genies), while the hostile were *afrits* or *ghuls*. But in the settled farming and trading communities of the oases the situation was different. Here, farmers and merchants came in contact with the Christian empires of Byzantium and Abyssinia and the Zoroastrian Persian Empire. As they did, they began to acquire monotheistic ideas. By the fourth century A.D. the people of southern Arabia had actually abandoned polytheism to adopt their own form of monotheism in which they worshiped a supreme god known as *al-Rahman* "the Merciful." In addition, there were many communities of Jews and Christians throughout the Peninsula, although the overwhelming majority of the beduin remained pagan.

The nomads of Arabia were not highly civilized by the standards of the time. But they had one supreme art which flourished in the desert: poetry. As in the Homeric age of ancient Greece, poetry was always intended to be recited aloud. An outstanding poet brought honor to his tribe; he immortalized its deeds with his words, and it was said that the beduin congratulated one another on three things—the birth of a boy, the emergence of a poet in their midst, or the foaling of a mare.

The Arab-American historian Philip Hitti has said: "Arabic literature, like most literatures, sprang into existence with an outburst of poetry, but, unlike many others, its poetry seems to have issued forth full grown." This is perhaps because of the special quality of the Arabic language—one of the glories of human civilization. The great Victorian traveler and orientalist Richard Burton noted that the very structure of the language, in which a combination of three letters, the triliteral root, on which a great edifice of subtly varying nouns and verbs is built, lends itself to poetry. "The language . . . leaves a mysterious vagueness between the relation of word to word, which materially assists the sentiment, not sense, of the poem. When verbs and nouns have—each one—many different significations, only the radical and general idea suggests itself. Rich and varied synonyms, illustrating the finest shades of meaning, are artfully used: now scattered to strike us by distinctness; now to form, as it were, a star, about which dimly seen satellites revolve."

When Philip Hitti wrote of full-grown poetry he was thinking primarily of the Seven Golden Odes known as the Muallaqat or "Hanging Ones" because, according to legend, they were suspended in the pagan shrine of the Kaabah. These are the most famous of the small body which has survived of the great mass of poetry of the period before the Prophet Muhammad. One of the seven authors was Antarah ibn Shaddad al Absi, known as Antar. Tales of the heroic Black Knight (he was the son of the Abyssinian slave-girl Zabibah) and his love for his high-born cousin Ablah are little known in the West but form as much a part of the cultural heritage of any Arab child as those of Hercules or Samson do for a westerner. These marvelous stories of chivalry, treachery, compassion, and cruelty give a brilliant picture of sixth-century Arabia. The characters, both men and women, are vivid and individual. The tales as they have been handed down are overlaid with Muslim characteristics, and they reveal a society with high ethical standards. The language is magnificent. Although all translation is imperfect, and none more so than that from Arabic, a recent version gives some of the flavor of the original as in this description of Antar's father first catching sight of Zabibah: "She was young and walked with all the spring and grace of Africa. Her skin was smooth as ebony, her wrists and ankles delicately formed as the bones of a gazelle. Her teeth, when she smiled, sparkled like hailstones in the sunshine after a desert storm, and her eyes burned brown like polished cornelian."

The wealth of central Arabia lay almost solely in its language. Some of the products of the Persian and Byzantine Empires, as well as their religions, had reached it through the caravan routes via the oases. Textiles, some items of food, wine, and probably the art of writing, reached the Arabs in this way. Society in the settled communities was complex and sophisticated only by comparison with the surrounding desert. The two most important communities were Yathrib (renamed Medina in Islamic times) and Mecca in western Arabia. Yathrib was agricultural, living off the cultivation of cereals and dates. Mecca was purely a trading community which by the end of the fifth century of the Christian era had overtaken all its rivals to become the commercial center of the Peninsula. Mecca benefited from the fact that the two alternative routes from Europe to the East—Mesopotamia via the Arabian Gulf and Egypt via the Red Sea—were disturbed and dangerous. The one through eastern Arabia was more difficult but more peaceful. Political organization amounted to a rudimentary form of democracy. The head of the tribe was either a *shaykh* (elder) or *sayyid* (lord) elected by the other elders. But he was hardly more than a first among equals, following rather than leading tribal opinion which was expressed through the *majlis*, or council of elders. Society was violent and only saved from anarchy by the tribal and personal laws of vengeance. There was no state or public law. Although it is known that there had been some ruling queens (such as the Queen of Sheba) in earlier times, and even that some tribes followed a system in which paternity was ignored and all inheritance passed through the female line, Arabia in the sixth century A.D. was indubitably a male-dominated society with patrilineal descent. The practice of killing infant girls, a burden on a poor society in need of warriors, was widespread.

Some time before the rise of Islam, Mecca came under the control of the Quraysh, a tribe from northern Arabia. It was into an impoverished branch of this tribe that the Prophet Muhammad was born about A.D. 570—the founder of a religion that changed mankind, created a great new civilization, and today has some 800 million believers who are increasing in number each year.

The essence of the Muslim faith is the belief in the oneness of God or Allah who is all-powerful and all-knowing. In the words of the Muslim sacred book, the Koran:

> God
> there is no God but He, the
> Living, the Everlasting.
> Slumber seizes him not, neither sleep;
> to Him belongs
> all that is in the heavens and the earth . . .
> He is the All-high, the All-glorious.

God is unique, "not begetting, not begotten," and no created being should be associated with Him. Worship is for Him alone. Muhammad is the last in the series of the Prophets of God who included Abraham, Moses, and Jesus. To Muslims he has made the final revelation of God's word; he is the Seal of the Prophets. So it is that although Muslims honor the two other great monotheistic faiths of Christianity and Judaism as divinely inspired religions, they consider that they have been superseded and succeeded by Islam. It was this and the fact that Muslims regarded certain Christian beliefs and practices, such as the doctrines of the Trinity or worship of the Virgin Mary and the saints, as detracting from the uniqueness of God or even as idolatrous, that caused the deep rift between Christianity and Islam. As Islam became a powerful conquering faith, its founder and the beliefs of his followers were constantly traduced by Christian apologists.

Muhammad's calling began when he was over forty. It was then, according to Muslim belief, that when he was meditating in a cave outside Mecca he heard the angel Gabriel saying to him:

> Recite: In the name of thy Lord who created,
> created man of a blood-clot.

Recite: And thy Lord is the Most Generous
Who taught by the Pen,
taught Man that he knew not
No indeed; surely Man waxes insolent,
for he thinks himself self-sufficient,
Surely unto thy Lord is the Returning.

From then on there followed a series of revelations by Muhammad to the small band of believers who gathered around him. These were ultimately written down to form the Koran (or Recitation). For Muslims the Koran is literally the Word of God.

Muhammad's first message to the people of Mecca was of the simplest: that they should abandon all forms of idolatry and surrender themselves wholly to the one almighty but compassionate God. It was this idea of total submission (in Arabic *Islam*) which later gave his followers the name of Muslims.

Even this modest proposal aroused fierce opposition, especially among the more prosperous Meccans who saw Muhammad's movement as a threat to the economically profitable cult of the Kaabah. After a decade of struggle, Muhammad moved with a few of his followers to Yathrib, three hundred miles to the northeast. His reputation as the leader of a movement that aimed to transcend tribal disputes was enough for the people of Yathrib to invite him to be their arbiter. The year of the migration or Hegira (*hijrah* in Arabic) was A.D. 622, and it became the starting point of the Muslim calendar. Yathrib became Medinat al Nabi, City of the Prophet, or Medina for short.

From now on Islam began to develop into a politically organized community as well as a religion with Muhammad as the acknowledged head of this community or *ummah*. He began to exhibit his qualities of political genius as he adopted all the powerful Arab traditions of personal honor, brotherhood, and tribal solidarity to strengthen the community of the Faithful. He also showed his ability to learn from his mistakes and to strengthen his authority through magnanimity in victory and willingness to compromise. His task was not easy because the first reaction of the fiercely individualistic Arab tribesmen was to be offended deeply by his calls for selflessness and surrender.

In 630 Muhammad was able to take over Mecca with little resistance. He ordered the idols to be overthrown and turned the Kaabah into a Muslim sanctuary, but in all other respects he treated the inhabitants with tolerance and liberality. In return nearly all the Meccans embraced Islam. By now the unification of the Arabian Peninsula was progressing steadily. Muhammad was the head of a state but it was a state of a unique kind, governed by the precepts of the Holy Book. These transcended, but did not destroy, tribal customs and traditions.

The essence of the message of the Holy Koran is that God has created man in order to worship Him and to act towards other men in certain ways. It contains the revelation of the will of God— what He has commanded and forbidden—and a warning that at the end of the world men will be judged by their acts. But God's mercy is infinite. His compassion is a constant theme throughout the Holy Book.

The submission of a Muslim to God does not mean passive resignation but active obedience. There are certain prescribed acts of obedience which are known as the Five Pillars of Islam. First, a Muslim should declare that "There is no god but God, and Muhammad is the Messenger of God." He should perform the five daily ritual prayers—wherever he finds himself, facing in the direction of Mecca—and prayers in the mosque on Friday (the Muslim day of public worship). He should give *zakat*, a tax of a certain proportion of his wealth to be given to those in need and to be used in various other ways. He should fast, from before sunrise to sunset for a month every year (the month of Ramadan), and he should make the Pilgrimage to Mecca, the *Hajj*, in accordance with a prescribed form at least once in his lifetime if his means allow it.

There is no question that Allah's commands as recorded in the Koran raised the status of women in Arabia at that time. It was not only that the killing of infant girls was strictly forbidden, but it was clearly stated that in marriage and divorce women should enjoy the same rights against their husbands as their husbands have against them. Women were given the right to own and inherit property. It is true that the woman's share of the property was less than that of the man and that the Koran states that in the family "men are a degree above them," but this merely acknowledges the fact that man is the head of the household—something that had been rarely disputed in most societies until the days of women's liberation. Contrary to a widespread belief in the West, there is nothing in the Koran to suggest that women do not have the same religious rights and duties as men or that women should be kept ignorant and uneducated. It was the scholars of Islam in later centuries who succeeded in interpreting or misinterpreting the Koran in such a way as to place women in subjection.

Another common Western view is that Islam is sexually licentious. In fact the Koran was somewhat puritanical by the standards of the time in its regulation of sexual relations. Marriage is urged on believers as necessary for procreation in a small society that has depended for survival on its manpower. This thinking is apparent in the permission for a man to have four wives and, according to certain interpretations which are not accepted by some Muslims, a number of concubines from among the females who were taken prisoners in war and made slaves. The Koran places a man under the obligation to treat all his wives in a precisely similar manner and with the same kindness and attentiveness, and "if you feel you cannot be quite fair [to all your wives, take] only one." Some twentieth-century Muslims have taken this to mean a clear preference for monogamy as the ideal since it is obviously impossible to treat all one's wives in exactly the same way.

If some modern Muslims, although by no means a majority of either men or women, feel defensive about the status of women in their society, they are fairly unanimous in regarding Western attitudes as hypocritical, swinging from one in which the sexuality of women was denied and the purity of the Victorian mother was protected by the existence of prostitutes to the present situation in which divorce and adultery are commonplace and many young couples feel that marriage has outlived its usefulness.

Apart from the detailed regulations of family life, the Koran contains a large body of ethical teaching and legal injunctions. All intoxicants, games of chance, and usury are forbidden. Dietary rules are similar to but less strict than those observed by the Jews, prohibiting the eating of pig meat or blood and animals that have died a natural death, had their necks wrung, or been sacrificed to others than God. Penalties are prescribed for crimes such as stealing, murder, and some minor offenses. Fraud, perjury, and slander are repeatedly and severely condemned, and some rules of social behavior are laid down. Slavery is permitted but some strict limitations are placed on the rights of owners who are commanded to treat their slaves well.

The Koran is not a code of law, and it does not contain all the rules which are necessary in all circumstances. Muslims therefore looked beyond it to the example of the Prophet and his Companions. Their words and deeds, known as their *Sunnah* or habitual modes of thought and action, were collected in the *Hadith* or traditions of the Prophet which were handed down through a line of reliable witnesses. Together the Koran and the *Sunnah* form the sources of the Islamic *Shariah*. This is normally translated as Islamic law but in fact it is much more than this. It is neither canonical law (Islam has no priesthood) nor secular law, for Islam makes no distinction between religious and state law. It is rather a whole system of social morality, prescribing the ways in which man should live if he is to act in God's will. If he contravenes the *Shariah*, his offense is against God and not the state.

This lack of a distinction between the secular and the religious—between what should be rendered unto God and what unto Caesar—is a characteristic of Islam. Another which is linked to the first is the absence of any hierarchy of clergy—no high priests or bishops and certainly no infallible Pope—who might claim to intervene between God and man. The nearest equivalent are the *ulama*, the "learned" or "doctors," corresponding to the "scribes" in Judaism, who in later Islamic societies acquired some of the same prestige and authority as the Christian clergy. But there was no question of regarding them as God's representatives, for such an idea would be regarded as blasphemy by a Muslim.

It is the *Shariah* which should guide the life of the individual Muslim. It is also the *Shariah* which creates the Islamic *ummah*, the community or brotherhood living together under obedience to the will of God. This community is open to all people regardless of race or color, and the sense of common membership of the *ummah* has always been and remains an immensely powerful concept in Islam. A Muslim may say his prayers alone at home but more commonly standing in a line in the mosque or perhaps in the open air in the field or desert. In the month of Ramadan he fasts with all his fellow Muslims throughout the *ummah* and when he makes the Pilgrimage to Mecca he does so with hundreds of his brothers (and sisters) during a special season of the year.

Above all, the supreme characteristic of Islam was and remains its unornamental simplicity, its absolute and unconditional monotheism. It was this, combined with the immensely powerful sense of unity which it imparted to the believers, that made it the irresistible force which conquered much of the world. It is also the reason Islam is growing faster than any other religion at the end of the twentieth century.

But the fact that the Prophet Muhammad, through his conviction, personality, and political skill, succeeded in imposing an astonishing degree of unity on his individualistic and generally unruly followers meant that a problem of leadership arose upon his death in A.D. 632. He left no sons and no instructions as to who should succeed him; the Muslim community was in a state of confusion and despair. Eventually it was agreed that Abu Bakr, one of the most respected of Muhammad's Companions and father of his young wife Aishah, should become *Khalifa*, i.e., Caliph or successor to the Apostle of God. He was succeeded by three more of the Companions—Umar, Uthman, and Ali, the Prophet's cousin and son-in-law married to his daughter Fatimah. Together these four Caliphs are known as the "Rashidun" or rightly-guided ones. It was under them that the amazing expansion of Islam took place, westward through Africa and northward and eastward into Asia.

But it was in 661, when Ali was assassinated by one of his own dissident followers, that the great division in Islam took place which survives to this day. In the main body of Islam—the people who came to be known as Sunnis—power passed to a family, the Umayyads, who came from the Meccan oligarchy but made Damascus in Syria their capital. They ruled as a virtual dynasty, although the principle that the Caliph ruled through the designation of the whole Muslim community remained. In 750 they were replaced by another dynasty, the Abbasids, who were descended from the Prophet's uncle. They moved the center of government to Baghdad on the Tigris in Iraq. The Abbasids continued to be Caliphs for five hundred years until the Mongols, led by Hulagu, the grandson of Genghis Khan, captured Baghdad in 1258 and put Mutasim, the last of the Baghdad Caliphs, to death. But long before this the great Abbasid empire had dissolved into a number of smaller states ruled by local dynasties or military groups who were often of Turkish origin. The authority of the Baghdad Caliphs had become a shadow. Yet the power of the local ruler could still be regarded as legitimate in the eyes of the Muslim Faithful if he used it to uphold the *Shariah* and defend the Muslim community. Their subjects, even when rulers were at war with each other, still had a strong feeling that they all belonged to the same *ummah*— the World of Islam.

But there was an important minority of Muslims who from the beginning never accepted the authority of the Umayyad Caliphs or regarded their succession as legitimate. The Shiites or "partisans" of Ali saw him as the direct successor of the Prophet as Imam or spiritual leader and the first of a line of Imams. Different groups of Shiites disagreed about who belonged to this line and when it ended but the majority regarded the Imams as having more than a role of political leadership—as being the infallible interpreters of the revelation given to the Prophet Muhammad. The last of their Imams disappeared in the tenth century A.D., but Shiites believe that he will emerge again at the end of the world to restore the rule of justice.

The division between the Sunnis and the Shiites remains the only great schism in the world of Islam. Perhaps one-tenth of the Muslims in the world today are Shiites. They are the majority among the Arabs of Iraq (although the Sunnis have been politically dominant there), and they are numerically important in Yemen, Syria, Lebanon, and eastern Arabia (including Bahrain). The fact that since the sixteenth century Shiism has been the ruling faith in Iran is of crucial importance in the relations between Iranians and Arabs.

4

Arabia Expands

*T*he first motive force behind the great outburst of the Arabs from Arabia following the death of the Prophet was the pressure of hunger and want. As such it was similar to earlier waves of migration northward from central Arabia. But soon this proved to be different. As the tide of conquest flowed on, a great empire was being established, and it was the minds and souls of men which were being conquered as well as their bodies.

At first the fighting was done mainly by the beduin Arab warriors who at this stage formed an elite class among the Muslims; the early Islamic state was essentially an Arab confederation. The idea that non-Arabs should become Muslims, although clearly sanctioned by the Holy Koran, was still so unfamiliar that any converts who were not full members by descent of an Arab tribe had to become *mawali*, or clients, of one of them. Persians, Egyptians, and North African Berbers became *mawali*. On the other hand, the "People of the Book"—that is, Jews and Christians—were tolerated and respected in their religion and personal lives. They did not enjoy full equality with the Muslims—today they would have been called second-class citizens—but in most cases they welcomed their Arab conquerors who treated them much better than their previous masters of the Persian Sassanid and Byzantine Empires.

These two superpowers of the seventh century A.D. were overthrown by the beduin Arabs with astonishing speed. The Arabs captured Damascus in 634 and Jerusalem in 638. When the

25

Caliph Umar entered the Holy City he assured its Christian Patriarch: "Verily, you are assured of the complete security of your lives, your goods, and your churches, which will not be inhabited nor destroyed by the Muslims. . . ." He also allowed the Jews who had been expelled by the Romans to return. He refused to pray in the Church of the Holy Sepulcher because he said believers would then turn it into a mosque. But Jerusalem, or Al Quds (the Holy) as it was called in Arabic, did become the third most sacred city to Muslims after Mecca and Medina—the place from which the Prophet departed on his night journey to the seven heavens. Two years after the capture of Jerusalem the Muslim armies had taken Egypt from the unpopular Byzantines. Their mounts consisted almost entirely of camels or horses. Because they had no siege equipment they could only take cities by frontal assault or blockade. Although they had never fought on the seas they built navies and challenged the formidable Byzantine fleet. Their most formidable opponents were the Berbers of North Africa—perhaps because they were not luxury-loving city dwellers but hardy nomad warriors like themselves. Eventually a lasting political fusion of Arabs and Berbers was achieved, and North Africa was the springboard for the invasion of the Iberian Peninsula which by A.D. 715 was almost entirely in Arab hands.

The Arabs remained only a small minority in the lands they conquered—perhaps no more than a few hundred thousand. They therefore left the existing administrative structures largely intact in these territories as they passed on for further conquests. But what they did bring was Islam and the Arabic language. Within a century of the death of Muhammad the great Arab/Islamic Empire stretched from the Pyrenees in the West and to Samarkand and the Punjab in the East, although the Arabs never succeeded in conquering the heartland of Turkey or in capturing Constantinople.

Two processes were at work within this empire: Islamization (through mass conversion to Islam) and Arabization. But although the two were linked they did not coincide. Within parts of the empire such as Syria, Iraq, and Egypt, large communities of Christians and Jews remained among the new Muslim majority and in most cases prospered. Similarly, there were those who were converted to Islam, including Turks, Persians, Kurds, and Berbers, who were not Arabized in that they did not adopt Arabic as their first language, although in every case Arabic, the language in which God had spoken to the Prophet, profoundly influenced their own tongues. It was only true in the very early days that all Muslims were Arabs in the sense of having pure Arab blood. This was no longer the case when the word "Arab" had to be extended to include all the Arabized people who had adopted Arabic but might have no Arab ancestors. It was even less true as Islam spread northward with the Turks into the Balkans, eastward into India, China, and the Malay states, and southward into black Africa.

Nevertheless, the extent to which the language of Arabian nomads imposed itself on the more sophisticated cultures of the ancient world is astonishing. Coptic, Aramaic, Greek, and Latin were ousted from areas where they had held undisputed sway for centuries. The vast structure of subtle, complex variations which made Arabic so suitable for poetry also made it the ideal vehicle for the expression of abstract and scientific concepts. Arabic absorbed many foreign words, but these were easily Arabized in a way that was not out of character with the language. But if Arabic covered these ancient cultures with its mantle it did not destroy them. Persian culture survived in its literature and as the language of statecraft and emerged invigorated through its synthesis with Arabic. Greek philosophy, science, and medicine were preserved for future ages through the Arab/Islamic civilization which absorbed and translated them.

The Arab conquerors were unskilled in all the arts of civilization except poetry, but in all fields they made use of the arts and skills of the people who came under their sway. The tent-dwellers of Arabia became great builders who developed a highly individual architecture of their own. Muslim artisans took over and developed all the crafts of working in metal, wood, stone, ivory, glass, and above all pottery and rug making, in which they made their greatest contribution. Because the prohibition of idols in Islam was applied to the plastic reproduction of the human figure,

Islamic art tended towards the elaborate development of abstract ornament. The Arabic script, often in the form of Koranic quotations, was incorporated into the exquisite geometric patterns which can be seen at their finest in the mosques and palaces of India, Persia, and Egypt.

The Golden Age of the Arab/Islamic Empire was the first century of the Abbasids, centered in Baghdad. The Abbasid Caliphs, of whom Harun al-Rashid is the most famous, were proud of their pure Arab descent, but their empire was a cosmopolitan synthesis of many elements. The Arab pretensions to natural superiority provoked a rebellious opposition from Muslims of other races who claimed that they had contributed as much to Islam as the Arabs. The Arabic language was dominant, but the power of the Arab tribal aristocracy was gone forever. What was vitally important for the future of the Islamic *ummah* was that the principle of racial equality was established under the Abbasid Empire. The rejection of distinctions based on color or race is of course enshrined in the Koran but, as we know from Christianity, the principle is not necessarily applied in practice even by the most pious. It would be wrong to say that Muslims are not conscious of race, but they are certainly much less so than Christians—especially Anglo-Saxon Protestants. It is one of the reasons for Islam's success in the twentieth century in converting people of the Third World.

The great empire based in Baghdad, a magnificent center of learning and the arts, declined as empires will. Rival Muslim powers, such as the heretical Fatimids of Egypt, Moorish Spain, and the Turkish Seljuks, arose and in turn lost their strength. At their peak they far outshone Western Christendom. Toledo and Cordoba, with their fertilizing Christian and Jewish minorities, were beacons of civilization when the rest of Europe was passing through the Dark Ages.

But in all these Muslim states power gradually passed from the hands of rulers who could claim physical or spiritual descent from the early Caliphs into those of new military dynasties who seized power for themselves. In the East these were mainly of the martial Turkish race. After four centuries of retreat, Christendom

Arabia Expands

began its counterattack, first in Spain, Sicily, and North Africa, and then toward the heart of the Islamic world itself with the First Crusade of 1096. When Godfrey of Bouillon captured Jerusalem in 1099 the Muslims were slaughtered in thousands. All the Jews who had taken refuge in their synagogues were burned alive by the Crusaders.

Although the world of Islam was racked by internal political dissension, its level of civilization in terms of tolerance, breadth of intellectual interest, and culture was far superior to that of the semi-barbarian invaders. Muslim doctors, for example, were appalled at the primitive medicine of the crusaders. The consequences of the series of invasions which were the Eight Crusades were largely negative: by the time the last Crusader Kingdoms had been eliminated in the early fourteenth century, Muslim rulers were much less tolerant of the infidel. Similarly, it was the final reconquest of Spain by the Catholic Kings Ferdinand and Isabella which led to the forcible conversion or expulsion of Muslims and Jews from the Iberian Peninsula.

While this titanic struggle was continuing between the Arab/Muslim world and the Christian powers of Europe, what had become of the original Arabs who had formed the vanguard of the first great Muslim conquest? Those nomadic tribesmen who had refused to settle down and allow themselves to be absorbed into the cosmopolitan empire of the Abbasids had preserved their poverty-stricken independence by remaining in the deserts, an object of fear and hatred to the people of the settled communities. In Arabia they took to robbing and terrorizing the caravans of pilgrims to the Holy Cities. As long as the power of the Abbasid Caliphs remained sufficient they were held at bay. Harun al-Rashid did much for the Pilgrimage, and his pious wife, Queen Zubaydah, had a chain of wells built from Baghdad to the Hejaz which can still be followed. But the decline of Abbasid power led to a breakdown in order with long periods of scarcity and famine. The people of Mecca had given up commerce to depend for their living on the Pilgrimage, and the men of Quraysh, *the Prophet's tribe*, had become statesmen and generals.

In A.D. 930 members of the rebellious Shiite movement of the Carmathians (Qarmations), who had originated in southern Iraq and gained control of much of Arabia, invaded Mecca and carried off the Black Stone of the Kaabah to Bahrain until they returned it in a broken condition after twenty years. Both the Holy Cities of Islam were a constant bone of contention between the rival dynasties in the Muslim world, but they managed to remain virtually independent for some three hundred years following the establishment of a Sharifate (i.e., lordship) of Mecca in A.D. 961. The Sharifs are by tradition descendants of the Prophet through his grandson Hassan, elder son of the Prophet's daughter Fatimah and Ali. Compared with other Muslim rulers the Sharifs generally led modest and simple lives in harmony with their surroundings, and eastern Arabia during this period saw some periods of relative peace and prosperity. Finally, in 1269 Sultan Baybars I of Egypt, an outstanding member of the strange slave dynasty of Mamelukes, established an effective Egyptian suzerainty over Mecca which lasted another 250 years until it was superseded by that of the Ottoman Turks.

During these centuries tens of thousands of the Faithful braved the perils of medieval travel to make the Pilgrimage and some of them left records of their journey. One of them was the Moroccan-born Ibn Battutah, who has been called "the traveler of Islam." After he made the *Hajj* in 1326 he reported favorably: "The inhabitants of Mecca are distinguished by many excellent and noble activities and qualities, by their beneficence to the humble and weak, and by their kindness to strangers. When any of them makes a feast he begins by giving food to the religious devotees who are poor and without resources, inviting them first with kindness and delicacy. . . . The Meccans are very elegant and clean in their dress, and most of them wear white garments, which you always see fresh and snowy. . . . The Meccan women are extraordinarily beautiful and very pious and modest. . . . They visit the mosque every Thursday night, wearing their finest apparel; and the whole sanctuary is saturated with the smell of their perfume." Ibn Battutah left Medina to cross the Peninsula to Baghdad, accompanying a vast host of fellow pilgrims who followed the route of Queen Zubaydah's wells.

5

Overlords and Invaders

*D*uring the fifteenth century, a great new Muslim power arose. This was the Ottoman Turks who, spreading out from the Anatolia region of present-day Turkey, had by 1517 gained control of all the Arab heartlands—Mecca, Medina, Syria, and Egypt. The Ottoman Sultan recognized the senior representative of the Sharifs as the princes of Mecca. For a long time the Turks showed little interest in Arabia as a whole, so that the Sharifs of Mecca, while acknowledging Turkish supremacy, were able to build up considerable power and prestige for themselves among the desert tribes. The Turks did, however, spend considerable sums on the improvement of the caravan routes and the repair and adornment of the Holy Places of the Hejaz. Later the Ottoman Sultans assumed the title of Caliph of Islam.

Along with the Hejaz the Turks gained control of Yemen, although they were expelled by the mountain tribesmen during the early seventeenth century. In eastern Arabia their hold was even lighter and in the Arabian Gulf they were forestalled by a new Christian maritime power—Portugal. In 1498 the great Portuguese mariner Vasco da Gama had reached India via the Cape of Good Hope and returned to Lisbon laden with spices. This was a momentous event with the greatest historical consequences. In reducing the importance of the overland trade routes from Europe to the East, this new route helped to turn the great commercial centers of the Muslim world into economic backwaters. It was

31

ultimately a major cause of the economic domination of the Muslim world by the West.

With their ambitions to build a great empire in India and the East, the Portuguese aimed to dominate the Red Sea and the Arabian Gulf. Fired by a combination of anti-Islamic fervor and commercial greed, they arrived in the Gulf some thirty years before the Turks. They attacked and pillaged the eastern Arabian coast from Muscat to Bahrain, leaving forts and garrisons to dominate the indigenous Arab trading and pearling communities. Throughout the sixteenth century the Portuguese controlled trade through the Gulf and the Straits of Hormuz. From time to time the Turks, with the help of local tribes, were able to challenge their supremacy. They drove the Portuguese out of Bahrain and Muscat. But ultimately it was the superiority of the Portuguese fleet that counted. The real challenge to the Portuguese came from two rival European maritime powers, England and Holland. By the end of the sixteenth century Dutch and English adventurers (or pirates) were beginning to compete for the spice trade. Early in the seventeenth century both the English East India Company and the Dutch East India Company were formed and, with licenses from the Shah of Persia, began to trade on a regular basis. Throughout the seventeenth century it was the Dutch who were dominant, but by 1750 it was the British who were supreme. In 1698 the English had agreed with the Dutch and the French to share responsibility for policing the Gulf waters, but the whole responsibility passed to the English. In the eighteenth century India became largely a British possession as the French and Dutch were ousted.

It was India which made Britain a world empire, and the coasts of Arabia lying along the route to India became a vital British interest. With the final expulsion of the Portuguese and also of the Persians from Bahrain and Oman, the Arabs were effectively in control of the whole eastern coast of Arabia at the beginning of the eighteenth century. But the Europeans were not to be excluded for long. In 1763 the Shah of Persia awarded the English East India Company agent the title of "Governor-General for the English Nation" in the Gulf. England's trading interests were becoming increasingly synonymous with political control. From 1770 onward the Royal Navy became increasingly active in the protection of maritime trade. Like the Portuguese before them, the English from time to time landed forces on the coast to establish control over the local tribesmen.

In 1798, when Napoleon's expedition to Egypt promised a real threat to British India, the English signed a treaty with the Ruler of Muscat to forestall any renewed French attempt to establish themselves in the Arabian Gulf. In the 1820s similar treaties were signed with other rulers along the Gulf coast. These treaties developed into annually negotiated truces. Later in the nineteenth century continued alarm at the aims of other powers, including Turkey, Persia, France, and Russia, caused Britain to conclude the so-called Exclusive Agreements with the Rulers of Bahrain (1861), the Trucial States (1892), and Qatar (1916). Under these the Rulers agreed never to cede any part of their territory except to the British government, not to enter into any agreements with any government other than the British and not to admit foreign representatives without British consent.

In 1839, on the other side of Arabia, Britain, for the same overriding purpose of protecting the route to India, landed and occupied Aden, a flourishing port with splendid fortifications in Roman times but now a decayed fishing village with no more than five hundred inhabitants. This annexation of what was nominally part of the Ottoman Empire inaugurated 130 years of British rule in Aden and increasing influence in the tribal territory of South Arabia (now the People's Democratic Republic of Yemen).

6

A Great Reformer

*T*wo hundred years ago the Arabian Peninsula was rich in tradition but little else. Muslims dreamed of making the Pilgrimage to the birthplace of their Prophet and their Faith but they were under no illusions about the discomfort and dangers they would face. Although the Western Christian countries were rapidly overtaking the Muslim world in material and scientific progress, the Ottoman Empire was still a great power capable of protecting the interests of the *ummah*. But western Arabia—the Hejaz—was a backward and poverty-stricken province of the empire, lacking the wealth and centers of learning that still survived in the great Muslim cities of the north such as Cairo, Damascus, and Aleppo. Only the people in Yemen, who had expelled the Turks, maintained a fair degree of prosperity, growing coffee and food, while the Arabs of Oman in the toe of the Peninsula were laying the foundations of a great naval empire which included the former Portuguese possessions of Mombasa and Zanzibar.

For Western Christians, Arabia was a land of mystery and fear. A few converts or slaves had been there and brought back scanty reports, but the pioneer of Western exploration of Arabia was the Dane Carsten Niebuhr who led scientific expeditions to Hejaz, Yemen, and the Arabian Gulf in 1762 and 1763. He brought back the news of a powerful new movement that had arisen in Najd in central Arabia and was rapidly spreading throughout the Peninsula.

The tribesmen of central Arabia had never been fully converted to the Islamic faith, and by the 1700s they had either
adopted various heresies or reverted to pre-Islamic idolatry. Some
who were still nominal Muslims raised saints above Allah in their
prayers, failed to pay *zakat* or make the Pilgrimage and even, it
was said, had forgotten the direction of Mecca when they said
their prayers. Worse still, some of the beduin of central Arabia had
revived the mystical cults of South Arabia while others worshiped
tombs, rocks, and trees, making vows to them and supplicating
them for favors.

In Wadi Hanifah in central Najd a false prophet named
Musaylimah had appeared in the Prophet's lifetime and been
defeated by the great general Khalid ibn al Walid. About a thousand years later the same Wadi produced a new man who was no
false prophet but a great religious reformer. He was Muhammad
ibn Abd al Wahhab, the son and grandson of holy men, who at an
early age, after much study and travel, began to preach the essential Muslim doctrine of Unitarianism or Tawhid. "We may revere
and imitate the good and holy men," he told his people, "but we
pray only to Allah." His movement gathered support but also made
enemies among local leaders when he attacked their ways. Eventually he was given asylum by Muhammad ibn Saud, Amir of
Diriyah, an oasis in the Wadi Hanifah. This alliance in 1744
between the Wahhabite movement and the House of Saud marked
the foundation of the future Kingdom of Saudi Arabia in the twentieth century.

Muhammad ibn Abd al Wahhab, who lived to the age of
eighty-nine, never claimed to be a new Prophet with some further
revelation of God's will. That he would have regarded as
blasphemy. But he called for a return to the purest form of early
Islam, basing his creed on the most severe of the four Sunni Muslim schools of law, the Hanbali. He maintained that it was not
enough for a Muslim to repeat the formula, "There is no god but
God alone, and Muhammad is the Messenger of God." He must
also say his prayers, fast in Ramadan, and give alms. Above all he
must renounce any form of idolatry or saint worship.

Ibn Abd al Wahhab's puritanical movement made many enemies among leaders in Arabia who had adopted less strict ways. But he also inspired a following of men who felt a new sense of pride and achievement comparable to that of the Companions of the Prophet. The alliance between the Wahhabi movement and the desert warriors of the House of Saud was formidable. In the second half of the eighteenth century Wahhabi rule spread throughout Najd, northward to the borders of Iraq, and into Al Hasa province on the Arabian Gulf. They then turned westward and in 1803 the Wahhabi/Saudi armies captured Taif and Mecca, destroyed many saints' shrines, and stripped the Kaabah of its ornaments. By 1806 the whole of the Hejaz was in their hands.

The Sultan of the Ottoman Empire was outraged at this development. His own troops were incapable of reversing the situation, but in Egypt a former officer in the Albanian division of the Ottoman army named Muhammad Ali had ruthlessly and efficiently consolidated his position as Viceroy of the semi-autonomous province. In 1811 Muhammad Ali sent an expeditionary force, first commanded by his son Tusun, which invaded the Hejaz in 1811 with the Sultan's approval. The Wahhabis fought back fiercely and inflicted some heavy reverses on Tusun's Turco-Egyptian army. Muhammad Ali replaced Tusun with another son, the brilliant general Ibrahim Pasha, and his superiority in equipment and tactics eventually enabled him to gain the upper hand. The bitter campaign ended with the defeat of Wahhabism. Ibrahim swept on to Najd and Hasa, destroying the Wahhabi capital of Diriyah. A century later the Lebanese-American writer and Arabian traveler Ameen Rihani discovered that Ibrahim was remembered as "Shaitan (Satan) Pasha . . . a double-barreled gun of evil—a Turkish Pasha and son of a slave mother." Abdullah, the head of the House of Saud, was taken to Constantinople and beheaded.

The Sultan's authority over the Holy Cities of Islam was restored, and for many years Turkish and Egyptian influence over both the Hejaz and Najd was unchallenged. The Saudi family set about restoring the ruined Wahhabi state. They made their new capital at Riyadh some fifteen miles away. A strong wall was built around the town which was supplied with a palace and a mosque. However, a new challenge arose to the Saudis in northern Najd, known as Jabal Shammar after its principal tribe. Here the Rashidi family of the town of Hail seceded from the former Wahhabi overlords and succeeded in establishing themselves as a powerful rival to the House of Saud. For some fifty years there was almost unbroken fighting between the two until in 1891 Abd al Rahman, head of the House of Saud, was forced to flee from Riyadh and take refuge with the Ruler of Kuwait. He was accompanied by the eldest of his five sons, the ten-year-old Abd al Aziz Al Saud, commonly known by the patronymic Ibn Saud, who was to prove to be one of the most remarkable leaders in the long history of the Arab people.

By the time he reached manhood, Abd al Aziz dominated his companions with his physical presence and personality. Over six feet two inches in height and a formidable horseman and warrior, he also possessed a charm and magnetism that few could resist.

In January 1902 the young Abd al Aziz succeeded in recapturing Riyadh in a daring night attack at the head of a force of barely thirty men. From there he set about restoring the former Wahhabi empire. He was helped by the fact that the Rashidi princes, although men of courage and skill in desert warfare, showed no political ability. Their failure to control the looting by their beduin warriors and their open dependency on Turkish support made them highly unpopular. They also showed an unquenchable tendency to murder each other. In contrast, the young Abd al Aziz, in addition to his proven fearlessness, already revealed his skill as a careful and cautious strategist, his magnanimity in victory, and his affection and loyalty towards his family. His father Abd al Rahman acknowledged his leadership but continued to give him wise, authoritative advice until his own death in 1927. Above all Abd al Aziz had an ideology in his alliance with the Wahhabi movement which the Rashidis, interested only in raiding for booty, lacked in good measure. Abd al Aziz, on the other hand, had learned the lesson of history, which was that while the Arabs had been inspired to great achievements under the impetus of religious fervor or outstanding leadership, the volatile character of a largely nomadic society meant that the gains were dissipated when the religious zeal cooled or the leader disappeared. His people needed a solid foundation to their society, and it was to this end that he founded in 1912 the first colony of Ikhwan ("brothers") at the oasis of Artawiyah. This was a military settlement, cultivating the land and dedicated to the service of God and the Amir. Within a decade some 100 similar colonies were founded, providing Ibn Saud with a formidable territorial army which eventually would conquer most of the Peninsula.

Rashidi power in Hail declined and, with the removal of the threat from the north, he was able to occupy the Turkish-held province of Hasa in 1913 with little difficulty. He could not go further because the entire Gulf coast was under British influence from Kuwait in the north (which had signed a Treaty of Protection with Britain in 1899) to Oman in the south. As Lord Lansdowne said in the House of Lords in 1903: "We should regard the establishment of a naval base or of a fortified port on the Persian Gulf as a very grave menace to British interests, and that we should certainly resist with all the means at our disposal."

In western Arabia the Ottoman Turks still maintained some degree of control. The opening of the Suez Canal in 1869 facilitated the dispatch of Turkish warships into the Red Sea. Ottoman domination was reimposed for a time in Yemen, although this proved as difficult to maintain as ever against the mountain tribesmen. In the Hejaz, the wily Ottoman Sultan Abd al Hamid had constantly to assert his authority against the intrigues of the Sharifs of Mecca. There were frequent disorders, foreign consuls were murdered, and there was little security for the suffering Muslim pilgrims. Abd al Hamid, who reigned from 1876 to 1909, had seen the loss to European Christian powers of most of his Balkan provinces and all the Arabic-speaking provinces from Egypt to Algeria. Only the Arab heartland of Greater Syria (including Palestine and Lebanon), Iraq, and parts of the Arabian Peninsula remained. Abd al Hamid was determined to consolidate his hold on what was left. He used force wherever necessary and maintained a vast web of spies to inform on potential rebels, but he was not without skill in political public relations. Pious and strict in his personal life, he appealed to his Muslim subjects by giving generously to mosques and schools. His shrewdest action was to build a railway from Damascus to Medina—the Hejaz Railway. This made it easier and safer for pilgrims to reach the Holy Cities; it also made it much simpler to send troops to the Hejaz to quell any disturbance.

Abd al Hamid's efforts to preserve his autocracy were foiled when in 1908 he was thrust aside by a group of reformers and military officers known as the Young Turks. Their revolt was at first greeted with wild enthusiasm by the mass of non-Turkish Muslims in the Empire who hoped that the new regime would give them real equality and democracy, as they had declared. These hopes soon turned sour as the Young Turks showed their determination to maintain Turkish domination in the Ottoman Empire. But in the brief honeymoon period between Turks and Arabs, the Young Turks took one important decision. This was to appoint Hussein ibn Ali, thirty-seventh in line of descent from the Prophet Muhammad and a member of the Hashemite family of Arabia, as Sharif of Mecca. Hussein had been held in an outwardly honored exile in Constantinople with his four young sons by Abd al Hamid, who regarded him as a potential troublemaker for the Empire. His judgment was to prove wholly correct. Hussein was autocratic, charming, and irascible; he had a deep sense of his own destiny.

At first Hussein acted cautiously with the Turks. He even conducted a successful expedition on their behalf to suppress a rebellion in the Asir province. On his return in triumph, the Turks encouraged him to extend their authority into the interior. He succeeded in taking Ibn Saud's favorite brother Saad hostage; and Ibn Saud was forced to accept a nominal Ottoman suzerainty to ransom his brother. By his action Hussein sealed the fate of his own immense ambitions. For the time being, events seemed to be moving in Hussein's favor. Having made himself indispensable to the Turks, he set about asserting with the Turkish Governor his rights as Sharif of an autonomous Arab province. The Young Turks considered deposing him, but in the face of strong opposition in the Hejaz they withdrew.

First Sultan Abd al Hamid and then the Young Turks had formed a close relationship with Kaiser Wilhelm's Germany to counterbalance the overbearing power of Britain and France which was constantly encroaching on the remains of the Ottoman Empire. Two months after the outbreak of World War I, Turkey joined Germany and Austro-Hungary against Britain, France, and Turkey's old enemy Tsarist Russia.

This was Hussein's opportunity. He sent out a feeler to the British authorities in Cairo in the person of his second son Abdullah to test their reaction to an Arab revolt against the Turks. He had already made contact with Arab nationalist societies in Syria and Iraq and felt that the prospects were encouraging. Any doubts he had about allying himself with Christian infidels against the Ottoman Empire, which was still after all the main protecting power for the Islamic *ummah*, were overcome by the prospect of leading a united Arab nation in the Arabian Peninsula and the Levant once the Ottoman Empire had collapsed.

As soon as war broke out with Turkey the British-controlled Indian government was convinced that the immediate occupation of Mesopotamia was essential for the security of India and the Gulf. An Indian Army brigade was landed at Basrah and began to advance toward Baghdad. Aware of the importance of securing the support of the Wahhabi ruler to the British cause, Sir Percy Cox, Chief Political Officer of the Mesopotamian Expeditionary Force, sent Captain W.H.I. Shakespear, as British representative at Ibn Saud's court. Captain Shakespear had already visited Riyadh in the winter of 1913-14 in the course of a great journey of exploration through northern Arabia, and he had excellent relations with Ibn Saud. In January 1915, however, Captain Shakespear was killed in a skirmish with the Rashidis while directing the fire of the Wahhabis's single mountain gun, dressed in his British uniform (which he always insisted on wearing). Another famous Arabian explorer, Harry St. John Bridger Philby, who also became a friend of Ibn Saud, has speculated that if it had not been for Shakespear's disappearance the whole course of the war in the Middle East and in Britain's relations with the Arabs might have been different. It might have been Ibn Saud's Wahhabi forces rather than the Sharif Hussein's son Amir Faisal and his friend Colonel T.E. Lawrence (Lawrence of Arabia) who would have attacked the Hejaz Railway and harassed the Turks on the flanks of General Allenby's armies. (Some years later Ibn Saud was asked by a British diplomat who was the greatest Englishman he had known. Without hesitation he replied: "Shagesbear!")

The consequence of this tragedy was that the responsibility for the direction of the war in Arabia fell upon the British authorities in Cairo. The Indian government's interest extended no further than the Gulf coast, and Ibn Saud was largely ignored for the rest of the war. In December 1915 the British signed a treaty with Ibn Saud recognizing the independence and territorial integrity of Najd (although ominously failing to define the Najd's frontiers with the Hejaz) and undertaking to pay a monthly subsidy of £5,000 with some arms. In return he was expected to keep up pressure on the Rashidis who had declared in favor of the Turkish Sultan.

In June 1916 the Sharif Hussein, after prolonged and indecisive negotiations with the British over the future of the Arab lands, finally launched the Arab Revolt by symbolically firing a rifle at the Turkish barracks in Mecca. The long campaign had begun which was to end two years later with the triumphant entry into Damascus of the Amir Faisal and T.E. Lawrence in the vanguard of the British troops under General Allenby.

The Sharif Hussein at once declared himself to be "King of the Arabs," but no one would recognize him as such. Britain and France would only regard him as "King of the Hejaz." The fact was that Britain and France had already entered into a secret agreement to carve up all the remaining Arab provinces of the Ottoman Empire into areas under either their direct military control or political influence. Since this was in clear contradiction of various promises and declarations they had made and were to make before the war ended in favor of the principle of independence for the Arabs in areas where they were the overwhelming majority of the population, the Anglo-French agreement caused bitter Arab disillusion after the Ottoman defeat. But these were troubles that could be overcome in time, as Britain and France had no intention of colonizing these lands and would eventually withdraw. Although very few realized it at the time, a much more insoluble problem was caused by Britain's promise to the Zionist Jews to support the establishment of a National Home for the Jews in Palestine.

T.E. Lawrence dreamed that a chain of Arab Hashemite kingdoms presided over by Hussein and his sons would emerge after the war under British tutelage. But as King of the Hejaz, Hussein was the only independent Hashemite to have emerged from the war. Britain established control over Iraq, Palestine, and Transjordan, and France over Syria and Lebanon. The Hejaz was considered strategically or economically unimportant enough to be allowed independence and could remain as a token of Britain's good intentions toward Arabs and Muslims.

7

The Struggle for Arabia

As far as the British were concerned, Ibn Saud's role in Arabia was to attack the Rashidis who had declared in favor of the Turks and offered a threat on the flanks of General Allenby's advance northward into Syria. He might have provided some effective assistance to the Arab Revolt in the Hejaz if he had been encouraged and provided with money and weapons. But the British were making their principal Arabian investment in Sharif Hussein, and he insisted on treating Ibn Saud as an unruly subordinate who must be kept in his place.

In October 1917 the British belatedly sent a permanent mission from Iraq to Ibn Saud in Riyadh. It was headed by a turbulent and eccentric thirty-two-year-old official named Harry St. John Philby who was to become one of the greatest Arabian experts. Having characteristically quarreled with his superiors, Philby left the British service to attach himself to Ibn Saud's court. He eventually became a Muslim and married a second wife in Arabia. His character was as complex and perverse as that of T. E. Lawrence although rather less glamorous. Garrulous and opinionated, he seems to have alternately amused and irritated Ibn Saud, but there can be no dispute about his contribution to the knowledge of the history and geography of Arabia. The well over a dozen books he left are indispensable sources although they are a long way from being masterpieces of English prose.

Partly through Philby's miscalculations, Ibn Saud's expedition against the Rashidis was delayed, and when it was finally carried out in 1918 it misfired. The British government was more than ever convinced that in Sharif Hussein they had backed the Arabian winner. The Turks had been finally defeated and the Rashidis were no longer a threat that needed to be countered. The government of India, which controlled the new British administration in Iraq, still supported the claims of Ibn Saud, but it was opinion in Whitehall which ultimately counted.

Ibn Saud's fortunes were depressed in the year following the war. Apart from being ignored in the postwar settlement of the remains of the Ottoman Empire, he suffered a personal tragedy in the loss of his eldest son Turki, two other sons, and his principal wife Jawharah in the Spanish influenza epidemic. But he soon showed that he was not to be ignored. In May 1919 the Sharif Hussein sent his second son Abdullah at the head of a strong expeditionary force to occupy the oasis of Khurmah which lay on the disputed border between the Hejaz and Najd. Feeling themselves safe in a fortified camp at Turabah, Abdullah and his troops were attacked at midnight by the Ikhwan. Abdullah and his staff escaped at the first alarm; the rest of his forces were slaughtered. The British government no longer underestimated Ibn Saud's importance.

In the winter of 1919 Ibn Saud was invited to send a representative to London. The mission was headed by Ibn Saud's second surviving son Faisal, then fourteen years old, whose dignity and personality left a strong impression. Apart from visits to the Houses of Parliament, the Bank of England, and the fleet, the official program included two Gilbert and Sullivan operas—a true test of the fortitude and politeness of the young Arab prince. Henceforth, Faisal was Ibn Saud's acting foreign minister.

The British might have better assessed Ibn Saud's significance in Arabia, but their principal concern remained with the partition of the former Arab provinces of the Ottoman Empire. Here disorder and confusion arose in the immediate aftermath of the war as a result of undertakings made by Britain and her allies to Arabs and Jews and to each other. Briefly, these were of three kinds. There were those to the Arabs, which the Arabs believed amounted to a promise to support the principle of their independence in areas where they clearly formed the overwhelming majority of the population. In this belief they were supported by various Anglo-French policy statements made before the end of the war which also accorded with the doctrine of self-determination preached by the American President Woodrow Wilson. However, these conflicted with an understanding between Britain and France, sealed in a secret agreement made in 1916, which effectively partitioned the whole Arab East into areas of either British or French direct administration or spheres of influence. Only the Arabian Peninsula, apart from the British-protected states on its fringes, was excluded because of its apparent political and economic unimportance.

The third undertaking was Britain's promise to the Zionists, in November 1917, to support the establishment of a Jewish National Home in Palestine. The consequences of this were understood by very few at the time; ultimately it was to create the most intractable of all the problems facing the Middle East in the twentieth century.

The results of so much deception and confusion of aims were soon apparent. The year 1920 was called by the Arabs the Year of Disaster. In Palestine the Arabs, for the first but not for the last time, rioted against the Zionists whom they believed to be coming to displace them from their homes. In Syria, the French used their overwhelming military superiority to expel King Hussein's third son Faisal who had been declared King of Syria by his followers. In Iraq the tribes of the Middle Euphrates rose in costly and violent rebellion against their new British rulers.

The British Prime Minister Lloyd George decided that a new approach must be made. In order to put an end to the disastrous rivalry between the India Office, responsible for British administration in Iraq and the Gulf, and the Foreign Office, which controlled Britain's main Middle East headquarters in Cairo, he put the whole problem of Britain's new semi-colonial Middle East empire into the hands of the young Winston Churchill who had recently been created Secretary of State for the Colonies. Having persuaded T. E. Lawrence to join his new Middle East Department, Churchill called a conference in Cairo in March 1921 of all the senior British Middle East officials, including Sir Percy Cox, the High Commissioner in Iraq, and his adviser, Miss Gertrude Bell, the formidable and eminent Arabian explorer and expert. The conference endorsed decisions which had in fact already been made in Whitehall. Prince Faisal, for whom Britain felt responsible since he had been ejected from Syria by the French, would become King of Iraq. Gertrude Bell returned to Iraq to ensure that the tribal leaders gave Faisal a triumphal reception. She succeeded, but some members of the British administration opposed the imposition of Hashemite rule in Iraq and favored a republic. One of these was Philby who left Iraq and a few years later also abandoned the Indian Civil Service to devote himself to Arabia and the cause of the chief opponent of the Hashemites, Ibn Saud.

But Iraq was not the only problem facing the British in the Middle East. The appointment as High Commissioner for Palestine of Sir Herbert Samuel, a prominent Jew who had been the first to propose the Zionist idea to the British Cabinet, was hardly calculated to reassure the fears of the Palestinian Arabs. Another difficulty was that King Hussein's second son Prince Abdullah, following his humiliation at the hands of the Ikhwan at Turabah, had arrived in the undefined territory which is now southern Jordan with a motley army of tribesmen and retainers and the declared intention of advancing to Damascus to avenge the treatment of his brother Faisal at the hands of the French. This objective was certainly impractical and probably spurious; Abdullah had expected to be King of Iraq himself and was resentful that the prize had gone to Faisal. But Abdullah could not be ignored, and the British felt some responsibility toward all the Hashemites.

Churchill traveled with Lawrence up to Jerusalem by train. First he attempted to reassure the Palestinian leaders that there was no intention of allowing Palestine, which was still over ninety percent Arab in population, to become a Jewish state. He also summoned Abdullah to meet him. After some hard oriental bargaining—in which Abdullah began by naming a price that he must have known could not possibly be accepted (such as that he should be made King of a united Transjordan and Iraq)—it was agreed that Abdullah should become ruler of the "independent" Emirate of Transjordan, with an annual British subsidy and British advisers, on the understanding that Britain would try to persuade the French to set up, at some time in the future, an Arab administration in Damascus with Abdullah at its head. Abdullah was quite aware that there was little chance of this happening. The new state was carved out of land just north of Arabia with a curious westward wedge-shaped projection which gave it a common border with Faisal's new Kingdom of Iraq. (This is known as "Winston's hiccough" on the ground that the frontier was being drawn by the Colonial Secretary with a ruler and pencil after an especially lavish luncheon in Jerusalem. The story is no doubt apocryphal but it symbolizes the popular feeling about the arbitrary manner in which Middle Eastern frontiers were demarcated.)

While Ibn Saud was far from pleased that his Hashemite enemies should be installed on thrones to the north, west, and south of Najd, there was nothing he could do about it. He was still dependent on the British subsidy, and the Hashemite lands were under British protection. But his fierce Ikhwan warriors were now aroused and difficult to control. Fortunately there was a target for their ardor in the old Saudi enemy, the Rashidis. Ibn Saud was aware that King Faisal of Iraq was in contact with the Rashidis, and he feared that the Najd might now be encircled by a hostile anti-Wahhabi alliance. Accordingly he launched a final campaign against the Rashidi capital of Hail. Ibn Saud was greatly helped by the bloodthirsty strife within the Rashidi clan. It was said that over the past century only two Rashidi rulers had died a natural death, and in 1920 the tradition had been maintained when the incumbent was murdered by his own cousin who was promptly hacked to death by loyal slaves. Furthermore, many of the Rashidi tribesmen were attracted by the Wahhabi faith; Ibn Saud took preachers along with his army. After a short seige, Hail surrendered and the twenty-year Saudi-Rashidi war was ended.

As usual Ibn Saud was magnanimous in victory. He prevented

his troops from looting Hail. He took all the surviving members of the ruling family to Riyadh where they lived the rest of their lives in comfort at his expense. He carried out the admirable Islamic tradition of marrying the widow of his principal rival and adopting her children as his own.

Ibn Saud, who had already been acclaimed by the Wahhabi chiefs as "Sultan of Najd and its Dependencies," was now in a much stronger position. In 1920 an expedition led by his fifteen-year-old son Faisal had added the southwestern highlands of Asir with their capital Abha to his territories. To the north of Najd he secured without much difficulty the allegiance of the people of Jawf. But this was followed by an incident that underlined a problem that Ibn Saud was to face for some years. Without his orders, a group of fanatical Harib tribesmen from central Arabia, advanced far northward into the newly-created Emirate of Transjordan where they massacred the entire population of a small village only fifteen miles from Amman. British planes and armored cars joined the local Bani Sakhr tribesmen in repelling the Ikhwan who in their headlong flight were massacred in their turn. The disciplining of his tribal warriors to prevent such incidents was one of the many difficult challenges Ibn Saud had to face.

However, the boundaries between Najd and both Kuwait and Iraq were still undefined. In fact Ibn Saud regarded border demarcation as ludicrous in an area where the nomadic inhabitants, who lacked any sense of nationality, were accustomed to wander over huge stretches of desert to find pasturage for their flocks. But the British protectors of Iraq and Kuwait were anxious to establish a frontier beyond which Wahhabi power would not be allowed to expand. Sir Percy Cox succeeded in reaching agreement with Ibn Saud on a frontier between Najd and Kuwait which provided for a chunk of territory as a Neutral Zone to avoid accidental disputes. But the long frontier with Iraq was a more difficult problem. An agreement known as the Treaty of Muhammarah which was worked out with Ibn Saud's representative was repudiated by Ibn Saud as being too favorable to Iraq. Ibn Saud therefore invited Sir Percy Cox to meet him at Uqayr. With some reluctance Ibn Saud agreed to the demarcation of a fixed frontier, and although Cox conceded the right of the Najd tribes to cross it for water and pasturage—provided neither side used the watering places for military purposes or attempted to fortify them—the Protocol of Uqayr, as it was called, effectively blocked any further expansion of Wahhabi territory into Iraq or Kuwait.

The Uqayr meeting also marked the beginning of a long and remarkable friendship between Ibn Saud and Ameen Rihani, an American writer and traveler of Christian Lebanese origin. Equally at home in New York and the Arab world, Rihani was in a unique position to explain the phenomenon of Ibn Saud to the Western world. His books are also highly readable, unlike Philby's turgid prose. "The Sultan Abdul-Aziz," he wrote, "is tall of stature, muscular, sinewy, and of noble proportions; has the Arab's complexion, but not the physiognomy—a swarthy face, without the high cheek-bones; has not the Semitic nose—his is straight but slightly upturned—and is quite modern in his beard and moustache, which he trims, Wahhabi-fashion. . . . He wears robes of white linen in the summer, of cloth in the winter, under a brown *aba* of camel hair; goes in sandals; perfumes himself profusely; and carries an unstained staff, which he uses as an aid to expression—with which he underlines a word, as it were, or emphasizes an idea. He has other aids to expression in his well-modelled hands, which are particularly elegant and eloquent in gesture; and in his dark brown eyes, which throw a soft light on the feeling in his speech when he is in good humour, and which influence his words when he is roused to anger. His mouth in the former state, like a red rose leaf, becomes in the latter like iron. The lips, shrunk and taut, white and trembling, the colour in a trice disappearing from them, suggest a blade of vibrating steel.

"Indeed, Ibn Sa'oud in anger changes completely and suddenly. All the charm of his features gives way to a mordant, savage expression. Even the light in his smile becomes a white flame."

He had made a similar physical impression on Gertrude Bell, who had met him on his visit to Basrah in 1915. But presumably she never saw him in anger because she wrote: "His deliberate movements, his slow, sweet smile, and the contemplative glance of his heavy-lidded eyes, though they add to his dignity and charm, do not accord with the western conception of a vigorous personality. Nevertheless, report credits him with powers of endurance rare even in hard-bitten Arabia." She was unaware that, although impressed by her knowledge of Arabia, he was embarrassed by her bossy and forward manner and her habit of saying: "Abdul Aziz, do come and look at this!"

Rihani held long conversations with Ibn Saud which were usually on politics, the favorite topic, as Rihani remarked, of all Arab rulers. Ibn Saud surprised him by his knowledge of world events. He was distressed by the fall of Woodrow Wilson who had recently been deserted by the American voters: "I do not think they did well. Wilson is a great man. And his is the credit for awakening the small oppressed nations of the world. Wilson showed them the way to freedom and independence. He has infused, especially into the people of the East, a new spirit. He has also made America known to us. We did not know America before Wilson." But he was scathing about the United States' apparently all-powerful wartime allies. "I liken Europe today to a great iron door, but there is nothing behind it." For that reason he did not blame America for retreating into isolation.

Rihani later rode across the desert to Riyadh where he was the Sultan's guest in his rambling mud-walled palace. When Rihani was struck down by malaria, Ibn Saud visited him every day, took his temperature with his new thermometer, and brought him quinine, biscuits, and "even books."

There was someone else in Uqayr whose presence was a portent. This was Major Frank Holmes, an adventurer and promoter from New Zealand who had worked before the war with Herbert Hoover in China and served in the British navy during the war. He had arrived loaded with presents, to try to persuade the Sultan to grant an oil concession to his tiny Eastern and General Syndicate. Ibn Saud was skeptical about both the possible presence of oil in his territory and the wisdom of allowing in Western capital and technicians. Sir Percy Cox also tried to dissuade Holmes, saying the time was not yet ripe and the British government could not afford his company any protection. Cox would have preferred that if a concession were granted it go to the powerful Anglo-Persian Oil Company (APOC) which controlled the Persian oilfields and in which the British government had a fifty percent share. The APOC was lukewarm, but Holmes was persistent. Rihani helped to persuade Ibn Saud that if he was going to allow in a Western company, he should prefer a small independent to a major in which a Western government had a large stake. Eventually Ibn Saud gave the concession to Holmes in 1923. Ibn Saud was delighted when he received the first annual rent of $2,000 both because he needed the money and because he regarded it as no more than a windfall which could not last.

A photograph of Rihani's shows the Sultan and Cox sitting in armchairs in the desert. A tubby pith-helmeted Holmes stands behind, close to the Sultan's chair. This enterprising, eccentric entrepreneur never acquired great wealth because he lacked the backing to develop the concessions he negotiated, but he was a true pioneer of Arabian oil exploration.

The trouble with limiting Ibn Saud's expansion toward Iraq, Kuwait, and Transjordan was that all Wahhabi ambitions were now directed against the Hejaz. The old King Hussein was by now thoroughly embittered toward Britain. The British government in return had virtually washed its hands of him since he had refused to sign a draft treaty in 1921 which would have meant accepting as an accomplished fact that Syria, Lebanon, and Palestine were all lost to the rule of his family. His annual subsidy from Britain had been discontinued.

Britain did help to arrange a conference at Kuwait that was intended to settle the outstanding differences between the Saudis and the Hashemites. But Britain made the mistake of proposing that Ibn Saud should give back Khurmah and Turabah—two oases east of Mecca—to King Hussein who claimed they were part of the Hejaz. This was certain to be rejected by Ibn Saud, but Britain had no intention of helping Hussein to recover this territory by force, as he was certainly incapable of doing on his own. The conference therefore ended in failure.

It was at this point that King Hussein decided to assert his patriarchal authority over his family by making a ceremonial visit to Transjordan which he still insisted on regarding as a province of his own kingdom. He arrived in style in Aqabah in January 1924 in a destroyer. There were no guns on shore to greet him with a royal salute so his own ship fired a salvo instead. With his flashing eyes, white beard, and imperious manner he was formidable, and the Emir Abdullah offered him due deference. But he was an acute embarrassment to the British authorities in Palestine who wished he would return to Arabia.

The old King's vanity and ambition then caused him to make a fatal error. Mustafa Kemal, father of the new Turkish Republic which he had raised from the ruins of the Ottoman Empire, decided, as part of his policy of secularization and westernization, to abolish the institution of the Caliphate which had been maintained by the Ottoman Sultans since the eighteenth century. Three days after the Turkish parliament decreed the perpetual abolition of the Caliphate, Hussein declared himself to have assumed the title of "Prince of the Faithful and Successor of the Prophet."

During the War the British had encouraged Hussein in the belief that they wanted the Caliphate to return to a man of Arab race such as himself. But they were no longer interested. There was some predictable support from pro-Hashemite loyalists in the Hejaz and Syria, but the reaction in the rest of the Islamic world ranged from indifference to rage.

The greatest fury was among Ibn Saud's Wahhabis. At that same moment the British government decided to end the nine-year-old annual subsidy of £60,000 to Ibn Saud so that he no longer had any motive for restraining his warriors even if he should have wished to. In fact expansion into the Hejaz was essential for the survival of the Sultanate of Najd. In September a ferocious Ikhwan force led by Sultan ibn Bijad of the Ghatghat colony fell upon the Hejaz mountain capital of Taif where King Hussein's eldest son Ali was in residence. Ali fled with his troops followed by some terrified citizens. In the confusion, some 300 civilians were massacred by the Ikhwan before the people of Taif surrendered and were granted amnesty. Bypassing Mecca to avoid meeting his enraged and contemptuous father, Ali retreated to Jiddah where he barricaded himself in with his forces. Hussein, who, whatever his faults, remained dignified and courageous to the last, wished to fight to the end. But the people of Hejaz insisted that he abdicate in favor of Ali who had a better chance of coming to terms with Ibn Saud and his Wahhabis.

So the old man sailed away with his household and what remained of his treasure (British gold and revenues from the pilgrimage) packed in gasoline cans. He went to Aqabah and from there, since the British feared that his presence might encourage the Wahhabis to seize this strategic port, to Cyprus where he died, an embittered exile, in 1931.

The Hejazis had little love for Hussein after his eight-year reign. But they were terrified of the Wahhabis and prepared to defend the fortified port of Jiddah. The Wahhabi forces entered Mecca without difficulty and destroyed the various tombs and monuments which they considered idolatrous in the Holy City. Ibn Saud arrived in December and entered Mecca wearing the white pilgrim garment. He restrained his troops from marching immediately against Jiddah and Medina, partly because of British protests following the massacre at Taif and the fact that he was uncertain of the discipline of the Ikhwan. This gave the people of Jiddah time to prepare their defenses and a desultory twelve-month siege ensued. During this time Ibn Saud overran much of the rest of the Hejaz and took the chance to reopen the pilgrim route. He had already begun to demonstrate that he could ensure the security of the Holy Places after centuries of disorder. If anyone could control the beduin tribes who preyed on pilgrims it was the Ikhwan. An English Muslim who made the *Hajj* in the year of 1925 was moved to write of Ibn Saud: "He is probably the best ruler that Arabia has known since the days of the four Khalifas."

Despite the superiority in arms held by the defenders of Jiddah, disease, hunger, and desertions reduced their morale. In

December 1924 they surrendered; Ali abdicated after a reign of fourteen months and retired to the court of his brother Faisal in Baghdad. Wahhabism was triumphant throughout the Hejaz. Only in the extreme northwest did the British authorities in Palestine retain any territory. There they sent troops and armored cars to occupy the strip of land between Maan and Aqabah. The excuse was that because the Turks had included it in the Vilayet of Damascus, it was now part of the British mandate for Palestine, although in King Hussein's time Britain had recognized it as part of the Hejaz. The reality was that it was considered essential for Abdullah's Emirate to have an outlet to the sea. Ibn Saud never recognized the annexation of Maan and Aqabah to Transjordan, but there was nothing he could do at the time to prevent it.

This was the moment in Ibn Saud's long career that most tested his powers of statesmanship. He controlled the Holy Places of Islam and had declared himself their trustee. How would the Muslim World respond? The great majority of Muslims who were not Arabs were certain to be skeptical that a tribal leader from central Arabia could succeed in establishing security in the Hejaz where generations of Sharifian rulers and the Ottoman Turks had so manifestly failed. Alarmed by the Wahhabi destruction of the tombs of the saints, the Persians and Indians sent delegations to the Hejaz to express their views on the future status of the region.

Ibn Saud acted with skill and caution. He appointed his second surviving son, Faisal, as Viceroy of the Hejaz and Abdullah Damluji, an Iraqi who had been ten years in his service, as Director of Foreign Affairs. He strictly forbade the Ikhwan elements of the Wahhabi army to enter Jiddah in order to prevent accidental clashes with the local population or resident expatriates. A start was made on providing transport and accommodation for Muslim pilgrims.

8

The Victory of Ibn Saud

Within a few weeks after having himself declared trustee of the Holy Places, Ibn Saud had impressed the Hejazis with his ability to maintain security and his willingness to adjust to what they regarded as their more sophisticated twentieth century ways. On January 8, 1926, their leaders approached Ibn Saud when he had completed his prayers at the Great Mosque of Mecca and formally asked him to accept their loyalty as King of the Hejaz. He agreed to rule, with God's help, through the Holy *Shariah*.

Ibn Saud was the Imam of his people as well as their King. This meant that he led them in prayer, and set them an example in religious devotion, but no more. Unlike the Sharif Hussein, or King Farouk of Egypt at a later date, he never aspired to the title of Caliph. He was only resolutely opposed to anyone else's taking the title.

The Soviet Union was the first of the powers to grant *de jure* recognition to the new Saudi regime, followed rapidly by Britain, France, and other European powers. The United States was to wait for a decade before it showed any interest in Arabia. The Soviet government saw Ibn Saud as an independent anti-imperialist force and hoped to use his new state as a channel of political and commercial penetration of the Middle East which was otherwise under British or French control. By 1938 the Soviets realized their mistake, and their legation in Jiddah was closed. Most of the staff disappeared in the Stalinist purges, with the exception of the lega-

57

tion doctor who was granted asylum and became a Muslim.

A formal treaty with Britain took two years to achieve because Ibn Saud refused to recognize the British mandates in Palestine, Transjordan, and Iraq until the problem of his claim to the Maan-Aqabah area was settled and agreement was reached on the restoration of the Hejaz railway destroyed during the war against the Turks. Ultimately, both these problems were shelved with the signing in 1927 of the Treaty of Jiddah under which Britain recognized "the complete and absolute independence of the dominions" of Ibn Saud who in return agreed to respect all the British treaties of protection with the Gulf emirates.

It was one thing for Ibn Saud's independence to be recognized by the powers. He still had to prove that he could control his vast, unruly territories. In the Najd he had learned how to handle the Wahhabi tribesmen but the Hejaz was different. Here his method was to make each tribal chief responsible for security in his own area and accountable to him while the Wahhabi army remained in the background as the ultimate sanction. The full rigor of the *Shariah* for crimes of violence or robbery was imposed, and security improved to the extent that the Hejaz became one of the safest places for individual citizens in the world, as it is today. This in addition to the measures he took to assist the Muslim pilgrims allowed their numbers to increase to 100,000 a year in the 1920s. The pilgrim fee of £5 per head in gold increased the revenues of the Kingdom far beyond anything he had known in Najd.

To administer the Kingdom Ibn Saud needed outside help, but he was determined to rely on Muslim Arabs, such as the Iraqi Abdullah Damluji, the Lebanese Fuad Hamzah, the Syrian Yusuf Yasin, and the Egyptian Hafiz Wahba, who had already acted as his diplomatic representative for some years and was to be ambassador in London for more than thirty years. However, he gave the key post of Finance Minister to a native of Najd, Shaykh Abdullah Sulaiman, who had been Ibn Saud's confidential secretary. He proved extremely able when the Kingdom faced acute difficulties a few years later. The only members of his family he entrusted with office were his eldest surviving son Saud, who became his Viceroy in Najd, and his younger brother Faisal, Viceroy of the Hejaz. Faisal had remarkable success in winning over the Hejazis who were naturally suspicious and resentful of the Wahhabis from Najd.

But if Ibn Saud was prepared to accept advice and remained highly approachable, he kept all executive power in his own hands (and did so until his death). At the same time he never laid claim to any oriental mystique of kingship. God was the only ruler, and his task was to ensure that His law was applied. Inevitably, however, there were differences with the stern Wahhabi shaykhs over interpretation of the law and, more precisely, over what was prohibited by the Holy Koran. On such matters as liquor and prostitution there was no doubt, and the Wahhabi Committee for the Commendation of Virtue and the Condemnation of Vice represented by the *mutawwiun* or religious police at once became active in the Hejaz. Tobacco was more questionable. In Najd it was prohibited together with the wearing by men of silk or articles made from the precious metals. Ameen Rihani noted that tobacco addicts in Riyadh hid away to smoke like guilty schoolboys. But in the Hejaz the tobacco trade was open and flourishing. Ibn Saud first considered confiscating and destroying all the tobacco stocks, but when the merchants complained about the enormous loss this would entail, he relented. They could dispose of these but import no more. However, by this time tobacco duty was recognized as an important item of state revenue and imports were discreetly allowed to continue. Tobacco, after all, (like coffee, which was nearly banned by strict Muslims in the Middle Ages) could not have been mentioned in the Holy Koran.

Nevertheless, some of the more extreme Wahhabis continued to oppose the use of tobacco. They also objected to radios, telephones, bicycles, and motor cars as infidel inventions. In extreme cases they were denounced as the works of Satan. When the first truck entered the exceptionally fanatical town of Hawtah, it was promptly burned by the inhabitants and its driver narrowly escaped with his life. Record players remained forbidden for many years and public cinemas are banned to this day.

Ibn Saud was determined that his kingdom should have those Western inventions that would strengthen it and make life easier for its people provided these did not undermine their way of life. Like all wise leaders, he did not try to force the pace but to use persuasion where possible. A gathering of religious shaykhs was convinced that the telephone was not the instrument of the devil when they heard on it a voice reciting the Holy Koran. (Thirty years later his son King Faisal had to use much the same methods to overcome objections to television.) On the use of radio and the motor car he was adamant because of their obvious necessity in holding the kingdom together. He told the *ulama* of Najd who came to see him that these were "two matters which I will not discuss because I am convinced of their great importance to me and to my country, and that they are permissible according to Islam." He also established a whole network of radio stations throughout his territories.

The need for radio—and indeed also for aircraft—was underlined in 1929 and 1930 when Ibn Saud faced a full-scale revolt of some of the Ikhwan. The warriors of the Ikhwan had fought and won for him in the Hejaz, but they were not all prepared to submit to his leadership. They denounced his Western innovations and also demanded the right to raid across the borders into Iraq and Transjordan, whose people they regarded as infidels. Ibn Saud knew this would be disastrous as these countries, which were British mandates, were defended by British planes and armored cars.

The dissident Ikhwan found their leaders in Faisal al Dawish, head of the tribe of Mutayr and chief of the original Ikhwan settlement at Artawiyah, and Sultan ibn Bijad of Ghatghat, conqueror of Taif in 1924. After four months of desultory warfare Ibn Saud defeated them in the battle of Sibilah. Sultan surrendered and died in prison. The King pardoned Faisal al Dawish whom he thought to be mortally wounded, but Faisal recovered among his tribe and with his allies resumed raiding against Iraq and Kuwait. Finally Ibn Saud took the field against them in person and defeated them soundly. Faisal sought asylum in Kuwait with the British, who handed him over to Ibn Saud. He died in prison a few months later.

This was the last revolt of the Ikhwan, who gradually faded away as Ibn Saud imposed his own authority throughout his territories. As Philby remarked: "Ibn Saud's creation of the Ikhwan movement in 1912, on original lines of his own devising, was a master-stroke of genius: only equalled by his own courageous liquidation of the organization eighteen years later, when it could be nothing but an obstacle to the consolidation of a position which he had built up so patiently and laboriously."

Ibn Saud had reached the limits of his territorial ambitions in the Peninsula, although the demarcation of boundaries with the British-protected states on the Gulf remained unsettled and was to produce problems in the future. The only immediate problem was in the province of Asir on the borders of Yemen. Following Ibn Saud's acquisition of the mountain districts of Asir in 1920, a civil war had broken out between rival members of the local ruling Idrisi family, relatives of the North African Idrisis, for control of the truncated Asir. The Imam Yahya of Yemen and Ibn Saud supported opposing sides. Ibn Saud's protégé won, and in return had to accept what amounted to a Saudi protectorate. The Imam had succeeded in occupying and annexing the Red Sea coastal plain of Tihamah, but had not given up his ambitions toward Asir and the neighboring valley of Najran. His aggressive actions provoked a brief Saudi-Yemeni war in 1934. Ibn Saud sent two invading columns, one led by Prince Saud toward the Yemeni capital Sana and the other headed by Prince Faisal along the coast. Saud was held up by the mountainous terrain but Faisal occupied the main Yemeni port of Hudaydah, where Ibn Saud ordered him to halt. Peace negotiations, in which Ibn Saud behaved with generosity and magnanimity, abstaining from any demands on Yemeni territory, led to a Treaty of Taif of "Muslim Friendship and Arab Fraternity" on May 20, 1934. This treaty was the basis of untroubled relations between the two countries for the next thirty years.

On September 18, 1932, the dual kingdom of Hejaz and

Sultanate of Najd were officially unified as the Kingdom of Saudi Arabia. The name of Saud is now so closely associated with that of Arabia that it is easy to forget that the formal link has only existed half a century. Ibn Saud's first instrument of unification for the Peninsula was the sword, which he used with extraordinary courage and daring. This was always combined with statesmanship and moderation in dealing with his enemies, except in cases of rank treachery. His third instrument was marriage.

Ibn Saud used to claim that he followed the Prophet in three things: prayer, scent, and women. The wearing of silk or gold ornaments is prohibited for Wahhabis but not perfume which the Prophet was known to use plentifully. Ibn Saud was also a great lover of women. Although, like all Arabs, he kept his domestic life strictly private and never discussed the women of his family with others, it is probable that he married something approaching three hundred wives during his lifetime. But this would include both the long-standing unions with wives such as Hissah Bint Sudairi, mother of seven of the forty-one royal princes who survived him, and those he married from important tribes in the Kingdom and divorced after a brief period. He also had a limited number of concubines; some of these were slaves and on occasion he gave them their freedom and married them.

For Ibn Saud, easy divorce played an important political role. Just as his marriage to the widow of his old Rashidi enemy helped to end the ancient feud between the families, so his marriage to the daughters of the heads of many Arabian clans assisted the unification of his kingdom. Even if he soon divorced one of them this was no disgrace. She retained an honored position, especially if, as was hoped, she gave birth to a royal prince.

All this was of course in accordance with Koranic injunctions on marriage and the treatment of women. He never had more than four wives at a time and in obedience to God's command that "if you fear you may not do justice to them, then [marry] only one," (Koran IV. 8.) he always tried to treat them with equal consideration.

It is hardly necessary to say that whereas this licensed

polygamy seems both morally shocking and socially undesirable to many non-Muslim Westerners, the Arabs of Arabia find Western promiscuity and openly tolerated adultery equally deplorable. They also would claim that their polygamy—and their easy divorce even more so—ensure that there are not the multitudes of women with no hope of getting married in their society. They have to acknowledge that easy divorce is the prerogative of the man in Muslim society, but they would not concede that complete equality between men and women in such matters is either desirable or attainable.

9
The Lean Years

*B*efore Ibn Saud conquered the Hejaz, his total revenue from all sources was about £150,000 a year; the British subsidy provided an additional £60,000 a year. After 1926 customs duties and the pilgrims' dues increased the Kingdom's income for a time. A small start could be made in providing medical services, sanitation, and schools to supplement the existing Koranic education. The nucleus of a regular army was created and provided with modern rifles and machine guns. A rudimentary transport and communications system was created; the number of motor cars increased from less than a dozen in 1926 to 1,200 in 1930. In that same year Ibn Saud obtained his first aircraft—four ancient British biplanes.

The Great Depression had disastrous consequences for even these modest efforts at development. The number of pilgrims fell from an average of 100,000 a year in the 1920s to 40,000 in 1931, 30,000 in 1932, and only 20,000 in 1933. Customs dues from imports associated with the pilgrims fell also, and at the end of 1931 the desperate Finance Minister Abdullah Sulaiman was forced to declare a moratorium on all the Kingdom's debts and to commandeer for ready cash the gasoline stocks of two private companies in Jiddah. One of these belonged to an outraged Philby. Major Frank Holmes's oil concession had lapsed as he ceased payments after two years. But the King had never expected him to find oil anyway.

By the autumn of 1932 the King was ready to overcome his

doubts about letting Western investment and non-Muslim technicians into his sternly traditional society. When Philby asked him why he was still hesitating, while bemoaning his country's poverty, he replied: ''Oh, Philby, if anyone would offer me a million pounds, I would give him all the concessions he wanted.''

The King's earlier assumption, generally shared by Western oil geologists, that there was no oil beneath his territory, had changed. After only six months' drilling the Bahrain Petroleum Company (in fact Standard Oil of California, incorporated as a Canadian subsidiary to get round the ban on non-British companies in the Anglo-Bahraini Treaty) struck oil in Bahrain in commercial quantities in May 1932.

Since Bahrain lies only twenty miles off the coast of Saudi Arabia, Standard at once became interested in Ibn Saud's eastern territories. The King had already commissioned an American mining engineer, Karl Twitchell, to study potential underground water and oil resources in the area. For the previous five years Twitchell had been making surveys of this kind in Yemen and Saudi Arabia, at the expense of Charles Crane, the distinguished U.S. businessman turned diplomat and philanthropist. Twitchell undertook to approach U.S. oil companies, and Philby, who had already been contacted by Standard, acted as go-between.

Realizing that competition would help Saudi Arabia's interests, Philby brought the Anglo-Persian Oil Company into the affair. But although APOC made an offer (through the Iraq Petroleum Company [IPC] in which it held a 23.75 percent share), it was never really in the running. The truth was that although APOC was anxious to keep new American companies out of the region, it already had more than enough oil of its own in Iran and Iraq. Stephen Longrigg, the IPC negotiator, was authorized to offer no more than £5,000 in rupees for a concession. After some hard bargaining, Standard was prepared to offer £50,000 as a cash advance against future royalties plus £5,000 a year in gold for the concession. On May 29, 1933, Standard Oil of California's concession was signed. Philby relates that the King, bored with the reading of endless clauses, dozed off more than once and only woke up with a start at the end to tell the Finance Minister: "Put your trust in God, and sign."

In this way the foundations were laid for the close relationship between Saudi Arabia and the United States which has so influenced the modern history of the Middle East. Philby, although British, played an important role in seeing that the concession went to an American rather than a British company. Patriotic in his way, Philby was an idiosyncratic rebel; his anti-imperialism made him believe that the United States rather than Britain deserved the concession. The King himself probably shared this view, although he was never anti-British. Like most Saudis he was mildly xenophobic, while always courteous to foreigners. But Englishmen like Shakespear and Cox were among the men he admired most. He consistently hoped and believed that Britain would not be defeated in World War II, against the views of most of his own counselors.

In 1936 Standard Oil of California (Socal) sold half its concession to the Texas Company, which had the world marketing outlets that Socal lacked but no oil of its own. In 1944 the California Arabian Standard Oil Company, or Casoc, as it was then called, changed its name to the Arabian American Oil Company (Aramco). In 1948 two other American Companies took shares in Aramco: Standard Oil (New Jersey) which took thirty percent and Socony Vacuum which took ten percent.

Aramco was a major force in Middle Eastern affairs but it was never a simple instrument of U.S. foreign policy. In fact it was often at loggerheads with Washington. On the whole this suited the State Department's interests when the United States, urged on by Congress, was providing massive support for the newly-formed State of Israel to which the Saudi government was always bitterly opposed. A clash between the oil lobby and the Zionist lobby in Washington was avoided, or at least postponed. On the other hand, the fact that American oil companies developed Saudi Arabia's major natural resource has profoundly influenced modern Saudi society. In fulfilment of its concession agreement, Aramco helped to train young Saudis. The trend inevitably intensified as the connection spread into other fields so that by the 1960s the great majority of Saudi Arabia's Western-educated technocrats were the product of American institutions of learning. This was in contrast to the Gulf states, where they tended to go to Britain.

Casoc at once began geological surveys of the promising great dome at Jabal Dhahran. The first well was drilled in April 1935, and oil was struck in commercial quantities in March 1938. "The lid was off!" remarked F. A. Davies, later chairman of Aramco. Casoc now had what was to prove to be the world's richest oil concession.

Jabal Dhahran and the surrounding desert at once sprouted wells, pipelines, and storage tanks. An oil-loading berth was built on a spit of sand in the Gulf called Ras Tanura. When the first tanker arrived to take on the first cargo, the King arrived to attend the celebrations. He camped in his tents outside the newly-planted American oil town with its air-conditioned houses, gardens, and shrubs. The King was so pleased with the company that he increased the size of the concession to 440,000 square miles, over half the area of the country.

The prospects for the Kingdom of Saudi Arabia had been transformed. But before the effect of the new wealth could be felt, World War II intervened to plunge the country into an even deeper crisis, made more painful by the new expectations that had been nourished. In 1939 Casoc produced about four million barrels of oil for which it paid about $1.9 million. But, with the disruption in world oil markets during the war years, royalties declined to about half that amount. At the same time the number of pilgrims, which had been picking up in the late 1930s, fell to a trickle, and a series of droughts increased the country's misery.

Once again the King was desperate, but this time, confident in the size of the country's oil potential, he felt able to ask Casoc for a loan against future royalties. The company was aware of its obligations toward the Kingdom and responded with a loan of $3 million but, feeling that it could not support the Kingdom's budget throughout the war, appealed to the U.S. government. President Roosevelt was sympathetic, but at that time there was no existing law under which the U.S. government could extend aid directly to the Saudi government. A solution was found through the British. The United States had not yet entered the war, but Britain was heavily involved in the Middle East and Saudi Arabia's sympathetic neutrality was vital. Britain was already providing Saudi Arabia with some £400,000 a year; it was agreed that Britain should increase this by using some of the $400 million U.S. Lend-Lease funds which had just been approved by the Congress. As the company's aid was reduced, British aid rose to about $12 million in 1942 and $16.5 million in 1943. However, the company then became alarmed that the British were using their aid to supplant U.S. and oil company influence. In March 1943 the British actually proposed a plan for a Saudi Arabian note issue with the creation of a Saudi Arabian Currency Control Board in London.

The oil company succeeded in impressing the U.S. government of the danger, and in February 1943 President Roosevelt signed a letter to the Lend-Lease administrator, Edward Stettinius saying ''that the defense of Saudi Arabia is vital to the defense of the United States.'' This made it possible for Lend-Lease aid to be provided directly to Saudi Arabia.

This appeal to the government on the part of the oil company had planted a seed in the fertile mind of Roosevelt's ebullient Secretary for the Interior, Harold Ickes. He proposed to the president that the government establish its own organization ''to acquire and participate in the development of foreign oil reserves'' in order to ensure America's strategic supplies. In this way the government-owned Petroleum Reserve Corporation (PRC) came into existence with Ickes as its unpaid president and chairman of its board. Ickes then proposed that the PRC should buy the whole of the California Arabian Standard Oil Company (Casoc). This proposal for a form of nationalization aroused the opposition of much of the oil industry. Moreover, since by then the Germans had been chased out of North Africa and the Axis threat to the Middle East had receded, the oil companies no longer felt the need for U.S. government protection.

The plan to buy Casoc was dropped. But Ickes then developed a new idea to build a huge oil pipeline from the Gulf to the Mediter-

---

ranean to provide an outlet for both Saudi and Kuwaiti oil. This would have the double advantage of ensuring a regular supply of cheap oil to the government and of leading inevitably to an agreement with the British, and so guaranteeing the position of U.S. oil companies in the area. This time Casoc was in favor of the idea, but the rest of the oil industry was still vigorously opposed to any government stake in the oil business.

However, the pipeline project in itself was sound. As soon as the war was over the partners in the newly expanded Aramco formed the Trans-Arabian Pipe Line Company (Tapline) and built the pipeline from the Saudi oilfields through Jordan and Syria to Sidon in Lebanon. It was opened in 1950.

As we have seen, King Ibn Saud consistently trusted in an Allied victory in the war. This was against the opinion of most of those around him, including Philby, who took a pacifist line before the outbreak of war and afterwards advised the King that the Germans would win and Saudi Arabia should remain neutral. In 1940 Philby unwisely decided to make a lecture tour of the United States; certain that the lectures would be defeatist and damaging, the British authorities had him arrested (or "kidnapped" in Philby's own words) on his way through India and returned him to spend six months in jail under Section 18B of World War I's Defence of the Realm Act.

Ibn Saud, on the other hand, insisted that Germany would be defeated. When his advisors greeted the announcement of the sinking of the British battleship *Hood* with applause he told them to wait and see, and when a few days later the German pocket battleship *Bismarck* was sunk, he made them stand up and clap again.

He was of course dependent on Anglo-American finance during the war, while German aid was purely hypothetical. Moreover, by the end of 1943 it was clear that he had been right and the Allies were going to win. When Churchill wrote of Ibn Saud in his war memoirs: "My admiration for him was deep, because of his unfailing loyalty to us," he was, as often, romantic in his judgment. Ibn Saud was loyal only to his faith and his people, and in his view, support for the Allies was in Saudi Arabia's interest. At the same time, he and his advisors (who included many "Northern Arabs": Palestinians, Syrians, Iraqis, Egyptians, etc.) had deep-grained doubts about Western motives and especially the position which concerned them most: the Balfour Declaration in favor of a Jewish National Home in Palestine. (Before the war a tentative agreement was worked out with Germany on the initiative of the King's Syrian Secretary, Yusuf Yasin, whereby the Germans would supply arms to Saudi Arabia, some of which it was understood would go to Palestinian Arabs who were in rebellion against the British Mandate. But with the outbreak of war the agreement was never implemented.)

Sir Reader Bullard, a prominent British Arabist and diplomat, recounts how he happened to call on the King in January 1938 on the same evening that the BBC Arabic Service was being inaugurated. One of the first items on the news bulletin concerned the hanging of an Arab in Palestine for being in possession of arms. The King told Bullard the next day that when he and his followers heard this they had all wept. "Now," he said, "as a ruler I know that the first business of a government is to maintain order. I also know that no man in Palestine has been punished by the British for his political opinions, but only for some offense against the law. Nevertheless, if it had not been for the Zionist policy of the British government, that Arab could have been alive today."

This fairly summarizes Ibn Saud's consistent attitude on Palestine. While he constantly advised the Palestinian Arabs against the use of violence, he adamantly rejected the proposal that the Zionists had rights in Palestine, still less that Britain had the authority to award them.

At the outset of the war, Philby devised a crackpot scheme with the Zionist leaders in London whereby Palestine would be partitioned and large numbers of Jews would be settled in the west of the country. In return a £20 million loan from Zionist sources would be provided to Ibn Saud who would become a sort of Arab overlord, or "boss of bosses" in Churchill's phrase to the Zionist leader Chaim Weizmann. Philby deluded himself into thinking that both Roosevelt and Ibn Saud would approve the scheme, but the King was in fact enraged by the suggestion that Weizmann could get him to sell Palestine for £20 million. When Colonel Hoskins, the head of a U.S. mission to Riyadh, raised the matter with Ibn Saud in 1943, he exploded with anger.

President Roosevelt's policy toward the Arab-Zionist dispute was to give vigorous encouragement to both sides. In October 1944 he told a convention of American Zionists that he knew how long and ardently the Jewish people had worked and prayed for the establishment of Palestine as a free and democratic Jewish commonwealth and added: "If re-elected I will bring about its realization." Four months later, on his return from the Yalta Conference, he proposed a meeting with Ibn Saud.

The health of the 65-year-old King had been declining. He was lame from arthritis and one eye was closed by a skin complaint. An American destroyer took him to see the invalid president in the Great Bitter Lake of the Suez Canal.

On a personal level the meeting was a success. The president gave Ibn Saud his spare wheelchair; he never used it because it was too small but he kept it as a souvenir. Their mutual esteem was strong, and when Roosevelt returned to Washington he told Congress: "Of the problems of Arabia, I learned more about the whole problem, the Muslim problem, the Jewish problem, by talking with Ibn Saud for five minutes than I could have learned in exchanges of two or three dozen letters."

But in the president's basic aim of persuading the King to agree to the large-scale settlement of Jewish Palestine he made no progress. Ibn Saud said that the sufferings of the Jews were the responsibility of Europe, not the Arabs. If necessary, they should be settled in parts of Germany but not in the poor and overcrowded land of Palestine. President Roosevelt ended by giving a promise that the basic situation in Palestine would not be altered without both Arabs and Jews being consulted.

As with President Wilson's declarations at the end of World War I, the Arabs were due for disappointment. Roosevelt seemed all-powerful to Ibn Saud, but, as president, he could not commit the United States to any permanent course. Within a few weeks he was dead and President Truman soon abandoned the attempt to balance U.S. policy between Arabs and Jews. This was something Ibn Saud could neither understand nor forgive. But for the time being the King was very warmly disposed toward Washington. From the canal he went on to the Fayyum Oasis, fifty miles southwest of Cairo, to meet Churchill. This encounter was much less of a success, although Churchill praised Ibn Saud as a "friend in need" in the dark days of the war. Unlike Roosevelt, Churchill refused to abstain from drinking and smoking in the King's presence. But this was a small matter. A lifelong Zionist, Churchill was not prepared to make any promises to Ibn Saud over Palestine.

Both the United States and Britain wanted Saudi Arabia to join the Grand Alliance against the Axis powers so that it could become a founding member of the new United Nations organization. They both hoped that the Saudi Kingdom would play a leading role in Arab politics after the war, although they certainly had an exaggerated idea of Saudi power and influence at this stage. But U.N. membership required a formal declaration of war against Germany and Japan, and Ibn Saud regarded this as absurd for his country, which had no quarrel with either. Eventually he succumbed to his friends' pressure; Saudi Arabia was represented at the San Francisco signing of the United Nations charter by the grave and dignified Prince Faisal, who acted as his father's Foreign Minister.

10

The Price of Affluence

As soon as the war was over, Aramco resumed the expansion of oil production. Work also began at once on the Tapline pipeline which was finished by the end of 1950. Oil output increased from the 65,000 tons in 1938 to 23 million tons in 1949. Revenues rose from half a million dollars to $39 million in 1949 and $56 million in 1950.

Although a million dollars a week seems negligible at a time when Saudi Arabia receives more than twice that amount every hour, it amounted to a revolution for the impoverished Kingdom of the 1940s. Ibn Saud's system of government, with his traditional Majlis al Shura, or Consultative Council of influential citizens, and the sprinkling of Arab advisors in key executive posts, had been adequate. In some of the regions, families related to the Saudis by marriage, such as the Sudairis in various places or the Jiluwis in the Eastern Province, held considerable autonomous power as regional governors. Ibn Saud's sons Saud and Faisal also marginally increased their responsibilities as Viceroys of Najd and the Hejaz. But all major decisions concerning foreign and domestic policy remained in the King's hands. There was no cabinet and no budget. Oil revenues were part of the King's Privy Purse, and he continued to dispense them with the same openhanded generosity to his family and to loyal shaykhs as when there were no more than a few hundred gold sovereigns in his coffers.

The effect on some of the royal princes, of whom there were now more than 2,000, was devastating. They wanted to acquire all the products of Western consumer society as soon as they saw them, and there were plenty of unscrupulous salesmen ready to provide them at inflated prices. This was the era when the world first began to hear of the "oil shaykhs." Ludicrous stories circulated in the Western press about Cadillacs imported and abandoned as soon as their ashtrays were filled, and ten-gallon cans of Chanel No. 5 left stacked in the sun or used as bathwater.

The King himself was too old to change his way of life. He built himself a new palace in Riyadh—rambling, in the traditional style of his ancestors—but he had no taste for luxury. His only recreations were hunting, horsemanship, and desert expeditions. He spent many hours in conversation with his friends, advisors, and visitors. Often the talk would be of religion or politics—both world events and Arabian affairs. In gayer moods it would be of women; he was fond of teasing those around him.

Although he had an inquiring mind, he had little interest in formal education, and perhaps his gravest fault was that he gave none to his sons beyond Koranic teaching. He was fortunate that some of them, such as Faisal, were of high natural intelligence which they were able to apply to their experiences in world affairs.

Ibn Saud may not have had extravagant tastes but he indulged some personal whims such as the building of a railway from Riyadh to Dammam on the Gulf. Aramco built it at a cost of $160 million against future royalties. It was totally uneconomic. However, it was the huge and growing appetite for luxury among his enormous family, which effectively included not only the Al Saud but collateral families such as the Jiluwis, Sudairis, and the Al al Shaykh, descendants of Muhammad ibn Abd al Wahhab, which brought the country close to bankruptcy despite the increasing revenues. In 1950 the King began asking why Saudi Arabia should still get only 21 cents per barrel of oil from Aramco when Venezuela had passed a law for a fifty-fifty share in oil profits between the companies and the government. (Aramco's profit was $1.10 per barrel.) Together with the State Department, which was worried about the communist danger in the Middle East, Aramco devised a scheme whereby additional payments to the King would be regarded as a foreign income tax which meant that they would not be taxable inside the United States. Ibn Saud received an extra $50 million a year which was lost to the U.S. Treasury. It was not a genuine fifty-fifty division of profits or anything like it, but could be presented as such and rapidly became the norm throughout the Middle East.

Although much was kept from the old King about the high-living behavior of some of the princes, he knew enough to sadden him toward the end of his life. This did not prevent him from continuing to pour out money to them, although he would accompany his gifts with lectures on the need to uphold the standards of their ancestors. An incident that could not be hidden from him concerned one of his sons who, on being asked to leave a party at the British Consul's in Jiddah because of his behavior, returned and shot his host dead through the window. The enraged old King wanted to have the prince put to death and was only dissuaded with difficulty by other members of the family. But he ordered that alcohol, which had previously been permitted in limited quantities to non-Muslims, should be prohibited throughout the Kingdom.

The last two years of the King's life were spent in virtual retirement in Riyadh. In the very last days of his reign he accepted the need for some kind of state structure and appointed a Council of Ministers. But it never met during his lifetime. Similarly, U.S. pressure persuaded him to allow the creation of the Saudi Arabian Monetary Agency (SAMA) under an American director. But it had no power and spending remained unbudgeted and uncontrolled. Some of the country's new wealth was spent on public works. Jiddah Port was expanded, airports built in Riyadh and Jiddah, and a few hundred miles of surfaced roads constructed. Increasing sums were spent on the still small nucleus of regular armed forces; Taif and Kharj became military training centers with American instructors to replace the earlier British military mission sent there during the war.

Aramco made a major contribution with schools, hospitals, roads, and a model farm in the Kharj district south of Riyadh. But most of the revenues at this stage went to fulfill the needs and whims of the royal princes. There was nothing resembling a comprehensive plan to raise living standards or provide schools and clinics for the mass of Saudis who were still poor, hungry, and unhealthy. To do so would have meant importing many foreigners to run these services, and Saudi Arabia had no administrative cadre to supervise them.

The old King was not willing to contemplate such an invasion and disruption of the Arabian way of life. The oil town of Dhahran in the Eastern Province had already seen a huge influx of foreign workers—Syrians, Palestinians, Sudanese, Indians—in addition to 1,200 Americans. Although Aramco was drawing increasing numbers of Saudis into its employment, the oil town remained largely isolated from the rest of the country, with its supermarket, cinemas, and television station, a Little America in Arabia. This was satisfactory to most Americans and Saudis.

Ibn Saud died on November 9, 1953, in Taif where he had gone to spend his last months. An immense crowd of mourners heard the prayers for the dead read over him in the city's great open prayer ground. His achievement had been immense; but because it was so great and he had done so little to prepare his heirs, his legacy was difficult to manage.

Prince Saud, who succeeded him, was physically as impressive as his father, courageous, amiable, and popular with the tribes. But he lacked Ibn Saud's shrewdness and statesmanship. He had traveled much more widely than his father but that was the limit of his political education. He had acquired high ambitions whereas Ibn Saud always knew the limits of Saudi power.

At home Saud's accession brought an acceleration of extravagant spending. As Crown Prince, his $11 million palace with myriads of colored fairy lights, many of them fused, had been notorious. Now two new ones—each costing $25 million—were built in Riyadh and Jiddah. Scarce water was piped across the desert to supply the gardens. A start was made on building schools and hospitals, which were staffed by Egyptians, Palestinians, and other Arabs, and on improving the facilities for Muslim pilgrims, but these efforts were haphazard and inadequate. Far greater sums were spent on direct subsidies to tribal leaders, money not likely to be devoted to public works or services.

Another demand on the royal revenues was caused by King Saud's increasing involvement in Arab politics. His main impetus was to pursue his father's resolute opposition to the ambitions of his old Hashemite enemies. After the assassination of King Abdullah of Jordan in 1951 relations improved with Abdullah's son Talal and his grandson Hussein, who succeeded his father after a brief reign. But King Saud's concern was to prevent both Jordan and Syria from passing into the orbit of Iraq. Nuri Said, the ambitious elderly Iraqi statesman, had plans, with somewhat ill-defined British backing, for a union of Iraq and Syria, and to this Saud was resolutely opposed. When Britain in 1954 succeeded in launching the ill-fated Baghdad Pact uniting the anti-communist "northern tier" regimes of Iran, Pakistan, Turkey, and Iraq, and then attempted to persuade Jordan and Syria to join the Pact, Saudi Arabia joined with the new republican regime of Egypt in denouncing the Pact. Instead of adhering to the Pact, Syria formed a joint military command with Saudi Arabia and Egypt in October 1955. Two months later King Hussein decided not to join the Pact when his country was swept by riots.

The Baghdad Pact was never popular with the majority of the public in the Arab states who regarded Israel as their enemy rather than the Soviet Union. This was the reason the staunch anti-communist crusader, Secretary of State John Foster Dulles, wisely decided that the United States should not join the Pact, although he had originated the idea. At the same time the Saudi-Egyptian campaign against the Pact, financed by Saudi Arabia, was highly effective in strengthening Arab opposition.

All this was expensive for Saudi Arabia. A $10 million loan was provided to Syria in 1955 and again the following year. The result of this foreign spending combined with domestic extravagance was to place Saudi Arabia in debt. This was a remarkable achievement considering that revenues had risen from $56 million in 1950 to $341 million in 1955. Aramco, which was reducing its production in accordance with its world marketing plans, refused to make any further advances against royalties and dissuaded foreign agencies from making loans to the Saudi government. As contractors' bills remained unpaid, international business confidence in the Saudi regime collapsed. The Saudi *riyal* fell to half its official value. Gold and foreign currency holdings of the Saudi Arabian Monetary Agency fell to a bare 14 percent of the note issue.

In 1956 the Arab political scene was transformed and radicalized by the Suez affair. Egypt's young revolutionary leader, Gamal Abdal Nasser, had already gained popularity throughout the Arab countries, especially among the younger generation, by his defiance of the West, which was still identified with imperialism. Instead of accepting that Egypt was a Western satellite, as it had so long been regarded, he had opposed the Baghdad Pact, bought arms from the Soviet Union, recognized Communist China, and vigorously supported the Algerian Revolution against France. In July 1956, he nationalized the Suez Canal Company. In the following October the two old colonial powers, France and Britain, committed the supreme folly of attacking Egypt in accordance with a prearranged plan with Israel. When the United Nations, led by the United States, forced Britain and France to make a humiliating withdrawal from the Canal Zone and Israel to remove its hold on Sinai and Gaza, Nasser became an Arab hero. The popularity of his radical nationalism became a threat to all the established Arab regimes.

Prince Faisal, as Saudi Foreign Minister, openly expressed support for Egypt's defiance of the West and thereby gained the reputation of being a sympathizer with Nasserism. But after the Suez War, events took a different turn. The Eisenhower-Dulles administration in Washington had effectively opposed the Anglo-French-Israeli invasion of Egypt but now identified the danger to the Middle East as triumphant Nasserism in alliance with the Soviet Union. The U.S. government at once set about mending its bridges to Britain and France and joined in their boycott of Egypt which became heavily dependent on the Soviet Union as a consequence. On January 5, 1957, President Eisenhower in a message to Congress promised military and financial aid to any Middle Eastern country "requesting such aid against overt aggression from any nation controlled by international Communism." This became known as the Eisenhower Doctrine, and it was a clear invitation to the Arab governments to declare themselves pro-Western and anti-Soviet.

While the Jordanian and Iraqi monarchies and Lebanon's right-wing President Camille Chamoun responded favorably, the Saudi reaction was less clear. King Saud was certainly alarmed by the radical republican trend in the Arab world, but it would not be easy to join an alliance with his old Hashemite enemies. Faisal was still expressing support for Egypt, but he was seriously unwell and undergoing medical treatment. It was at this point that an invitation arrived for King Saud to make an official visit to the United States. The U.S. government had surprisingly decided that it would be possible to build up Saud as a popular rival Arab leader to Nasser.

The visit was marred by a frigid reception in New York City and the refusal of Mayor Wagner to greet him, although President Eisenhower and Mr. Dulles did their best to make it up to him with extra warmth in Washington. King Saud explained that if he was to stand as the representative of an alternative policy to Nasser's neutralism, the United States must provide support in practical and visible terms. President Eisenhower agreed to substantial arms supplies, technical assistance, and a $250 million loan. In return King Saud promised to renew the U.S. contract for the use of the Dhahran airfield for five years and to explain the Eisenhower Doctrine to the other Arab leaders.

In fact King Saud never endorsed the Eisenhower Doctrine unequivocally. He seems to have believed somewhat naively that he could persuade Nasser, if not to accept the Doctrine, to remain neutral. But Nasser's opposition was relentless. He saw it, like the Baghdad Pact, as an attempt to perpetuate Western domination of the Arabs and dragoon them into hostility toward the Soviet Union.

This was the popular view, and King Saud was not prepared

to take a public stand against the tide. However, he did act in other ways. When King Hussein of Jordan decided to confront his own leftward-looking government and an incipient pro-Nasser revolt in the army, Saud responded to Hussein's request to send some of his troops into Jordan. In May 1957 he paid a state visit to Baghdad, the center of pro-Western anti-Nasserism in the Arab world, and finally made peace with his former Hashemite enemies.

Nasser's response was to launch his immensely powerful propaganda machine against Saud. Ahmed Said, Director of Cairo's Voice of the Arabs and possibly the best known figure in the Arab world after Nasser, poured out scornful invective. He had abundant material in Saud's personal extravagance and the arrogant misbehavior of some of the Saudi princes and shaykhs. A regular program called "Enemies of God" pointed to the wide gulf between the professed Islam puritanism of the Saudi regime and the habits of many of its members.

Prince Faisal spent the second half of 1957 in the United States undergoing two operations. He returned via Egypt where he had several meetings with Nasser; his public statements, although careful and cautious as was his way, expressed support for Nasser's neutralist policies. He returned to Saudi Arabia and a warm welcome from his brother Saud but, without any open rift, he was clearly distancing himself from Saud's policies.

In 1958 Nasser's career as an Arab nationalist leader reached its apogee. In February, Egypt's union with Syria, "the throbbing heart of Arabism," was declared. Three weeks later the Middle East was rocked with charges by the head of Syrian Military Intelligence of a plot by King Saud to have Nasser assassinated in order to prevent the Syrian-Egyptian union from taking place. The Damascus and Cairo press followed this up with detailed reports of the suppression of striking Aramco oil workers and the presence of a U.S. military air base at Dhahran.

Although these reports were colored by Cairo's propaganda machine, they contained strong elements of truth. They were certainly widely believed, and as a pro-Nasser mood swept the Middle East there was a serious possibility that the Saudi

Despite modernization and the introduction of new technologies, religious and cultural tradition is maintained in Arab states. (top) An oasis in Bahrain with an ancient burial mound in the background. (left) 300-year-old minarets remain standing among ruins near Manama, capital of Bahrain. (above) A traditional Kuwaiti sailing vessel. *MEPHA photos*

(above) The Kaabah is considered by Muslims to be the house of God built by the patriarch Abraham and his son Ishmael. (right) Aerial view of the Holy City of Mecca and the Great Mosque. *Camerapix photos* (opposite page, top) Muslim pilgrims perform the Tawaf, an obligatory seven circuits of the Kaabah, in the courtyard of the Great Mosque of Mecca. (lower left) Twin minarets of the Great Mosque dominate the Holy City, and a devout pilgrim reads Koranic verses while performing the Tawaf. *Camerapix photos*

Changes brought about by industrialization can be observed throughout the oil-producing Gulf states. (left) Riggers readying a drill in a Qatar oil field. (below) Complicated pipe structure at the Ras Tanura refinery in Saudi Arabia. *MEPHA photos* (opposite page, top) The Dubai drydock and ship repair complex was completed in the late 1970s at Port Rashid. *Costain photo* (center) The Jubail-Yanbu pipeline under construction in Saudi Arabia. *MEPHA photo* (lower left) A plaque commemorates the discovery of oil in Bahrain in 1932. *MEPHA photo* (lower right) A tanker loads oil at a Kuwaiti sea island loading facility. *Bechtel photo*

THE BAHRAIN PETROLEUM COMPANY LIMITED
DISCOVERY WELL IN BAHRAIN AND THE GULF AREA

JABAL AD DUKHAN Nº 1.

SPUDDED IN....OCTOBER 16, 1931
STRUCK OIL......JUNE 1, 1932
INITIAL FLOW RATE-400 BBLS/HOUR

(above left) Towers rise above the Kuwaiti landscape. (right) A graceful minaret contrasts with a multi-storied office building in Kuwait. (below) A private home in a style reminiscent of desert tents. *MEPHA photos* (opposite page) Modern apartments for rent in Dubai. (top right) Construction company signs give evidence of multinational activities. (bottom) A street scene in Kuwait. *MEPHA photos*

Foreign workers have been imported to meet expanding industrialization throughout the Gulf states. Korean workers (above) assemble at a Bahrain construction site. *MEPHA photo*

(opposite page) Foreigners and Arabians team up on road construction crew (bottom) and a truck stops at a construction site check point (center) in Saudia Arabia. *MEPHA photos* (above) A contemporary project in Kuwait offers modern, comfort-able, low cost housing. *MEPHA photo* (below) Nearly completed, the Sharjal Hotel in the United Arab Emirates is an example of the contemporary architectural design of new construction in the Gulf region. *Bech-tel photo*

(above) Young girl in contemporary dress contrasts with woman in traditional clothes in this Bahrain market street scene. (right) Workers lay sewer pipe as rapid growth of construction and cities brings change to this Saudi street. *MEPHA photos*

Diners in the Gulf states can choose their fare from among many of the cuisines of the world, including American fast foods (top) or elegant continental style served in modern hotels (left). *MEPHA photos*

Under a 20-year contract to the Bechtel Companies of the U.S.A. the largest engineering and construction complex in the world is underway in Jubail, Saudi Arabia. In 20 years, the industrial site will hold a community of nearly 400,000 people. It will include oil refineries, petrochemical, fertilizer, aluminum, steel, and other industrial plants. A two-port complex will make Jubail a premier Gulf port.

More than 7,000 workers were on the site in 1981 and more than 30,000 will be there by the mid-80s. (above) Ceremonial arch beam at 1977 inauguration of project. *Bechtel photos*

(top) Advanced design is displayed in the striking administration and classroom building of Kuwait University. (bottom) Lights illuminate a modern mosque and contemporary office buildings in central Kuwait. *MEPHA photos*

(1) King Abdul Aziz ibn Saud (1932-1953)

(2) King Faisal bin Abdul Aziz al Saud (1964-1975)

(3) King Khalid bin Abdul Aziz al Saud (1975-)

(4) Heir apparent Prince Fahd bin Abdul Aziz al Saud

(5) Shaykh Khalifah bin Hamad al Thani, Emir of Qatar   *MEPHA photo*

6

7

8

(6) Shaykh Zayid bin Sultan al Nihayyan, President of the United Arab Emirates and ruler of Abu Dhabi *MEPHA photo*

(7) Shaykh Isa bin Salman al Khalifah, Emir of Bahrain *Camera Trends photo*

(8) Shaykh Rashid bin Said al Maktoum, ruler of Dubai *MEPHA photo*

(9) Shaykh Jabir al Ahmed al Sabah, Emir of Kuwait *MEPHA photo*

(10) Shaykh Saad al Abdullah al Salim al Sabah, heir apparent and Prime Minister of Kuwait *MEPHA photo*

9

10

monarchy could be overthrown.

It was then that the Saudi royal family and the senior *ulama* allied to it, decided, out of a rational sense of self-preservation, that action should be taken. Prince Abdullah ibn Abd al Rahman, the brother of Ibn Saud, who carried high prestige as the senior member of the family, took soundings and found a consensus that Saud should abdicate in favor of Faisal. But Faisal, who had promised his father never to take action against Saud, refused. It was decided that Saud should remain King in name only but delegate all his powers to Faisal. Saud accepted without hesitation; he had no choice.

On March 25, 1958, Mecca Radio interrupted a reading from the Koran in its Ramadan program to announce that the King had handed over his powers to the Emir Faisal.

11
Faisal in Power

*F*aisal took swift action to tackle the country's critical condition. With advice from the International Monetary Fund and the World Bank, of which Saudi Arabia was now a member, he set about restoring the nation's finances. Proper budgets were introduced for the first time, and sharp cuts made in the largest single item of expenditure—the Privy Purse—which was progressively reduced by two-thirds. Faisal himself was a man of simple and austere tastes. His home was modest compared with Saud's desert Versailles. He frequently drove himself to work or, if not, sat in front with the driver and without his brother's large armed bodyguard.

Commercial banks were obliged to maintain 15 percent of their deposits as statutory reserves with SAMA, which for the first time began to perform some of the functions of a central bank. Within eighteen months the country had returned to solvency. Gold and currency reserves rose from $24 million to $186 million and prices fell. The riyal was officially devalued to a realistic level.

In foreign affairs Faisal's policy was to end Saud's attempt to rival Nasser's influence. He withdrew the Saudi troops from Jordan and cut off the subsidy to King Hussein. Nasser, who had welcomed his advent to power, stopped the attacks on the Saudi monarchy by the media of the new United Arab Republic. In July 1958 the Iraqi monarchy was overthrown by an army-led coup, and the young King Faisal, his uncle Crown Prince Abdul Ila, and Prime Minister Nuri Said were massacred. Nasser's radical republicanism

85

was triumphant in the Arab world but Saudi Arabia was less vulnerable. Faisal swiftly recognized the new regime in Iraq.

The reputation that Faisal had gained as a radical neutralist was in many ways misleading. Certainly he did not wish to see any of the Arab states, least of all Saudi Arabia, as a satellite of the West, but he also detested communism—which he consistently identified with Zionism. In his austerely traditional view of Islam he believed, like his father, that the Koran provided an adequate consti-tution and that the simple duty of the ruler was to uphold the *Shariah*. In fact he was politically ultra-conservative and many of Nasser's policies, which included suppression of the fundamentalist Muslim Brotherhood and close friendship with the Soviet Union, alarmed him, although he understood the reasons for them and on sound strategic grounds chose not to oppose them publicly.

Inevitably, Faisal's austerity was unpopular in some quarters. The middlemen who had been making huge profits by fulfilling the needs of the spendthrift princes were indignant. Saud had been prodigal in his gifts as well as his own spending, and the tribal leaders were angered that their subsidies should be reduced or cut off altogether. Thus although Faisal was infinitely more astute and intelligent than his brother and although his restoration of Saudi finances made it possible to initiate a real program to provide schools and hospitals, Saud retained some of the loyalties that had been the basis of his father's power. He was able to achieve a temporary comeback.

In order to recover his powers, Saud made an improbable alliance with some of the younger princes led by his brother Amir Talal, who professed superficially progressive ideas, and their allies among the intelligentsia who wanted rapid secular reforms. He promised to introduce a constitution and representative institu-tions such as elected municipal councils, perhaps even a parlia-ment. The coalition of anti-Faisal forces consisting of liberals and disgruntled tribal leaders was incongruous, but it enabled Saud to enforce Faisal's resignation as Prime Minister in December 1960. Saud became Prime Minister with Talal as his deputy and Finance Minister.

But Saud's career as a democratic and constitutional monarch was short-lived. A constitution providing for the right to form trade unions and a parliament which would be two-thirds elected, was announced on Mecca Radio, but the King refused to sign it. After nine months Prince Talal resigned and went into opposition. In 1962 he and three other princes went into exile in Cairo and announced the formation of the Front for the Liberation of Arabia. The event was given maximum publicity by the Egyptian media, for by then the dispute between Egypt and Saudi Arabia had been resumed with greater intensity.

It was now Saud's health which deteriorated, and he spent long periods abroad for treatment. The immense and costly retinue he took with him attracted the attention of the Western media as well as the Egyptian newspapers. Faisal resumed some of his powers in the King's absence; the country was ruled by an uneasy coalition of pro-Saud and pro-Faisal factions.

In September 1962 an event occurred in Arabia that brought an unprecedented challenge to the Saudi monarch. A group of Yemeni army officers overthrew the Imam Badr, who had just succeeded his father Ahmed, and declared a republic. Nasser at once sent a large expeditionary force to their support. The Imam fled to a mountain fastness in Northern Yemen where he was joined by members of his family who rallied their forces to fight back.

Nasserism had suffered a shattering setback a year earlier with Syria's secession from the United Arab Republic. The Yemeni affair provided Nasser with new opportunities. For the first time a republic had been declared in the Arabian Peninsula. From Yemen support could be given to the radical nationalists who were in revolt against Britain in the Federation of South Arabia (now the People's Democratic Republic of Yemen) which had recently been formed out of Aden Colony and Protectorate. A new radio station in Sanaa called the Voice of Free Arabia declared that the whole Peninsula would be liberated. It was unsparing in its attacks on the Saudi monarchy.

The threat to the Saudi regime was now serious. Although the regular armed forces had been built up to 40,000, with a 400-

strong American training mission, and they were well supplied with modern equipment, they were highly inexperienced. Their loyalties also seemed uncertain as two of Saudi Arabia's very few trained air force pilots defected to Cairo. At the same time Saudi Arabia was involved in the republican-royalist Yemeni civil war through its support and sympathy for the royalists. Egyptian aircraft were attacking Saudi border areas where the Yemeni royalists were concentrated.

In view of Saud's obvious incapacity to cope with this dangerous situation, the royal family once again rallied to oblige him to hand over full powers to Faisal. This time Saud, whose health was rapidly deteriorating, was unable to make a comeback. The family waited until 1964 to enforce his abdication. His sons and what remained of the pro-Saud faction in the royal family attempted to forestall the abdication by a last-minute effort to restore friendly relations with Egypt. But this failed and Saud went into exile. Sick and frail, he turned up in Cairo with his vast entourage in 1966. The Egyptians secured some propaganda advantage out of his presence and even took him for a tour of the republican-held areas of Yemen. He died in Europe in 1969.

Faisal acted with his customary quiet promptitude. Within a week of taking power he issued a Ten-Point Program which promised the promulgation of a Basic Law for the government of the country "drawn from the *Koran* and the Traditions of His Prophet and the acts of the Orthodox Caliphs, that will set forth explicitly the fundamental principles of government and relationship between the governor and the governed, organize the various powers of the state and the relationship among these powers, and provide for the basic rights of the citizen, including the right to freely express his opinion within the limit of Islamic belief and public policy."*

Other points provided for the formation of a Consultative Council, a new structure of local government, an independent judiciary with a Judicial Council, and various measures to improve

*Full text translation *Saudi Arabian Radio Broadcast* November 7, 1962 quoted in Gerald de Gaury *Feisal* London 1966, p. 148.

social services and encourage economic development. The Program also declared the final abolition of all slavery throughout the Kingdom. Since the only slaves that remained were domestic slaves who normally remained in the same family's employment after they had been freed, this decree did little to change the existing situation. The slave trade had long ceased, and domestic slaves were treated as members of the family. But the fact that slavery still existed in Saudi Arabia surprised many Westerners and provided useful material for Sanaa Radio.

As soon as Faisal was again firmly in command, it became apparent that Saudi Arabia had certain advantages in its prolonged struggle with Egypt for influence in the Arabian Peninsula. Although it would be some time before the measures that were undertaken to strengthen Saudi Arabia's defenses were to become effective, Egypt soon found itself in acute political and military difficulties in Yemen. It was relatively easy for the Egyptian expeditionary force, which was eventually increased to some fifty thousand—equivalent to the entire Saudi armed forces—to secure control of the main towns for its Yemeni republican allies. But the troops from the valley and delta of the Nile were quite inexperienced in mountain guerrilla warfare which was a way of life for the Yemeni royalist tribesmen, and the Egyptian commanders had underestimated the difficulties. The cost to Egypt in casualties and money was high, and it was always possible for Saudi Arabia with its superior financial resources to outbid Egypt in winning support from the many Yemeni tribes whose loyalties were wavering. Above all, it was difficult for Egypt to secure the establishment of a Yemeni government that was not evidently dependent on Egyptian support. Egypt began to appear in the guise of a neo-imperialist power, and Saudi Arabia recovered much of the initiative.

Faisal suffered a setback in December 1962 when President Kennedy's administration decided to recognize the Yemeni Republic and was followed by some fifty nations. These did not include Britain which in its struggle against the various nationalist groups in South Arabia discreetly but undeniably favored the royalists. A close working relationship developed between Britain and Saudi

Arabia, and in 1965 Britain signed a £120 million contract to provide Saudi Arabia with an entire air defense system.

U.S. recognition of the Yemeni Republic, on the other hand, created a cloud in U.S.-Saudi relations for a time. The United States had hoped that the secure establishment of the Republic would lead to the speedy withdrawal of Egyptian troops, but this was not to be. However, Washington did not withdraw recognition from Sanaa for fear that it would cause the Republic to lean too heavily on the Soviet Union. The United States did send in mid-1963 a squadron of F-100 Ds to the Kingdom for six months, ostensibly for training measures, but in fact as a deterrent to further Egyptian air attacks.

Faisal showed his readiness to compromise up to a certain point. In 1964 he sent observers to a royalist-republican peace conference held in Sudan that was also attended by the Egyptians. But the ceasefire that was agreed upon failed to hold. As de facto monarch he represented Saudi Arabia at the Arab summit meeting called by Nasser in Alexandria. On the surface courtesies were restored between the Saudi and Egyptian regimes, but there was no mutual confidence. In the following year it was President Nasser who, faced with the mounting cost of the apparently endless Yemeni civil war and difficulties at home, decided on his own initiative to visit Jiddah to meet Faisal and reach an agreement. In addition to an immediate ceasefire, this provided for the formation of a royalist-republican provisional government to be followed a year later by a national plebiscite by which time all Egyptian troops would be withdrawn.

But this settlement also failed to hold. As part of the agreement a royalist-republican conference was held at Harad in North Yemen in November 1965. This broke down ostensibly because of the Yemeni royalists' denial of republican claims that the Yemeni monarchy had been permanently abolished and replaced by the republic. The deeper reason was that Faisal, now King de jure as well as de facto had decided to go over to the offensive against Nasserism.

Hitherto when Faisal had been in control of the country's foreign policy, his overriding aim had been to avoid exposing the highly conservative Saudi regime to unsettling trends. He eschewed all adventurous initiatives and kept what later came to be called a low profile. Until the Yemeni civil war this strategy was markedly successful. As we have seen, he even managed to maintain reasonably cordial relations with Egypt.

Now that Nasserism had arrived in the Arabian Peninsula this was no longer possible. He still did not indulge in abusive political language, which would have been quite contrary to his nature, but he did go over to the attack. His objective was to form an undeclared alliance of all the conservative anti-Nasser forces in the region and even beyond. Against the "Arab socialism" which was being preached from Cairo he proposed a loose form of Islamic unity. He did not deny or oppose the call for Arab unity, but he emphasized the traditional and religious elements in Arabism. Over the question of Palestine he laid more stress on the need for Jerusalem to return to Muslim control than on the demand of the Palestinian Arabs to return to their homes.

Faisal launched his new initiative during a visit to Iran while the Harad peace conference in Yemen was still in progress. In a speech to the Iranian Majlis (parliament) he called for unity against the alien forces threatening the Islamic world. Although he did not mention Nasser's Egypt, everyone knew this was his target. The Shah of Iran, who detested Nasser, was delighted. Faisal followed this up with a series of visits to Muslim countries during which he proposed the holding of a conference of Muslim heads of state to match the Arab summit meetings which had been organized by Nasser. He implied that Egypt was responsible for the growing Soviet power and influence in the Arab world.

Faisal was not proposing any formal alliance of Muslim states; even so the visible results of his campaign were meager. Only Muslim governments outside or peripheral to the Arab world, such as Morocco, Pakistan, Somalia, and Iran, were prepared to give him open support. On the other hand, conservative elements in the Arab world opposed to Nasserism now looked to Faisal for leadership. Ironically, these included some right-wing Lebanese Christians. The response from Cairo was a bitter denunciation of this "reactionary Islamic pact" which was compared to the defunct Baghdad Pact.

Faisal's campaign was cut short by the Six-Day War of June 1967. The shattering defeat by Israel of Egypt and its eleventh-hour allies—Syria and Jordan—created a wholly new situation. Nasser was not toppled, but the influence of Nasserism was broken, if not destroyed. Faisal attended an urgent Arab summit meeting in Khartoum at the end of August at which he took the lead in proposing that the leading Arab oil states—Saudi Arabia, Kuwait, and Libya—should provide substantial aid to Egypt and Jordan to restore their shattered economies and defenses. At the same time, in private meetings with Nasser, he reached a swift agreement on Yemen which meant that the Egyptian forces would be withdrawn.

Faisal's brand of Pan-Islam conservatism appeared to be dominant. He still made no claim to be a popular Arab leader, still less to replace Nasser. He never abandoned his withdrawn, aristocratic demeanor to appeal to the masses. When the Arab heads of state arrived in Khartoum it was the defeated Nasser rather than the quietly triumphant Faisal who drew the cheers from the crowd. But this is unlikely to have distressed him; he held all Nasser's political trump cards.

However the shifting currents of the Arab world never ran in one direction for long. The June war had provoked a wave of anti-Western feeling throughout the Arab states. This was directed specifically against Britain and the United States, who were wrongly accused of intervening directly in the war on Israel's side but correctly regarded as responsible for Israel's existence. The radical anti-Western trend among the Arabs was for a time intensified.

Even in the Arabian Peninsula the defeat of Nasserism did not have the results that many expected. The Yemeni republicans, instead of collapsing after the departure of their Egyptian allies, rallied their forces and threw back the royalist onslaught against Sanaa. The civil war dragged on for two more years, with severe hardships on both sides. The royalist leadership became internally divided, and Saudi Arabia reduced its support for the royalist cause. Peace came in 1969 with a compromise whereby the republic was retained although several prominent royalists were co-opted into the regime. The Imam Badr and his family withdrew into permanent exile. In South Arabia—or South Yemen as most of its Arab inhabitants called it—the situation was considerably worse from the Saudi viewpoint. Britain had already announced its departure by the end of 1967 from the former Aden Colony and Protectorate, with its military base. Britain was hoping to leave behind a Westward-looking Federation of South Arabia which it had constructed out of the petty sultanates and shaykhdoms in the region and fused with Aden Colony. Instead the extremist National Liberation Front, having defeated its more moderate rivals, proceeded to topple all the sultans, including those in the Hadhramaut or East Aden Protectorate where Faisal had established close ties with the hereditary rulers. In this way the first Arab state with undeniable Marxist leanings was born on the soil of Arabia. The Saudi monarchy, with its overstretched and still very limited military forces, had been able to do nothing to prevent it. In North Yemen, Saudi Arabia, as the main supplier of finance, could exert considerable and increasing influence. In South Yemen—soon to be the People's Democratic Republic of Yemen—it had no influence at all.

Elsewhere in the Arab world the trend did not seem to favor Faisal's Islamic conservatism. In Sudan in 1969 the right-wing parliamentary regime was overturned by a radical army group led by Colonel Jaafar Nimeiry who established Nasserist-type institutions and swiftly turned to suppression of the traditional Islamic political leadership. A few months later a considerably more radical and stridently Nasserist young Libyan colonel named Muammar Qaddafy overthrew the pro-Western King Idris. Meanwhile the Palestine Liberation Organization established jointly by the Arab governments in 1964 declared its independence in the wake of the Arab defeat in 1967 and chose its own leader in Yasser Arafat. Although Arafat, head of Fatah—the main constituent in the PLO—was no left-wing extremist, several of the associated groups in the organization were openly Marxist or Maoist in orientation. Moreover, the declared objective of the PLO, which was the establishment of a secular democratic state in Palestine in which Muslims, Christians, and Jews could live in equality, was not attractive to the King of Saudi Arabia.

Although for all these reasons it would have been an exaggeration to speak of Saudi hegemony in the Arab Middle East, there is no question that Faisal's prestige and influence in the region increased in the wake of the June 1967 war. Except in South Yemen, the Arab extreme left was nowhere established in power, and the Aden regime was isolated. Even Nasser softened his attitudes toward the West before his death in 1970. Saudi Arabia remained militarily weak, but it had become the principal paymaster for the Arab states in their confrontation with Israel. This applied also to the PLO which received contributions from individual Palestinian Arabs but also depended heavily on Saudi finance. Faisal used his influence in the PLO to favor Fatah against the left-wing Palestinian guerrilla groups.

There remained one powerful inhibiting factor for Saudi policy in the Arab world which still exists today. This is that while the Saudi rulers identify the twin dangers to Arabs and Muslims as Zionism and communism—and Faisal considered them virtually synonymous—it was undeniable that the United States, Saudi Arabia's main Western ally, and not the Soviet Union, was the principal supporter of the Zionist state. Faisal's strategy was to favor Pan-Islamic movements over the Arab alliance. In the aftermath of the 1967 war, he managed for some time to postpone holding a second Arab summit meeting which was certain to take an extreme anti-Western stand. He then scored a major success when on his initiative a Pan-Islamic summit meeting was held instead in Rabat. The immediate reason for this meeting was the burning of the Al Aqsa Mosque in Jerusalem—the third holiest place for Muslims and now under Israeli control. The conference decided to hold regular meetings of Islamic Foreign Ministers and to establish a permanent Islamic Secretariat in Jiddah.

When the second Arab summit was finally held in December 1969, Faisal made a large contribution to its failure by refusing to

Faisal in Power

increase his financial support to the confrontation states by the amount they desired. At this stage he was ignoring demands by Egypt and the other socialist Arab states that he should use the "oil weapon" against the West and Israel. The Arab summit was a failure; a tired and disillusioned Nasser clutched at the only straw available. This was the Rogers Plan proposed by the U.S. secretary of state and providing for an immediate ceasefire on the Suez Canal, where Egypt and Israel had been fighting a fierce "war of attrition," as the starting point for a general settlement. Faisal quietly favored this plan which was bitterly denounced by the PLO and the radical Arab states.

In September 1970 the activities of the PLO in Jordan—especially of the left-wing groups that rejected Arafat's authority—led to a confrontation with the Jordanian Army and ultimately to the removal of all the PLO military bases from Jordan. In the uproar in the Arab world which accompanied the Jordanian civil war, both Libya and Kuwait cut off aid to the Jordanian government, but Saudi aid was continued unobstrusively. The death of Nasser in 1970 at the close of the summit meeting that he called in Cairo to try to resolve the Jordanian-PLO dispute removed Faisal's old rival from the scene. Although there had been some superficial improvement in their relations, and attacks by the Cairo press on Saudi Arabia had ceased since 1967, neither of the two leaders trusted the other.

As a result of Anwar Sadat's succession as head of state after Nasser's death, Egypt began a long process of moving away from the Soviet Union toward the United States. Faisal welcomed this and soon established much closer and more confidential relations with Sadat than he had ever held with Nasser. This brought several clear advantages to Saudi Arabia; there was no longer any question of Egypt supporting left-wing movements in Arabia or elsewhere in the Arab world. Within two years President Sadat ejected all the Soviet military advisors from Egypt, thereby ending the most important Soviet presence in the Arab states.

At the same time this trend placed increased responsibilities on Saudi Arabia. It had been one thing for Faisal to refuse

Nasser's demands that he use the oil weapon; with Sadat this would not be so easy.

During the 1967 war, Saudi Arabia had briefly joined the other Arab oil states in cutting off supplies to Britain and the United States. But the weapon was ineffective; there was no world oil shortage, and neither of these countries took much oil from Saudi Arabia. In addition, the revenues were needed to help the defeated Arab states, as even Egypt had to concede. By 1973 the situation was quite different. There was no longer a world glut of oil but a shortage. The governments of the oil-producing countries were using their improved bargaining position and the increased self-confidence and experience acquired over the years to oblige the oil companies to accept their direct participation in oil production. The Saudi Minister of Petroleum was Shaykh Ahmad Zaki Yamani who had held the post since 1962. He had replaced the stridently radical Abdullah Tariki who lashed the oil companies with his tongue. Yamani was soft-spoken but much more formidable. Educated in law at New York and Harvard Universities, he was thirty-two when he took office. He had already established one of the first private legal practices in the Kingdom.

While the oil companies were issuing warnings that Saudi Arabia might use the oil weapon, the majority of U.S. government experts were inclined to disagree. They based their calculations on Saudi Arabia's heavy dependence on U.S. technical, and especially military, assistance and its detestation of the Soviet Union. When Faisal sent increasingly urgent messages to Washington through the oil companies that American interests throughout the region were in danger they were greeted with skepticism. As one Aramco man reported: "Some believe that His Majesty is calling wolf where no wolf exists except in his imagination." This showed a complete misunderstanding both of Faisal's character and his position. He certainly detested communism, but he hated Zionism equally and regarded them as synonymous. He took his position as Keeper of the Holy Places of Islam with deadly seriousness, and when he said that his one desire was to pray in Jerusalem before he died he should have been believed. But his position in the Arab world was also misunderstood. His friendship with the United States was certainly valuable, but this had to be balanced against the feelings of the Arabs, including those of his own people. The dangers of pro-Americanism could outweigh its advantages.

Some time in 1972 President Sadat made the decision to exchange his alliance with the unpredictable Libyan Colonel Qaddafy for a close understanding with Saudi Arabia. As he prepared, in coordination with Syria, to launch an assault against the Israeli forces in Sinai in order to break the Middle East stalemate, Saudi Arabia was the only country he informed of his plans.

On October 8, 1972, Egypt attacked across the Suez Canal. As the Israeli forces reeled under the blow, the United States began a huge airlift of arms at Israel's urgent request. October 17, the Saudi Foreign Minister Omar Saqqaf was in Washington to hand President Nixon and Secretary of State Kissinger a letter from King Faisal saying that if the United States did not stop supplying Israel within two days there would be an embargo on oil. Nixon replied that he was committed to supporting Israel. On the same day the Organization of Arab Petroleum Exporting Countries (OAPEC), meeting in Kuwait, decided that its members should reduce oil production by five percent a month. To nearly everyone's astonishment, the normally ultra-cautious Saudi Arabia went further by announcing that it was cutting back its production by ten percent and adding for good measure a total embargo on all oil for the United States and the Netherlands, which it identified as the most ardent supporters of Israel.

At this stage the United States was the least directly affected of the industrialized nations because only about 7.5 percent of its oil imports came from Arab sources. But the implications of the Saudi gesture were momentous. The United States' closest friend in the Arab world had not only taken drastic measures against it but had obliged the U.S.-owned oil company to see that they were carried out.

But the Saudis were aware that the oil weapon could not be put to unlimited use. It was blunt as well as double-edged in that if it caused the collapse of the economies of the non-communist industrialized world, the governments of the Arab oil states could hardly survive. There was also a real possibility of a Western invasion of the oilfields. On October 17, the height of the war, the Arab oil exporters meeting in Kuwait had declared that they would continue to cut back oil production "until the Israeli withdrawal is completed from the whole Arab territories occupied in June 1967 and the legal rights of the Palestinian people restored." But this could not be sustained; by the end of 1973 the Arabs had removed their restrictions on the sale of oil to Europe, and by March 1974 they had lifted the embargo against the United States.

Nevertheless, the power relationship between the West and the Arab oil states was permanently changed. The European countries and Japan showed this by adopting attitudes toward the Palestine problem which grew steadily closer to the Arab view. The United States, with its heavy political commitment to Israel and a dependence on Arab oil which, although growing, was still less than that of the Europeans, was more reluctant to change. It restored its broken relations with Egypt and Syria and at least outwardly adopted a more even-handed attitude toward Arabs and Israelis. But its new approach to the Arabs was mainly a response to the enthusiastically friendly overtures from Egypt. Faisal characteristically maintained his reserve and when Kissinger went on to Riyadh after receiving a bearhug from President Sadat, the King gave the Secretary of State an icily polite reception. It remained true that the U.S. administration from now on had to give increased weight to Saudi Arabia's view on the Middle East and avoid taking its friendship for granted.

One of the main reasons for the new relationship between the Arabs and the West was the enormous increase in oil prices and the consequent shift in income in the Arabs' favor. Oil prices quadrupled within two months and the revenues of the oil producers rose in proportion. By 1975 Saudi Arabia's gold and currency reserves had become greater than those of the United States and Japan combined and second only in the world to those of West Germany. Saudi Arabia, with over 30 percent of OPEC's output of oil and some 35 percent of the proved reserves of the non-communist world, was the single most important producer. It had also become a major financial power, with the capacity for influence in all the international money markets by means of its policies.

As usual, King Faisal used this new power with great circumspection. Because of its relatively small population and the enormous size of its income in relation to its immediate needs, Saudi Arabia had no interest in accelerating the increase in its revenues. In this it was different from Algeria and Iran which felt the need for every extra dollar. The Shah of Iran in particular, with his boundless ambitions to make his country a major industrial and military power, was the leading hawk in OPEC. Iran did not take part in the Arab use of the oil weapon, but the Shah had learned the lesson and was fully prepared to exploit its results. King Faisal, in contrast, was now primarily concerned that any further sudden increases would cause a major depression, perhaps even economic collapse, in the West. His instruction to Shaykh Yamani, who in any case agreed with his view, was to restrain the increase in prices. In the following years Saudi Arabia therefore became the leading dove in OPEC. It was often obliged to threaten to break up the organization in order to get its way.

Faisal's diplomatic skill and unobstrusive firmness immensely increased Saudi Arabia's prestige and influence. Without a trace of flamboyance he had become an international star personality. Among the Arabs his tendency was always toward moderation and conciliation rather than confrontation. With the exception of quasi-Marxist Democratic Yemen, which he always refused to recognize, he maintained relations with other Arab regimes of which he certainly disapproved. At the crucial Arab summit meeting in Rabat in October 1974, it was he who led the other Arab states in persuading King Hussein of Jordan to join them in recognizing the PLO as the sole representative of the Palestinian people. His argument was that since the United Nations had given the PLO quasi-official status the Arabs could hardly do less. Having refused to break with King Hussein throughout the latter's troubles with the PLO, he was in a unique position to influence Hussein's decision.

Faisal's tragic assassination on March 25, 1975, by a mentally unstable nephew was a major political catastrophe. Since the assassin never explained his motives, there was widespread speculation that he was acting for some foreign agency ranging from extremist Palestinians to the CIA. But since there was no attempt from any quarter to follow up the King's death with political action, it seems certain that he was acting alone. Whether he was spurred by vague leftist political ideas or revenge in a family feud is equally unknown.

As always happens in moments of crisis, the family rallied and acted swiftly to ensure a smooth succession. As prearranged, Faisal was succeeded by his brother Khalid, and another brother Fahd became Crown Prince and First Deputy Prime Minister. Khalid had been chosen by the family at the time of Saud's abdication. Deeply respected for his personal integrity, he was known to have neither the experience nor taste for diplomacy or administration. Overall responsibility for the country's policies was left to Crown Prince Fahd, although King Khalid showed more readiness to exert his influence as head of state than had been expected.

12

After King Faisal

The loss of Faisal's exceptional personal ascendancy meant that Saudi Arabia's policies were no longer so clearly predictable. Two tendencies were detected within the royal family: a "modernizing" one represented by Fahd and his full brother Sultan, Minister of Defense, and a more traditional and conservative tendency represented by the King and a fourth brother Abdullah who commanded the National Guard. These were differences of emphasis rather than principle and were often exaggerated by outsiders. However, the family's skill at keeping its disagreements private tended to encourage the speculation that it was the family's determination to prevent any internal rivalries from developing that prompted the decision not to single out any one of the King's brothers as next-in-line in succession to Crown Prince Fahd.

The lines of King Faisal's foreign policy were maintained and have been continued to the present: conciliation and mediation within the Arab world, support for common action by Islamic states, friendship with the West, and vigorous anti-communism. The special relationship with the United States is employed to press for an American Middle East policy more favorable toward the Arabs and especially Palestinian rights. Some members of the Saudi regime would favor establishing diplomatic relations with the Soviet Union for tactical reasons, although this is unlikely during the King's lifetime. Saudi Arabia remains almost unique among Third World countries in having no direct links with Moscow. On

101

the other hand, since Faisal's death Saudi Arabia has been able to pursue a more conciliatory policy toward the semi-communist regime in South Yemen which Faisal declared anathema. The objective, which has so far had only limited success, has been to wean South Yemen away from the Soviet camp. There are others among the princes and the non-royal ministers who feel that Saudi Arabia is not sufficiently outspoken in its criticism of U.S. policy. Certainly Crown Prince Fahd has said in many public statements, especially when visiting the United States, that Saudi Arabia has no intention of using the oil weapon and that cooperation rather than confrontation with the West is the best way to make Western policies more favorable to the Arabs. But it may be recalled that King Faisal and his ministers were making such statements in 1972. In certain circumstances Saudi Arabia would have no alternative to using the oil weapon, although not necessarily in the same form as in 1973.

In one important respect Saudi Arabian policy has become more flexible. King Faisal could never bring himself to mention Israel's right to exist or the various UN resolutions which all imply that the greater part of Palestine will remain in Zionist hands. Early in his reign in an interview published in the *Washington Post* on May 25 King Khalid declared his acceptance of Israel's right to live within its pre-1967 borders and this has since been the official stand of the Saudi government.

In its widely acknowledged role as the principal mediating force in the Arab world, Saudi Arabia played an important part in bringing the Lebanese civil war of 1975-76 to an end. With some help from Kuwait, it arranged a summit meeting at which President Sadat of Egypt and President Assad of Syria at least temporarily settled their differences. This was an essential step before any agreement could be reached on establishing the Arab "Force of Restraint" to keep the peace in Lebanon. Syrian troops already in Lebanon provided the bulk of this force, but the 750 soldiers contributed by Saudi Arabia were a crucial element as they were generally trusted by the two sides in the civil war. The fact that anti-Muslim Lebanese Christians were ready to place their trust in the Wahhabi rulers of Saudi Arabia was on the face of it surprising. But it was consistent with Saudi Arabia's deliberately restrained and conciliatory role in inter-Arab disputes.

Saudi Arabia's diplomatic strategy both toward the West and the Arabs met its most severe test as a result of President Sadat's unexpected unilateral decision in November 1977 to confront the Israeli leadership in Jerusalem in an effort to secure a general settlement of the Arab-Israeli dispute. Characteristically, the Saudi government did not condemn the Egyptian president outright, despite its hurt anger that he had taken this action without consulting his ally and principal source of funds. A Saudi government statement acknowledged that a state had the right to use any means to recover lost territory, as Egypt was doing, but did not have the right to abandon vital Arab interests in the process.

As Egypt then proceeded, with the help of forceful American mediation to reach the Camp David Agreements of November 1978 and then to conclude a Peace Treaty with Israel in February 1979, the Saudi dilemma became evidently more acute. The United States was in effect a full partner in the Israeli-Egyptian agreements, and it strongly encouraged both Saudi Arabia and Jordan to join the negotiations. The Saudis had no belief that the Camp David approach could achieve a real settlement with Israel or the minimum of justice that the Palestinians might accept, but, unlike the more militant Arab states, it was not prepared to denounce the United States or call for President Sadat's overthrow. Any successor regime in Egypt was likely to be worse from the Saudi viewpoint.

However, the strain in Saudi Arabia's friendship for the United States was apparent, with irritation on both sides. Following the conclusion of the Egyptian-Israeli Peace Treaty, Saudi Arabia attended an Arab meeting in Baghdad to adopt countermeasures. To the surprise of many, Saudi Arabia agreed to common action to boycott and isolate Egypt. It was able to avoid declaring an anathema on the United States, but the Saudi delegates to the meeting noticeably avoided taking a lead, and the firm hand of King Faisal was noticeably absent.

Saudi Arabia is the dominant power and the natural leader in the Arabian Peninsula. The policies of its government, whether in the political, economic, or social fields, affect the whole region. But although the smaller Arabian Gulf states acknowledge Saudi Arabia as their big brother, they have their own strongly individual personalities. They have much in common but their experiences and circumstances are different in significant ways. Kuwait, a commercial port at the head of the Gulf for two centuries, was the first to become immensely rich through oil. Bahrain island, although less wealthy, has much the longest experience as a trading center while Abu Dhabi, with virtually no economic history of its own, has become a great focus of modern business within two decades.

It is therefore worth looking at each of these states in turn. The fact that the survey does not cover the whole of the Arabian Peninsula does not mean that the two Yemeni states (the Yemen Arab Republic and the People's Democratic Republic of Yemen) are not of great interest or that their people will not play a major role in the future of Arabia. It is only that their lack of oil resources means that they are not undergoing the revolutionary changes which make Saudi Arabia and the Gulf region unique. Oman, which is also omitted, *is* an important oil producer, but it is only in very recent times that it has emerged from a long period of almost total seclusion to establish links with its neighbors. An adequate survey of Oman's history and special conditions is beyond the scope of this survey.

13
Kuwait

*I*n the early 1950s highly colored reports reached the general public in the West of the first "oil shaykh." Through ruling "a few square miles of desert" that happened to contain some oil, he was said to be amassing an immense fortune. This was the Ruler of Kuwait, Shaykh Sir Abdullah al Salim Al Sabah, knighted by Queen Elizabeth II in her first birthday honors. Iran, Iraq, and Saudi Arabia were all producing oil, but Kuwait was different because of its tiny population of 200,000. It was the first of the oil "city-states."

Known affectionately as "Najd by the sea," Kuwait is a small wedge of territory between Iraq and Saudi Arabia that has survived as an independent state, partly through the fierce will of its own people and partly because various international interests have converged to preserve it. The Al Sabah, who have ruled Kuwait for some 250 years, are descended from the clan that dominated the great Anazah beduin tribe of Arabia, who were driven northward by drought and famine early in the eighteenth century. Another clan which came with them, the Al Khalifah, went on to become the rulers of Bahrain.

The Al Sabah chose the site of the present city at the entrance to a great sweeping bay because of its sweet water. The name they gave it is the diminutive of *kut*, the fort which was the only building among their tents in those early days. They managed to persuade the local Ottoman Turkish governors, who exerted a rather loose control from neighboring Basrah, to leave them in

105

peace and beat off an attack by a powerful predatory Arab tribe from Persia. The story that the head of the tribe's objective was Mariam, the beautiful daughter of the Shaykh of the Al Sabah may be colorful embroidery but "Ana Akhu Mariam" (I am Mariam's brother) became the state war cry, and no Sabah princess was ever allowed to marry outside the family.

From their former nomadic life the Al Sabah and their companions soon settled down to become merchants, seafarers, and pearl-fishers. By 1760 they had a fleet of some 800 dhows based on Kuwait port with camel caravans carrying trade southward to Riyadh and northward into Mesopotamia. The port flourished even more when the English East India Company made its base at the head of the Gulf in Kuwait after the Persians had temporarily occupied Basrah in 1776.

During the second half of the nineteenth century when the Ottoman Turks were attempting to assert their authority over eastern Arabia, the Rulers of Kuwait were conciliatory and accepted from them the post of *qaim-maqam* or provincial governor. But in 1896 Mubarak, one of the brothers and a man of different mettle, seized power in a palace coup. His passionate desire to avoid Turkish annexation caused him to turn to the British. Although cautious, they were concerned about Germany's growing alliance with Turkey and its declared aim to extend the Berlin-Baghdad railway southward to the Gulf. Britain regarded this as an unacceptable threat to its Indian Empire. In 1899 Britain agreed to provide Kuwait with support and protection in return for the Ruler's undertaking not to alienate part of his territory to another power. This was one of the Exclusive Agreements, similar to those Britain concluded with emirates and shaykhdoms on the fringes of Arabia, which effectively kept out everyone else for nearly fifty years.

The Turks did not give up their claim, and negotiations with Britain continued. But with the outbreak of World War I, Kuwait declared for the Allies, the British landed troops in Basrah to occupy Mesopotamia, and the Turks withdrew.

The time of Mubarak the Great (reigned 1896-1915) was one

of great prosperity. These were the golden years of the pearl trade. The population increased in the first decade of the century from about 10,000 to 35,000. It was during these years that the two first schools were opened to teach the sons of merchants reading and writing and some arithmetic.

It was from Kuwait that the young Abd al Aziz ibn Saud, whose family had taken refuge there some years earlier, set out to recover his lost territory of Najd from the Rashidis. Mubarak sponsored and helped him and later, when Ibn Saud was Sultan of Najd, encouraged him to declare for the Allies against the Turks. However, this did not prevent Ibn Saud's fanatical Ikhwan warriors, who regarded the Kuwaitis as intolerably loose-living, from making repeated raids on Kuwait territory in the years following the war. The Kuwaitis built a wall and defended themselves with spirit. Relative peace was not restored until the conference in 1922-23 between Britain and Ibn Saud to settle the frontiers between Iraq, Najd, and Kuwait. Britain, acting as spokesman for both Kuwait and Iraq, in effect gave away two-thirds of the desert territory claimed by the Sabah family to Ibn Saud in return for his abandoning to Iraq equally large areas of what he regarded as Najd. Britain told the unhappy Ruler of Kuwait, Shaykh Ahmad, that Ibn Saud could not be prevented from seizing the territory if he wished. At least this provided reasonable insurance against Saudi claims to Kuwait itself. No such certainty applied to the Iraqis who did not feel morally committed by British undertakings on their behalf when they became independent in 1933.

Kuwait prospered throughout the 1930s despite the decline in the pearl trade because Kuwaiti merchants benefited from the new oil prosperity in Iraq and Iran. The Anglo-Iranian Oil Company (formerly APOC and later BP) for some time took little interest in Kuwait itself as a possible source of oil; it already had enough oil on its hands in the two neighboring countries. However, when Gulf Oil began bidding for a concession through Major Frank Holmes, the eccentric New Zealander who had earlier obtained concessions both from Ibn Saud and the Ruler of Bahrain, BP became alarmed and enlisted British Colonial Office support to keep out any non-British company. But Gulf Oil was able to obtain the State Department's backing for the "open-door" policy, especially after Andrew Mellon—one of the company's owners—became U.S. Ambassador to London in 1931. The Ruler now understandably enjoyed the spectacle of major British and American companies competing with one another. Eventually BP and Gulf decided that the best thing to do was to join forces and apply together for a concession. This was granted on December 23, 1934, to the Kuwait Oil Company, jointly owned by BP and Gulf Oil. It was understood from the beginning that the British would concentrate on administration in the company and the Americans on production.

The first well was drilled in 1936, and in 1938 the huge oil field at Burgan, south of the city, was discovered. World War II intervened and exports only started in 1946. The transformation of the first oil shaykhdom had begun.

In 1937 the British traveler Freya Stark had still been able to write of Kuwait: "So perfect a small town, everything being right in the right surroundings, the lovely place and people...I know of no place with such a charm of remoteness that is yet not solitude...."

The remoteness and solitude were soon a memory. Kuwait might be receiving ten cents a barrel less than Iran, Iraq, or Saudi Arabia because its royalties were not tied to gold, but its small population ensured that revenues per head were much higher. The Ruler who succeeded in 1950, Shaykh Abdullah, was a farsighted man with a shrewd understanding of both Kuwait's potential and limitations. Although a social and religious conservative, he was not afraid of rapid development and the dangers of disruption it implied. Before the oil, Kuwaitis had been wealthy enough to lay the foundations of civic development. Now they could think of providing schools and hospitals for everyone.

Kuwaiti society was always a synthesis between the town merchants and the beduin of the surrounding desert. The trading connections made it easier to welcome the non-Kuwaiti Arabs who were needed if Kuwait were to develop rapidly. Palestinians,

Egyptians, Syrians, Iraqis, and others poured into the country; Kuwait soon became the first of the oil shaykhdoms whose people were in a minority in their own land. Despite the Kuwaitis' lack of xenophobia, this created many delicate problems. The Arab immigrants had the right to all the benefits of the new Kuwaiti welfare state but, except for the tiny minority who acquired Kuwaiti citizenship, no political rights. However much they prospered, they felt themselves second-class citizens.

The Sabah family kept executive power in their own hands, and as cabinet government developed in the 1950s, they held all the key posts. But their power was far from being absolute. The leading merchant families, who lent them money before the oil boom and grew considerably richer afterwards, have always had influence. In 1921 they even persuaded the Ruler Shaykh Ahmad to accept a council of advisors. Ahmad soon got rid of it and ruled as before, but it set an important precedent. Within the family itself a careful balance has always been maintained between its Jabir and Salim branches who normally alternate in the Rulership. As in any family, its members are of varying caliber. Some showed energy and ability in government while others enjoyed an extravagantly aristocratic life-style which cast doubt on the future of shaykhly rule.

Change was so rapid in the 1950s that it left everyone a little breathless. In 1958 the skeleton of the great modern city that exists today was just discernible among the construction sites. The year before, the old mud city wall had to be torn down; only the gates were preserved as symbols of the past. Some planning opportunities were lost in those years, and several foreign contractors were ruthless in exploiting the Kuwaitis' lack of experience of modern business methods. But the Kuwaitis were quick to learn as they always have been.

At that time the key question was whether Kuwait could become independent. To the outside world, and especially the other Arab states, Kuwait was little more than a British colony. It was argued that Britain had originally created Kuwait for political reasons and was now preserving it for economic reasons.

In fact, if Kuwait had asked to abrogate the 1899 treaty at this time, Britain could hardly have refused. What held Kuwait back was the lack of Kuwaitis. They had to be able to man all the government departments, including a diplomatic service, if their independence was to have much meaning. Although the number of Kuwaitis with university training was rapidly increasing, there were still no more than a few hundred, and many of these were likely to devote themselves to business.

Nevertheless, in June 1961 the Sabah family felt confident enough to take the plunge, and the 1899 Anglo-Kuwaiti agreement was terminated by mutual consent. Kuwait became a member of the United Nations and the Arab League. Almost immediately Kuwait's very existence was threatened as General Abd al Karim Qasim, the unpredictable ruler of Iraq, claimed Kuwait as part of his territory and threatened to occupy it by force. Shaykh Abdullah appealed to Britain, which landed troops, but two months later these were withdrawn and replaced by a joint Arab League force. Kuwait had skillfully demonstrated that, if the other Arab states had formerly regarded Kuwait as an artificial entity, they now wanted its independence. This was the best guarantee for the country's future. Since then Kuwait has wisely refrained from taking sides in inter-Arab disputes and has remained neutral even when the dispute between "radicals" and "conservatives" has been at its strongest. It has managed to remain on terms with all sides, frequently offering itself as a mediator.

Nothing did more to enhance Kuwait's position than the efforts it made from an early date to share its wealth with its less fortunate fellow Arabs. In the year of independence the Kuwait Fund for Arab Economic Development was set up by the dynamic young Finance Minister who is now the Ruler, Shaykh Jabir al Ahmad, to provide low-interest, long-term loans for projects that other Arab governments regarded as vital, such as the expansion of the Suez Canal or Beirut port, railways in Sudan, and irrigation in Tunisia. Apart from the Fund, Kuwait helped to build schools and hospitals in other Gulf states that had no oil revenues. It also made several huge loans, which were in fact gifts, to powerful

Arab governments such as the Egyptian and Iraqi. Cynics could say that Kuwait was paying for its independence, and there was undeniably a political element in many of these gifts. But the important fact was that Kuwait was setting an example in spreading its wealth.

Within six months of independence the ruling family took another bold and imaginative step by deciding on constitutional government. An elected Constituent Assembly agreed on a permanent democratic constitution, and in January 1963 the first parliament was elected by Kuwaiti males over twenty-one. Inevitably, it was dominated by the leading merchant families, but there was a small group of radical nationalists who had influence far beyond their numbers.

This remarkable experiment in parliamentary democracy in a small Arab shaykhdom has not been an entire success. The executive branch which increasingly includes young technocrats from outside the ruling family, has found it factious and disruptive. In seeking to promote Kuwait's national interests, the National Assembly has sometimes prevented the government from making important decisions such as in relations with the oil companies. In 1975 the cabinet resigned saying that parliament was making government impossible. The Ruler dissolved the National Assembly and suspended certain clauses in the constitution. But the ruling family was apparently determined that the experiment would be resumed under a revised constitution, and a splendid new parliament building was constructed. New elections were held in February 1981.

Kuwait has now enjoyed oil wealth for just one generation—a short span in the life of any community even if it was founded 250 years ago. Roughly speaking, the first half of this period—until the death of Shaykh Abdullah in 1965—was devoted to providing the country and its people with all the facilities and services of a developed country: roads, a modern port and airport, housing, schools, and hospitals. In 1932, over 4,000 people died in a smallpox epidemic in ten days; in 1949 there were still only four doctors in Kuwait, and there were 4,600 children in school. By

1967 there were 400 doctors in the government health system and 120,000 children in school. From the beginning, education and health services were provided free to immigrants as well as to Kuwaitis. These public services still have to go on expanding because of the population explosion (200,000 at independence; 1.3 million in the 1980 census). The educational budget today is rather more than total oil revenues in the late 1950s. There are now more schoolchildren in Kuwait than the total population in 1950. But the significant fact in Kuwait's modern history is that within the first fifteen years of oil revenues, poverty had been virtually abolished, Kuwaiti children were decently housed, well fed (sometimes overfed), free from disease, and going to school, both boys and girls. The country's small and compact population had made it possible to conduct what amounted to a laboratory experiment in removing the effects of poverty and deprivation from a group of human beings.

Kuwaitis were now able to look at wider horizons. There was of course no sudden change, but in the mid-1960s they became noticeably more ambitious. They were also more assured in their attitude toward wealth, as multi-millionaires became a dime a dozen in Kuwait; other people in Arabia were now the *nouveaux riches*. Intellectual and cultural life was becoming more varied and sophisticated. The University of Kuwait, founded in 1964, has put down roots and today has the comfortably well-worn look of an ancient institution. Publishing houses proliferated, and Kuwaiti newspapers, relatively free from censorship, began to carry weight and influence well outside the country's borders—especially with the decline of the Cairo and Beirut presses in the 1970s. Despite a total ban on alcohol imposed by parliament, against the Ruler's advice, Kuwaitis are less puritanical than their Saudi neighbors. Cinemas and theaters flourish. Kuwait has already produced one important film director, and Kuwaiti actors and musicians make television programs which are shown throughout the Gulf.

The adolescent township that existed in 1958, with one main street, with two main buildings, and a few shopwindows with goods displayed at random, has now developed into a great metropolis. Extensive garden suburbs spread out into the desert and a vast network of Los Angeles-type superhighways, under constant expansion, can barely cope with a quarter of a million private cars. A cosmopolitan social life is centered on the city's luxury hotels of which there are now a dozen but never enough to meet the demand. There are many parks and sports stadiums—even an ice-skating rink—and the municipality plans a whole new series of leisure centers on the seashore. There is a conscious attempt to lure Kuwaitis away from spending the summer months abroad, as so many do at present, by making life at home more attractive.

Kuwait City can hardly expand any more because it is built on a tongue of land—something the first nomad settlers hardly envisaged. Planning consultants are advising building new cities on the coast that may be north or south, but in any case far enough away not to become dormitory suburbs of Kuwait City. Somehow the three million population expected by the end of the century must be provided for.

All this is at immense cost to the state. The provision of water alone both for human consumption and the trees and gardens is a heavy burden. Although some brackish water comes from underground supplies, most comes from distilled sea water, of which Kuwait has one of the highest capacities in the world: approaching 100 million gallons per day now and expected to exceed 200 million by 1985.

In the early days, as the oil company seemed only to tap the soil to find wonderfully accessible oil in abundance, Kuwaitis thought little about the future. But by the time of independence the prospect that even their oil must run out one day was very much on their minds. How could the life of their great city be preserved?

There are broadly three approaches to the problem and all have been adopted, whether consciously by the state or instinctively as self-preservation by individuals. The first is simply to extend the life of the oil and gas fields and to make as much use as possible of these resources for Kuwaitis. Kuwait has long taken a lead in this matter; in its lifetime the National Assembly was constantly urging the government to take a tougher stand toward the oil companies. Kuwait has insisted on taking an increasing number of the decisions affecting the oil industry into its own hands.

The second possible insurance for the future was to set up alternative industries to oil. In the 1950s many felt this was quite impractical. First the home market on which industrialization must be based was far too small even if it was growing rapidly. Then it seemed unlikely that the Kuwaitis, with their strong merchant tradition, would ever put their money and enterprise into new industries. The only existing industry was the traditional one of building dhows.

In 1961, at the time of independence one revolution had already taken place in Kuwaiti attitudes. Three years earlier no Kuwaiti would have considered investing his money in something he could not see, such as a shop or cinema or, more usually, an apartment building. Nor was there a rush to take up the shares of any new company that was formed. In the 1960s the government was able to stimulate a variety of new industries by setting up joint enterprises—that is with the state in partnership with private capital. These were concentrated in sectors that were thought either to be too large for private capital alone, such as petrochemicals, or socially desirable, such as food (fisheries and flour mills) or transport. The National Industries Company, 51 percent state-owned, has a variety of plants producing building materials, batteries, detergents, etc.

Not all investors needed the state to participate, and some private enterprises have been set up on their own. Kuwaiti contractors were the first to do so, taking advantage of the oil boom, and there are now over 80 contractors in the Kuwaiti Contractors' Union. But at least for the manufacturing industry the government has had to help. Some 25 miles south of Kuwait the Shuaybah Industrial Area was set up in 1964 on four square miles of land, with the government providing power, water, and a major port. This now shows every sign of taking off and expanding. One method used by a Kuwaiti businessman Qutaybah al Ghanim was to import an entire Kirby Building Systems plant from Houston, together with 240 American workers and set it up at Shuaybah. The factory has now been Arabized and sends exports throughout the region.

Not all private industry succeeds, and the government often has to step in either by increasing its share or taking over altogether—as with the Kuwait Oil Tanker Company, established in 1957. In early 1978 the Kuwait stock market was so enfeebled that the government had to move in to support it by buying shares in hitherto private companies. But the important fact remains that no one today would regard the concept of an industrialized Kuwait as ridiculous. The local market is growing faster than was expected, and the whole Gulf region offers opportunities to exporters.

Kuwait can try to spin out its oil and gas reserves as long as possible; it can attempt to establish alternative industries. A third course is to invest its surplus oil revenues to provide income when the oil runs out. But this investment would be a supplement to rather than an alternative to the other policies. No Kuwaiti wishes to contemplate his country living entirely on income from investments like a wealthy spinster aunt. Yet it obviously makes good sense to look after these investments and increase them. For some twenty years the government has been building up a State Reserve out of budget surpluses, and in 1976 a so-called Reserve Fund for Future Generations was established which received ten percent of all state revenues and cannot be touched for 25 years. In 1980 Kuwait's total reserves were somewhere between $30 billion and $40 billion. In view of the huge increase in revenues as a result of the rise in oil prices in the 1970s the figure might have been expected to be even higher. But the inflation in the price of goods imported from the industrialized countries, combined with the cost of constantly expanding services for the Kuwaiti public, has more than kept pace with the increase in revenues. Nevertheless, the income from Kuwait's investments from what can be regarded as savings is now approaching the equivalent of twenty percent of oil revenues. Most of these savings are invested abroad. Some are looked after directly by the Ministry of Finance which has its own Investment Office in London, others are channeled through Kuwaiti investment companies in which the government has shares. In the early days the money was kept very liquid either on deposit or in short-term loans. (Most Kuwaitis twenty years ago were convinced that they were financing London itself because their government had bought Greater London Council stock.) Today the tendency is to build up more tangible assets in property or portfolio shareholding. Kuwait owns a chunk of the Champs Elysées, a share in the German Daimler Benz, another in the British Lonrho, a hotel complex in Atlanta, Georgia, and other pieces of property from Brazil to Japan. Often these investments arouse local resentment. The cry of an "Arab takeover" is heard. Kuwait therefore tends to avoid publicity in the West and reserve any self-advertisement for its often highly adventurous investments in the needier Arab countries—Sudan, Egypt, and Morocco.

Kuwait has acquired a well-deserved reputation as the shrewdest and most sophisticated of the big Arab overseas investors. The Saudi Arabians may now have more funds at their disposal, but the Kuwaitis have some ten to fifteen years' advantage in experience. In 1961 one wondered how far the West realized that Kuwait's Fahd Street, still partly unpaved and covered with drifting sand, was destined to become one of the world's major financial centers. In 1969 the World Bank placed the first Kuwaiti dinar bonds privately through the Kuwait Investment Company. Five years later the first publicly quoted international bond issue was launched, and since then the Kuwaiti bond market has grown steadily. A Kuwait Stock Exchange, the first in the Gulf, was inaugurated in 1977.

Yet one still has the impression that Kuwaitis are hovering on the brink of the shark-infested sea of international finance. They have not answered the question of whether they want the Kuwaiti dinar to become an international currency and whether their economy would be large enough to sustain it. "Internationalization" would require various new laws and regulations. The Stock

Exchange, for example, although it has one of the highest turnovers in the world, is still limited to the shares of Kuwaiti companies. With its modest rows of plastic-covered benches it gives the impression of a social club for Kuwaiti businessmen rather than a professional market. Everyone knows each other, and settlements are made on a personal basis, with clients sometimes refusing to deal with each other because of some half-forgotten family feud.

The Kuwait Stock Exchange might be regarded as a symbol of the country's dilemma: how a tiny state can play an international role while keeping its national character. There are several choices confronting the nation, and all of them are difficult. If it aims for economic growth as it has done in the past, it will have to continue to rely on immigrants to do much of the work. Something may be done by concentrating on capital-intensive, highly automated industries, but this alone cannot provide the answer. Kuwaitis may be able to take over all the major responsibilities but this will not resolve the problem; the non-Kuwaiti majority will resent their second-class status in a country they have helped to build. One alternative would be to grant full Kuwaiti citizenship to all the long-standing immigrants, but this would premanently change the character of the nation to a degree that ancestor-proud Kuwaitis would find hard to accept.

There is one reason why the problem may be lesser than it might appear. Between one third and a half of the non-Kuwaiti residents—perhaps 250,000—are Palestinian Arabs. The vast majority of these do not want Kuwaiti citizenship because this would mean abandoning their claim to return to Palestine. On the other hand, the presence of such a large foreign minority in a small city-state might be regarded as a threat. The government has become alarmed at times at the high rate of Palestinian immigration and has tried to limit its numbers. But the Palestinians have a strong interest in the survival and stability of Kuwait, as their prosperous community provides much of the funds for the Palestine Liberation Organization. Yasser Arafat himself spent some years there as a successful contractor.

It is not only the Palestinian Arabs who benefit from Kuwait's survival. The Kuwait Fund for Arab Economic Development, which since 1974 has been making loans to non-Arab Third World countries as well as to Arab borrowers, was a pioneering institution that has provided a model for others. Through this and other channels Kuwait was devoting over five percent of its GNP to aid—certainly one of the highest rates in the world.

Yet the institution in which the ruling family takes the greatest pride, and the one which demonstrates best the kind of role that Kuwait can play in the area, is KISR—the Kuwait Institution for Scientific Research. This was established in 1958 and now has a budget of $40 million and a staff of 330, many of them distinguished Arab-Americans. KISR tackles all Kuwait's main problems which are also those of the whole region: solar energy, desalination, arid-zone agriculture, marine biology, and pollution. It is through research and experiment of this kind that Kuwait's future is most likely to be assured. The Kuwaitis are very conscious of the fact that theirs is the oldest and most experienced of the oil city-states. They have a special responsibility for discovering the role they can play in the world when their oil reserves are depleted.

14
Bahrain

*T*he archipelago of low-lying islands that today forms the State of Bahrain is one of the most ancient trading centers in the world. Standing some fifteen miles off the coast of Arabia, the main Bahrain Island has supported a settled population for at least five thousand years. The name Bahrain means "two seas." The origin of the name is uncertain; it was originally applied not to the islands but to the mainland across the way, now the Eastern Province of Saudi Arabia.

Under the name of Dilmun it became during the Bronze Age (about 2800 B.C.) the center of a powerful empire that dominated the trade routes between the Sumerians of Mesopotamia and the ancient cities of the Indus Valley.

Dilmun or Bahrain was always envied by others. The Sumerians described it as a holy land blessed by Anki, the god of sweet water, and in their version of the story of The Flood, they told how the survivor was granted immortality and settled in Dilmun. In about 600 B.C. it was swallowed up by the Assyrian Empire. The Greeks called it Tylos, and two of the ships of Alexander's fleet called there on their way back from India. By the time of the coming of Islam, Bahrain was occupied by settlers from Arabia and dominated by the Persian Empire. These original inhabitants are known as Baharinah and are said to be descended from Arabs taken by King Nebuchadnezzar into Mesopotamia who later managed to flee from there to settle in Bahrain. In the ninth year of his leadership the Prophet Muhammad sent a letter to the local

119

Arab ruler Al Mundhir ibn Sarwah inviting him to adopt the new faith, and present-day Bahrainis are proud of the fact that their ancestors were among the first outside the Arabian Peninsula to embrace Islam. At the time of the Sunni-Shia schism in Islam, the Baharinah adopted the Shiite faith.

During the thousand years that followed, Bahrain knew some periods of prosperity. In the fourteenth century Ibn Battutah found ''a fine and considerable city, with gardens, trees, and streams. Water is procured at little cost: it suffices to dig the ground with the hands, and water is found. In this place are palm enclosures, and pomegranates, lemons and cotton are cultivated. The temperature is very high and there is much sand which often buries the dwellings.'' But Bahrain was constantly invaded and occupied by covetous powers in the region—Persians, Turks, Portuguese, Wahhabis, and Omanis. Many of the suffering Baharinah were forced to leave and became scattered throughout the region. In the eighteenth century Sunni Arabs came over from mainland Arabia and in 1783 were able to eject the Persians who had ruled the island for thirty years. Among them was the Al Khalifah family (who had come southward after helping the Al Sabah to found Kuwait) who founded the dynasty which rules Bahrain to this day. At times the Rulers of Bahrain have declared unwilling allegiance to Muscat, the Wahhabis, the Ottoman Turks, or the Persians, but they have always regarded themselves as independent.

The indigenous population of Bahrain is therefore both Sunni and Shiite. Since they rarely intermarry they show physical differences that long-standing residents claim to be able to distinguish easily. There are also a substantial number of Bahrainis of Persian origin as well as a black African strain inherited from former slaves.

During the nineteenth century, Bahrain was affected by the gradual extension of British hegemony in the Gulf. The Ruler adhered to Britain's General Treaty of Peace with the neighboring states of the Trucial Coast; he signed a similar anti-slavery agreement with Britain in 1835. It was not until 1861, however, that Britain, in consequence of the political claims to Bahrain being put forward by Persia and Turkey, agreed to protect Bahrain against external aggression in return for acknowledgement of British suzerainty. This was extended by the further Exclusive Agreements of 1881 and 1892 by which the Ruler agreed not "to cede, sell, mortgage or otherwise give for occupation any part of his territory save to the British government." The British navy served to keep the Turks at bay until they finally left the area in 1914. The British at first interfered hardly at all in Bahrain's internal affairs. The Ruler from 1869 was Shaykh Isa ibn Ali, a powerful and venerable figure who was opposed to all modernization or reform. He refused to import steel beams for his new *majlis* because they were dangerous and rejected the use of mules on the ground that they were contrary to nature. Gradually the British tried to edge him towards change through the Political Agent they appointed in 1900. But by the 1920s this was no longer enough. British hegemony in the Gulf was being increasingly challenged by the new ruler of Persia, Reza Shah*, and Britain was looking increasingly to Bahrain as its main center of influence. In 1923 they "persuaded" the aged Shaykh Isa to give way to his son Hamad.

The action was bitterly resented by many Bahrainis; Ibn Saud always regarded it as deplorably high-handed and constantly referred to it in later years. Nevertheless, it did lead to a marked improvement in Bahrain's internal administration.

On August 10, 1925, an advertisement appeared in the personal column of *The Times*: "Young Gentleman, aged 22/28, Public School and/or University education, required for service in an Eastern State...." The job was to be Advisor to the Ruler of Bahrain, and it went to an impecunious young upper-class Englishman named Charles Belgrave after he had been interviewed and approved by the British Resident in the Gulf, the senior British official in the region. He held the post for more than thirty years during which he helped establish a local police force and various government services that made Bahrain the most efficiently administered state in the region. In this he was greatly assisted

*Reza Shah, father of the late deposed Shah, was a colonel of the Cossack brigade who carried out a coup d'etat in 1921, first becoming Commander-in-Chief, then Prime Minister, and finally Shah in 1925.

when the Bahrain Petroleum Company (Bapco) discovered oil in 1932. Bapco was actually part of Standard Oil of California but was incorporated in Canada to get around the Exclusive Agreement with Britain.

Bahrain was never to be more than a tiny producer compared with Kuwait, Saudi Arabia, or Iran. Reserves are small and the search for new fields has been disappointing. Nevertheless the few million dollars a year of revenues brought in by the oil—soon to be supplemented by income from a huge refinery built mainly to process Saudi oil—made a significant difference in the lives of Bahrain's small population (about 80,000 in the 1930s). The revenues were generally used with prudence—they were not large enough in any case for gross extravagance—and because they began twenty years before those of the other Arab oil states, Bahrainis had the education and business experience to take advantage of the prosperity of the whole region when it arrived. It could be argued that Bahrain is the most fortunate of the Arabian oil states in that it has become gradually better off rather than suddenly immensely rich. Development did not require the import of a huge foreign labor force.

Bahrain was also lucky in that the oil industry saved it from the worst effects of the collapse of the pearling industry. Customs revenues before the oil were less than £100,000 because of the general poverty of the region, made worse by the world depression. Pearling was Bahrain's main source of livelihood, employing about 20,000 Bahraini males in the 1920s.

The pearls of the Gulf had been known since classical times as the most exquisite in the world, although the Greek geographers referred to them unglamorously as "fishes' eyes." They may be white, golden yellow (popular in South America in modern times), "black" (actually gunmetal blue), or rose pink, the most precious of all. Life was hard for the divers during the five-month summer season which they spent away from their homes. They had no more equipment than a wooden nose-clip, which enabled them to stay under for about a minute, and leather guards for fingers and toes against the sharp coral rocks. Sharks and poisonous jellyfish just had to be avoided. The "pullers" who hauled the ropes to let them up and down in the water had an easier time, but they received half the divers' share of the profits. They received no wages but an advance on future profits from the ship's captain, who in turn borrowed from the pearl merchants, usually at exorbitant rates of interest. Most of the divers were in debt and many were elderly men who had to go on diving to survive.

In 1932 Belgrave persuaded the Shaykh to limit the rates of interest and size of advances and introduce proper accounting. But by then the pearl industry had begun a steady decline toward extinction. First the luxury trade was hit by the world recession, and then the Japanese discovered how to culture pearls by introducing a scrap of foreign substance into the oyster which covers it with nacre. The pearl merchants could all tell cultured pearls from the real ones on sight, but few who bought them could make the distinction.

The oil industry enabled Bahrain to survive the slump and to prosper, especially when large-scale oil production began after World War II in neighboring Saudi Arabia, Qatar, and Kuwait. Bahrain was fitted for the role of entrepôt and services center for the region. Shaykh Salman, who smoothly succeeded his father in 1942, continued to rule with the help of Belgrave as his Advisor. But at the same time the younger generation of Bahrainis who had been to the new schools and quite possibly also to a university in Beirut or Cairo was beginning to resent the semi-colonial atmosphere on the island. In the early 1950s the heady waves of Nasserist Arab nationalism began to emanate from Egypt. These young Bahrainis formed clubs which became centers of political opposition.

Charles Belgrave's personality helped to provoke opposition. Dedicated and incorruptible, he was a self-confessed Tory imperialist of the old school. (As a retreat he built himself a modest house on the small Jida island which was used as a prison and where he contentedly worked in the gardens alongside the chained convicts.) Like Lord Cromer in Egypt half a century earlier, he dismissed the young nationalist leaders with contempt. What they lacked was the "character-building" of a good English public school.

Trouble began in 1952 with a serious Sunni-Shia split over representation on the Municipality, but Sunnis and Shiites soon joined forces to seek political reforms. Eight of them formed their own Higher Executive Committee to ask for trade unions, a labor law, and a modern legal code. Soon they went further to demand an elected parliament and the dismissal of Belgrave.

The Ruler agreed to some of their demands but, as usual in such cases, this did not satisfy the nationalists who were always one step ahead. Belgrave advised the Ruler to stand firm and not to recognize the Committee, which he said represented only themselves. On the other hand, he was indignant that the British Political Agency was in contact with the Committee and taking the line that Bahrain must change more rapidly with the times.

Matters came to a head in 1956. In February, Arab nationalist feeling reached a new pitch as King Hussein of Jordan dismissed General Glubb, his British Commander-in-Chief. At this point the British Foreign Secretary visited Bahrain, and his car was stoned by a huge hostile crowd demanding Belgrave's dismissal. The enraged British Prime Minister, Anthony Eden, was convinced that this was part of a Pan-Arab, anti-British plot organized from Cairo. From then onward the British Political Agency ceased to have much sympathy for the Committee, although the Committee, convinced that it still had the support of the British government, maintained its demands.

The Ruler agreed to recognize the Higher Committee, which changed its name to the Committee of National Union, but in other respects he hardened his attitude. He reiterated his confidence in Belgrave, and when Belgrave announced his retirement in 1957, he appointed another Englishman to the newly-created post of Secretary of Government as well as several more British to strengthen the police force. Tension rose to its height during the Suez crisis of November 1956, when there were serious pro-Egyptian and anti-British riots; several were killed and property was destroyed, although the landing of British troops prevented any damage to the oil installations. Saudi Arabia, regarding Bahrain as a British interest and afraid of sabotage of its pipelines, cut off oil supplies to the refinery for four months until Israel was obliged by U.S. pressure to withdraw from Sinai.

Those of the Committee of National Union who failed to escape were arrested and charged with conspiring to overthrow the regime. Three of them were sentenced to fourteen years' imprisonment and deported in a British warship to join the shade of Napoleon Bonaparte in St. Helena. They became the object of a prolonged campaign for their release by a few British politicians and journalists.

All political activity virtually ceased. Clubs and newspapers were closed. It was only after some years, as the high tide of Nasserism receded, that the atmosphere became more relaxed. The ruling family was helped by the increasing prosperity which diverted the attention of many of the brighter young Bahrainis into business. "Our political passions are being smothered in dollars," as one of Bahrain's leading young technocrats said a few years later. In 1961 Shaykh Salman died and was succeeded by his son Isa, the present Ruler. The custom of the last five generations of nominating an heir apparent rather than leaving the choice of succession to be made by the family on the death of the Ruler, as in most other Gulf States, has greatly assisted Bahrain's stability.

The British attitude during the decade after Suez was curiously unreal. Superficially nothing had changed; if anything, the British seemed more determined than ever to hold on to their position in the Gulf now that the Suez affair and the 1958 revolution in Iraq had destroyed what remained of British power elsewhere in the Arab world. Bahrain was now very much the British headquarters in the region—especially as Kuwait moved toward independence. The British naval base was moved there from Persia in 1935 and the British Residency in the Gulf from Bushire in 1946. The Political Agent in Bahrain also had responsibility for Qatar and the Trucial Coast.

Even as late as the late 1950s visitors were astonished to find something resembling the British Indian Raj in the early years of the twentieth century. There were abundant old colonial types of all ages who stared in astonishment at any suggestion that Britain might one day leave the area. The oil company Bapco (which though U.S.-owned was British-administered) still had no Bahrainis among its senior staff, and the question whether Bahrainis ought to be allowed as guests in the Bapco Club was still under discussion.

Throughout the 1960s successive British governments reaffirmed their intention of staying on in the Gulf indefinitely. It was argued that this was essential to defend British and other Western interests and incidentally to prevent Persians and Arabs from being at each others' throats as they were certain to be if Britain departed. However, in 1968 the British Labour Government, beset by economic problems, made a sudden about-face and announced its intention of leaving the area forever by 1971.

The Ruler was both surprised and upset by this decision. Nasserist Arab nationalism was no longer a threat, but Baathists and other radical elements were active in the Gulf area, and there was an apparent threat to all the ruling shaykhs from the Marxist opposition in Oman which had formed PFLOAG—the Popular Front for the Liberation of the Arabian Gulf. A much greater immediate threat to Bahrain was the long-standing Iranian claim to sovereignty over the island which the Iranians held had been accepted by Britain in 1869. Officially Iran referred to Bahrain as its fourteenth province and refused entry to foreigners with Bahraini visas on their passports. With encouragement from Saudi Arabia and Kuwait as well as Britain, Bahrain at once began to discuss plans for a federation with the other small Gulf Emirates—Qatar and the Trucial Coast states. However, it was soon apparent that no federal formula could be devised that could both give Bahrain due weight as the most populous and advanced of the member states and be acceptable to others. Meanwhile Britain, in a highly constructive farewell gesture, succeeded in persuading the Shah of Iran to drop his claim to Bahrain. A face-saving formula was devised whereby Iran accepted the verdict of an inquiry by a senior

UN official in Bahrain that showed that the great majority of the population wanted Bahrain to be an Arab state.* Accordingly, Bahrain decided to opt for complete independence, which was declared on August 15, 1971. The British Residency in the Gulf, for so long a seat of power, became the new Bahraini Ministry of Information.

At independence, the Ruler for the first time delegated some of his powers. A cabinet was formed in which only about one third of the ministers were members of the ruling family, although in key posts. The British advisors were officially reduced to civil-service status although they retained crucial positions in charge of the security and intelligence services.

Following the precedent of Kuwait, Shaykh Isa decided that his rule should develop into a form of constitutional government. In 1973 a 44-member National Assembly was elected by adult male suffrage. However, as in Kuwait also, the new parliament eventually made life impossibly difficult for the executive branch. A minority of vocal radicals formed an alliance with their more conservative colleagues to assert the sovereignty of parliament. After only twenty months' existence of the National Assembly, the cabinet asked the Ruler to dissolve it, and government has since been carried on by the Emir's decree.

The parliamentary clauses in the constitution have only been suspended and could be revived, as it has been in Kuwait. Meanwhile, despite the obvious dangers, Bahrain enjoys a high degree of stability which is due to several factors of which the efficiency of the security forces is only one, and not necessarily the most important. The ruling family is genuinely popular and wholly integrated into the life of the community. It is not separated from the people by any extravagant display of wealth or power. The island and its population are small enough (total area 225 square miles with about 300,000 inhabitants in 1980) for the Ruler to remain highly accessible, as he would wish. This is not intended to suggest that Bahrain is free from social and political tension. After

*In 1979, following the Shah's overthrow, a prominent Iranian Ayatollah revived the claim but, to the relief of the Bahrainis, he was repudiated by the government and received no support from Ayatollah Khomeini.

a series of strikes in 1975 the government disbanded all labor unions and banned all strikes. Five years later it was beginning to make cautious moves to restore union rights, but the government felt confident enough to choose its own pace.

Undoubtedly the most serious threat to stability is the Sunni-Shia division. The Shiites include both the descendants of the indigenous Baharinah and of more recent Persian immigrants; together they form about 60 percent of the population. Although care has been taken to give the Shiites a share of political and administrative authority and there are a number of prosperous Shiite merchants and businessmen, their community is still poorer and less influential than that of the Sunnis. Since early 1979 the problem has been exacerbated by the Iranian Revolution. Although Ayatollah Khomeini himself has tried to appeal to all Muslims for Islamic regeneration rather than specifically to his fellow Shiites, this has not been true of many of his closest followers. In any case the Ayatollah's radical hostility toward other Islamic regimes was bound to have some attraction to those who feel themselves to be the underdogs. There were Shiite demonstrations which led to rioting in the autumn of 1979 and again in the spring of 1980. The Bahraini authorities expelled a Shiite shaykh who claimed he was Khomeini's representative in Bahrain.

The strongest potential antidote to Shiite grievances lies in the contrast between the order and prosperity in Bahrain and the anarchy and economic hardships in Iran. The prosperity must be shared by the whole population, and in general this is so in Bahrain even if the Shiites are less well off than the Sunnis.

The economic development of the past twenty years—and especially the last five—has certainly been phenomenal. The well-ordered but leisurely colonial town that was Manama in the days of Belgrave has become a great commercial center at an international crossroads which measures up to Singapore, Hong Kong, or Beirut before its self-destruction. In October 1932 Belgrave recalled the excitement in Bahrain when the first Imperial Airways plane landed on what is now the Manama racecourse on its way to India. When the pilot tried to take off, the plane sank into a covered ditch and had to be hauled out with ropes. Today Bahrain Airport is one of the best known in the world, a scheduled stop for airlines operating between Europe, India, the Far East, and Australia. In 1976 it was the first airport to receive the Concorde on a regular flight. Although the other Gulf states have now caught up, Bahrain led the way in telecommunications with its earth station, linked to the Intelsat Four Satellite, making direct dialing possible between the Gulf and much of the world. In 1973 Bahrain had the first color television in the Gulf.

Bahrainis realize that being first is not enough. Their neighbors can all build their own ports, airports, and communications systems so that they do not have to rely on Bahrain as an entrepôt and services center. Moreover, although Bahrain was the first Gulf state to produce oil, it is also the first whose oil production has begun to decline. Yet Bahrainis have turned this into an advantage. Diversification of the economy away from oil is not only advisable but imperative, and Bahrain has the inestimable advantage of a developed infrastructure and a local labor force that can fill at least some of the country's needs. Bahrainis have less reluctance to work with their hands than their more affluent neighbors.

Bahrain's traditional industries for many centuries have been fishing, pearling, weaving, and boat building. These all survive but on a much reduced scale. The catch of fish is poor and the demand for the bigger dhows has fallen away, although the skilled craftsmen now make the smaller *jalibuts* (''jolly-boats'' to English eighteenth-century sailors) which can be fitted with engines. But Bahrain's links with the sea have been brought into the twentieth century by the giant Arab Shipbuilding and Repair Yard (ASRY). Bahrain was chosen as the site by the Organization of Arab Petroleum Exporting Countries (OAPEC) who financed the project, and the yard was built on a spit of sand attached to Muharraq Island by an artificial causeway. It is managed by the Portuguese firm Lisnave. (As Bahrainis like to point out, the invaders of three hundred years ago are now returning peacefully.) In the first two years after it was opened in 1977 it repaired 300 ships which can take up to

500,000 tons. Some 60 percent of the 1,300 employees of ASRY are Arabs, and the aim is to make this 90 percent by 1984. It has a training center which has turned out 500 skilled workers in two years. There is a brisk demand for their services, and nearly half of them have found employment elsewhere. The Bahraini chairman of ASRY points out that this is not to be deplored, as one of the objects of the whole scheme was to provide trained manpower for the Gulf.

Bahrain's other major industry outside oil is aluminum smelting. Aluminium Bahrain (Alba), started in 1972, produces 50 percent above its original capacity of 120,000 tons a year in spite of some past labor troubles. Both ASRY and Alba have given rise to a whole range of secondary industries—light engineering, repair, and maintenance. There are a number of other small independent factories turning out building materials and consumer goods. But Bahrain's future depends more than anything on the provision of services. During the Lebanese civil war the government made a positive decision to bid for Bahrain to become an alternative to Beirut. In 1975 it allowed the establishment of "offshore banking units"—known as OBUs—which means that they pay a license fee but are not subject to Bahraini taxation or statutes. They cannot compete for local business but can take large deposits from governments and other banks and provide loans. This operation has been a huge success. More than fifty banks, mostly major international licenses, have established OBUs in Bahrain and their total assets in 1979 had already exceeded $23 billion, making Bahrain the equal of Singapore as a banking center of this kind. In addition there are some twenty foreign companies taking advantage of similar exemption from currency and exchange control to make Bahrain the center of their Middle East operations. The hugh exhibition center at the entrance to Manama attracts up to 500 international companies at its trade fairs.

There are other reasons why Bahrain could be described as the "Beirut of the Gulf." Twenty years ago the only hotel accommodation was the modest British airlines hostel, the Speedbird. Today there are so many luxury and first-class hotels that there is anxiety about filling them. But tourists—both Arabs and expatriates—pour in from the rest of Arabia, attracted in part by Bahrain's relatively relaxed social laws. The sale of alcohol is allowed, and restaurants from East and West, bars, and discotheques have sprung up around the hotels. (Unfortunately, but not surprisingly, some foreign visitors try to press Bahraini liberalism too far by wearing clothes that would raise eyebrows in Greenwich Village. The Bahrain Police set up a "Decency Patrol" to tour the suqs (bazaars) and hand out warnings to scantily-dressed expatriates). The worries about empty hotel rooms are likely to disappear as international travelers are beginning to stop over for a few days in Bahrain. Even more visitors may come when the projected causeway is built to link Bahrain with Saudi Arabia. Already the Thursday planes are crammed with weekending Saudis. The twenty thousand who came in 1979 would probably increase two or three times if they could come by road. The building of a billion-dollar causeway, to be financed by Saudi Arabia, has been long delayed since it was agreed upon in the time of King Faisal, but it is scheduled to start in 1981 and take about two years.

The analogy with Beirut should not be pressed too far. Bahrain, the only island Arab state, has its own strong personality, which has been shaped by the Gulf rather than the Mediterranean. It belongs to Arabia and not the Levant. Despite the Sunni-Shia division its society is blessed with a natural unity which Lebanon sadly lacks. Class divisions have been softened by the high standard of social services. Economic growth has been rapid but steady rather than hysterical, except in 1975-76 following the boom in oil prices when, in the words of one minister, "Bahrainis lost their heads for two years." Public housing for the less affluent fell behind in the wild construction boom of villas for the wealthy. The money supply rose by 65 percent in one year. Then the government caught its breath and clamped on controls. Inflation declined and even rents began to fall.

To a returning visitor, one sad thing about this cheerful and amiable island is the decline in the green vegetation which has always singled the island out from its neighbors. Many Bahrainis are curiously indifferent to the fact that the natural springs have been overused, that about half the 900,000 palms have been allowed to die, and that the property boom has eaten away much of the very limited fertile land. One school of thought in the region holds that it is a process of Darwinian natural selection and inevitable in a society of enterprising people who need the land for other economic uses. But there are other views, and the government is attempting to reverse the trend by encouraging investment in agriculture while conserving the precious natural water supplies. This is essential if the "Island of Two Seas" is not to turn to desert.

15
Qatar

*T*here are few Westerners—even champions of radio quiz competitions—who would succeed in pointing out the State of Qatar on the map. Kuwait became known as the first of the Arab city-states to acquire great wealth, Bahrain is often in the news as a stopping place on the route to the East, and the name United Arab Emirates is self-explanatory. But Qatar? In fact, however, this 4,000 square-mile desert peninsula pointing northwards into the Gulf has established itself as an independent state with a strong individual personality while remaining one of the two or three smallest members of the United Nations. At the same time it has not allowed its great wealth to go to its head. If it has one of the highest per capita incomes in the world, it is because the population which shares its oil revenues is so small—perhaps 220,000 of whom less than 65,000 are Qataris. The Ruler, Shaykh Khalifah al Thani, could easily address the entire nation in the magnificent new sports stadium outside Doha, the capital.

The clan of Al Thani, a branch of the famous tribe of Tamim, came to Qatar from the Yabrin oasis in the southern Najd in the eighteenth century. They were Wahhabis—that is supporters of the puritanical reformer Muhammed ibn Abd al Wahhab who was the ally of the House of Saud. Qatar was then well known as a center of the pearling industry based on its fortified ports of which Zubarah in the northwest of the peninsula was the most important. There were regular trade links with India and China, but this

133

was hazardous because control of the sea lanes was disputed with the Arab fleets by first the Portuguese and later the Dutch and the British. One of the most famous Qatari sea captains was Rahmah ibn Jabir, who conducted daring raids from the sheltered inlets (aerial photographs have recorded passages he carved through the reefs) until he was finally killed in a battle off Dammam in 1826.

The Al Thani were nomadic herdsmen when they arrived in Qatar, but they turned to the more settled and lucrative trade of pearling and fishing. Gradually they established their authority over the other tribes who shared the peninsula among them. The ruling family of Bahrain, the Al Khalifah, claimed suzerainty over Qatar at that time, and the Al Thani devoted much of their energies to rejecting Bahrain's overlordship. By the middle of the nineteenth century Qatar was effectively ruled by the Al Thani under their Shaykh Muhammad ibn Thani from his capital al-Bida (later Doha). When the British traveler W. G. Palgrave visited Qatar in 1862, toward the end of his great journey from Gaza to the Gulf, he described Shaykh Muhammad as "a shrewd wary old man, and renowned by prudence and good-humoured demeanour, but a hard customer at a bargain." Five years later his position as Paramount Shaykh of the Qatari tribes was strengthened through a treaty with Britain, the dominant power in the Gulf, under which both parties agreed to keep the peace at sea.

Shaykh Muhammad was succeeded on his death in 1872 by his son Shaykh Qasim (often transliterated "Jasim" because the "Q" in the Gulf is pronounced "J"). Poet, devout Muslim, and skilled tribal diplomat, Qasim outshone his formidable father as a leader. Under him the Qatar peninsula crystallized into a distinct political entity. Much of his energy and political skill was devoted to keeping a balance between the influences of Britain and the Turks, who in the 1870s made a determined if belated attempt to assert the authority of the Ottoman Empire in eastern Arabia to compensate for the loss of its European provinces. In 1872 he allowed the Turks to establish a small garrison in Doha, but he resisted all their attempts to supplement it with administrators. He agreed to be the local *qaim-maqam* or Ottoman district commissioner but strengthened his position by refusing to take any salary. In 1893 he defeated a Turkish force in a sharp encounter at Wajba on the coast. However, he did not break with the Turks but continued to play them skillfully off against the British.

Qasim died at a great age in 1913 and was succeeded by his able son Abdullah. Two years later the Turks, having entered World War I on the side of the Germans and lacking any sea power in the Gulf, were forced to withdraw their tiny garrison from Qatar. The British moved in and in 1916 signed an Exclusive Agreement similar to those it had concluded with Kuwait, Bahrain, and the Trucial States. This meant that the Ruler of Qatar agreed not to cede any territory except to Britain, not to enter into agreements with other countries or admit their representatives. In return Britain offered military protection.

In the 1920s pearl fishing and nomadic herding provided Qatar's tiny population with a primitive subsistence. But in the 1930s world recession and the Japanese development of cultured pearls brought disaster. The Qataris were reduced to near starvation as any middle-aged or elderly Qatari will recall today. "The bulk of the inhabitants are on the verge of destitution," reported the British Political Agent in Bahrain in 1931. "People have sold the rafters of their homes to maintain themselves." Some desperately sought work in Saudi Arabia or Bahrain. But in 1935 the Ruler granted a concession to a company called Petroleum Development (Qatar), later renamed Qatar Petroleum Company (an offshoot of the Iraq Petroleum Company with the same Anglo-U.S.-French owners). This company struck oil in 1939 and, after the interruption of World War II, production began in 1949. When the official inauguration was held in February 1950 a toast was drunk, but the managing director's instructions to provide champagne were written in Latin to avoid offense.

The outlook was at once transformed. Qatar is only a modest producer. In the 1950s company officials were discussing whether they should consider themselves the "smallest of the big producers" or the "largest of the small producers." The fact remained that the tiny size of the country's population gave it a per capita income comparable to that of Kuwait. The discovery of two additional fields offshore in the 1960s—one by QPC and the other by Shell—coupled with the oil price rises of the 1970s have given Qataris one of the highest incomes in the world. (A Swiss bank solemnly produces annual statistics that show either Qatar or Kuwait edging ahead of the other in per capita income. In fact it is only a crude measure with a wide margin of error.)

Shaykh Abdullah abdicated because of his age in 1951 and died two years later. This provoked a family crisis among the Al Thani. The next twenty years formed a sort of interregnum dominated by Shaykhs Ali and Ahmad, uncle and cousin of the present Ruler Shaykh Khalifah. Shaykh Ali abdicated in 1960 in favor of his son Ahmad, and Shaykh Khalifah became Deputy Ruler and Prime Minister. Khalifah, a vigorous and energetic personality with strong views about Qatar's need to look to the future, was constantly frustrated by his indolent cousin the Ruler who spent much of his time away from Doha either falcon hunting or visiting his various properties abroad. Ahmad had an attractive sense of humor. Reclining on the deck of a launch which was speeding up the Thames on a fine summer's day he is said to have remarked of the crowds who waved from the banks: "I see that the natives are friendly."

During the 1950s and 1960s a start was made on providing Qatar with the services it lacked almost entirely. The first primary school was opened in 1952 and the first hospital in 1959. But a large slice of Qatar's still modest revenues was spent on luxurious but generally uncomfortable palaces by the highly individualistic members of the ruling family.

The crisis came after Britain announced that it would be leaving the Gulf in 1971 and was therefore canceling its treaties of protection with the Gulf states. With encouragement from Saudi Arabia and Kuwait, Qatar entered into negotiations with Bahrain and the Trucial States for the formation of a federation. But ultimately Bahrain and Qatar decided to remain outside the United Arab Emirates. A major reason was the difficulty of finding a formula that would not have meant the federation's being dominated by Qatar's long-standing rival Bahrain, whose population was equal to that of the rest together. Qatar therefore opted for independence. At the time it was generally considered to have only the bare minimum of population required to sustain a fully independent status.

Shaykh Ahmad was not in Doha but Geneva when he proclaimed Qatar's independence. Five months later, in February 1972, Shaykh Khalifah took over the Rulership in a bloodless coup which had the approval of most of the rest of the family.

In contrast to his languid cousin, Khalifah exudes energy. His occasional brusqueness with his own officials and expatriates who are helping with the country's development is due more than anything to his impatience that results are not being achieved more quickly.

Because it is so small, Qatar can be run as a large family business. The Ruler can, and sometimes does, call in the leaders of any section of society to deliver praise or blame. However, the country does have a constitution which provides for an Advisory Council to help the Ruler govern. This now has thirty members who "should represent all the people of Qatar." They must be over 24 years of age and persons of "respectable social standing, of good judgment and have competence in various fields." They are at present all appointed by the Emir rather than elected, but it is worth pointing out that whereas the Rulers of Kuwait and Bahrain have both felt constrained to end their experiments in representative democracy at least temporarily, Qatar has been able to uphold its constitution. The Council meets once a week for eight months a year in its own new conference-style chamber. It does not initiate legislation, but all new laws have to be referred to the Council before they are promulgated by the Emir. The Council can also initiate its own debates on social and cultural affairs and ask for policy statements from individual ministers. The discussions are usually lively and inevitably well informed.

In fact although the Emir is in appearance an absolute ruler, there are some real limits to his power. One is the members of his own family. Many of these are strong, self-willed personalities, including some of the females who belie the myth of docile and complacent Muslim women. Another power in the land is the merchant class. Only two merchant families—the Al Mana and the Darwish—were prominent before the oil came when both had members who were right-hand men to the rulers. The opportunities provided by the oil boom have created other merchant-barons.

But if the Emir is not all-powerful, his personality is omnipresent in Qatar. Every new development tends to reflect his character. As a passionate Qatari nationalist he can be said to have three aims which are all interlinked and which would be the same for anyone in similar circumstances: diversification of the economy to reduce dependence on the sale of crude oil; Qatarization to reduce dependence on foreign experts; and, by no means of least importance, improvement of the environment and quality of life in Qatar.

The achievement of this last objective faces formidable problems. When Palgrave visited Qatar in the 1860s he wrote: "To have an idea of Katar my readers must figure to themselves miles and miles of low barren hills, black and sun-scorched with hardly a single tree to vary their dry monotonous outline: below these a muddy beach extends for a quarter mile seaward in slimy quicksands, bordered by a rim of sludge and seaweed. If we look landwards beyond the hills, we see what extreme courtesy may call pasture land, deary downs with twenty pebbles for every blade of grass."

In the 1960s, a century after Palgrave's visit, the oil had been flowing for some years but there was little change. Only a gay little pink-and-white clocktower standing near the Emir's palace showed the shape of things to come. Today, against all the odds, Doha has the makings of a fine city-port. Part of the bay has been filled in so that a spendid corniche road could be built. This is to be extended to an entirely new residential district that is being built on land reclaimed from the sea—the West Bay Development—with a striking pyramid-shaped Sheraton Hotel, foreign embassies, beach club, and marina. The temptation to make that would almost certainly have been the wrong decision to build an entirely new capital has been avoided. The heart of old Doha remains even if most of it has been pulled down. Flowering shrubs and trees line the streets; there are several public gardens including a splendid new zoo being built just outside the city. Private gardens also flourish as people have been surprised to discover how many things will grow within their compounds on even the parched soil of Qatar. Palgrave would have been astonished. The *piece de resistance* is the Qatar National Museum, undoubtedly the finest in the region and comparable to the best in the world. It is housed in a restored palace complex of the nineteenth century Shaykh Abdullah overlooking the harbor and displays the architecture, culture, and tradition of Qatari life—both of the beduin and the settled people of the coast. The aquarium shows some of the abundant varieties of fish in the Gulf, and a small lagoon displays several types of dhow which are now nearly extinct. (''Dhow'' is a general term used by Westerners for Arab craft but is not employed by the Arabs themselves.)

But admirable and indispensable though the Museum may be to maintain and strengthen Qatar's links with its own past, it is hardly the building which arouses the most interest among Qataris in the 1980s. This is the Center, a vast enclosed market owned by one of the Ruler's cousins which claims, no doubt correctly, to be the largest department store in the Gulf. When this opened in 1978 it went through a difficult year until its managers realized that they were relying too heavily on luxury items for the ''carriage trade'' and for non-Arab customers. Now that it has a majority of middle-priced items likely to appeal to the bulk of Doha's Arab population the Center is booming. On my last visit my middle-aged Qatari driver, who was old enough to remember when no one in Qatar had enough to eat, went regularly to the Center to buy French bread for his family although he always supplemented it with Persian bread from the still flourishing traditional *suq*.

The Ruler is especially fond of roses, but his ambitions go much further than this. He is apt to say that he would die happy if Qatar were self-sufficient in food. On the face of it this seems an impossible dream. It is true that the produce of the small enclosed farms dotted about the Peninsula was capable a few years ago of providing the population with fruit and vegetables at certain seasons of the year. But the water table has fallen alarmingly. In May 1980 an order had to be made that no new wells were to be drilled and the country's sweet water reserves--barely half its proved oil reserves—were to be sealed off. The use of distilled sea water for agriculture is still quite uneconomic as the crops produced cost five or six times the present variety. The huge and increasing quantities that are distilled are needed for industry and domestic use. Daily consumption of water is the amazing quantity of 150 gallons per person—about four times the European average. Thirty years ago the ordinary Qatari would have considered himself fortunate with a single gallon a day.

The Ruler urges his own officials and the dedicated FAO advisors to find a solution. There are various possibilities over the horizon such as the 100 percent purification of effluent water so that it can be used to grow food, not only, as at present, trees and shrubs. Cheaper methods of desalinating sea water may be developed. There is a possibility, still no more than a twinkle in the eye of John Pike, the FAO Coordinator in Qatar, that when the vast offshore natural gas reserves are tapped, the great quantities of heat produced from freezing the gas will be used to distill sea water which could cover the north of the peninsula with a network of irrigation canals. One thing is certain: the Ruler will not abandon his dream of a self-feeding Qatar.

The search for an alternative to the sale of crude oil as Qatar's main source of livelihood is especially urgent because oil reserves are only about four billion barrels and are likely to run out by the end of the century. Fortunately, Qatar does have an extra resource in the huge offshore natural gas field known as the North West Dome. This has reserves estimated at 100 trillion cubic feet which is more than the great Dutch Groningen field before it was exploited to fuel European industry. Qatar has not yet decided how or when to tap this resource; it can afford to wait until its markets are assured and the price of natural gas rises, as assuredly it will. Meanwhile the North West Dome can be regarded as an insurance policy.

But even 100 trillion cubic feet of gas is a finite resource that one day would be exhausted. Other industries have to be developed, and even if most of these are almost inevitably dependent on oil as a raw material at least they mean that Qatar itself is making fuller use of its own natural wealth. The new industrial center is at Umm Said, thirty miles south of Doha on the coast. Here there are natural gas liquefying plants, petrochemicals, fertilizers, and a huge integrated iron and steel complex. All of these suffered severe teething troubles when they were started in the 1970s—especially the fertilizer plant which was the first. In 1977 a great fire destroyed one of the natural gas plants, and it is now being rebuilt by a Japanese company. The difficulties have largely been overcome with the benefit of experience. At Umm Said port ships load Qatari ammonia and urea to fertilize the crops of India, China, and Malaysia. The partly Japanese Qatar Steel Company (QASCO) is the first of its kind in the Gulf to use natural gas as a fuel. It is proud of its low costs which compare favorably with those in the West, and it exports its manufactured steel to the other industrializing countries of the Gulf.

The measure of Qatar's development lies not only in these few giant projects which are owned by the state in partnership with foreign companies but in the services and light industries that are growing up around them. It was just two months before the first tanker arrived to take off Qatari oil in 1950 that a group of ten leading merchants opened Qatar's first bank. Now three out of the country's thirteen banks are Qatari-owned and there is one Qatari insurance company. But Qatar has not attempted to challenge Bahrain and Kuwait as a financial center, and the country still has a long way to go to develop the institutions it needs to service its own private sector. This is now showing signs of taking off. A few years ago virtually all the repair and maintenance work was carried out by foreign firms. Now some Qataris are entering the field of shipping and machine repair in partnership with foreign companies. They are even looking to export their services to the Gulf states although they can expect strong competition from the Bahrainis.

Qataris would naturally like to be in charge of their own explosive development as far as possible. But their shortage of manpower is as acute as in any of the Gulf states—even if the population has tripled since the time oil was discovered. Moreover they need to be trained for responsibility. Education has a short history in Qatar; the first primary school was only opened in 1952. Now there are over 130 schools, with plans to double their number over the next decade. There is a vocational training center, a College of Trade and Industry, and a teachers' training institute which was expanded into a university in 1977. Qatar is even in a position to offer education to some of its neighbors, such as the Omanis who had no schools until 1970.

Many felt that the opening of the University of Qatar, crammed into four secondary schools, was premature. The splendid new campus, with its pre-cast concrete buildings, will be completed by 1982. But the university is an essential focus of national life and the impetus behind the demand for it was too strong. The university vice-chancellor is a distinguished Egyptian from Cairo's ancient Islamic University of Al Azhar, and much of the faculty is Egyptian. But education is the field in which Qataris are taking over most rapidly. In 1954 there were no Qatari teachers. Now about 25 percent of the teachers are from Qatar, and in primary schools the proportion is as high as 90 percent. In the university, half the faculty will be Qatari by the mid-1980s.

Hitherto young Qataris have had to go abroad for their higher education. In 1980 there were about fifty in the United States, a hundred in the United Kingdom, and nine hundred at various Arab universities. A new generation of young Qataris with university or technical education is now ready to take over some of the jobs that were held either by older, less qualified Qataris, sometimes in sinecure positions, or by expatriates. Inevitably this can cause resentment, especially when the fresh young Qatari expects to step straight into a senior managerial position. But on the whole it is working smoothly. The Qataris tend to create honorific advisory posts for the Palestinians, Egyptians, Sudanese, and other Arabs who have served them well over the years.

Inevitably some of the young Qataris who return home from abroad find life in Doha dull and constricting—a view that is shared by many of the expatriates. Alone among the people of the Gulf emirates, Qataris are Wahhabis like the Saudi Arabians, although the atmosphere of Qatar is far from being ultra-puritanical. The development of social and cultural activities has been remarkable in view of the tiny indigenous population. Where there were no newspapers twenty years ago there are now two Arabic dailies, an English weekly, shortly to become a daily, several weeklies, and a cultural monthly magazine, edited by a dynamic Sudanese, which distributes over 60,000 copies. Qatar television relies heavily on material imported from other Arab countries but also manages to produce its own programs. Some of these can be highly ambitious attempts to wed modern techniques to Arab traditions, with varied but often stimulating results. The traditional arts and crafts of the Gulf are encouraged but so also are painting and drama which seems incongruous in a Wahhabi state. Qatar has begun to produce a few interesting painters and there is an embryonic but flourishing theater.

Considering its short history as a separate state, Qatar has a strong and recognizable identity which shows no sign of being swamped either by the foreign majority of its population or by the products of Western civilization. But in spite of Qataris' intense local pride there can be no question of isolationism. Qataris like to call their country "the finger of Arabism in the Gulf." There could hardly be a more passionate Qatari nationalist than the Ruler, but several visiting Western dignitaries who comfortably assumed that Qatar would care little about Palestine have been startled to receive from him a magisterial lecture on the problem. Qataris share in the general feeling among Arabs that a distorted picture of them and the Muslim religion is received in the West; the Qatar government has been active in putting forth suggestions to the other Arabian Gulf states as to how this might be remedied. It has proposed, for example, the creation of a network of information centers in major non-Muslim countries and the sponsoring of films, books, and translations to illuminate the heritage of the Arab and Muslim peoples.

16
The United Arab Emirates

*T*he instep of the boot-shaped Arabian Peninsula is the five hundred miles of low-lying coastline between the Qatar Peninsula and the small Musandam point which stands at the entrance to the Gulf. It consists of shallow inlets or *khors*, sandbars, coral reefs, mud flats, and a myriad small islands. Behind this the desert stretches back to merge with the Empty Quarter of Arabia except at the northern end where the belt of gray and rugged Omani mountains reaches the sea.

The whole region is parched except where rain on the mountains has created small fertile valleys or percolated beneath the soil to form a few inland oases—such as the Buraymi complex on the edge of the Empty Quarter. On the shore in places groundwater seepage allowed tiny populations to settle. Where the sandbars were sufficiently firm, as at Dubai, Sharjah, or Ras al Khayhmah, small ports grew which traded up the Gulf and into the Indian Ocean.

The labyrinth of shoals and reefs, navigable only by the most expert and experienced, provided the ideal base for piracy and the Pirate Coast was its name to the Portuguese, Dutch, and British sailors when they invaded the Gulf.

In the nineteenth century the tribes inhabiting this coastal region were known as the Qawasim (pronounced *Jawasim*, the plural of Qasimi). Brave and merciless, they were greatly feared by the Europeans. Sir John Malcolm, a British envoy of the Indian government, was warned by his Arab servant: "If you are their captive, and offer all you possess to save your life, they say, 'No! it is written in the Koran that it is unlawful to plunder the living, but we are not prohibited in the sacred work from stripping the dead'; so saying, they knock you on the head."

At the beginning of the nineteenth century the captains of the British vessels of the East India Company had orders only to act in self-defense against the Qawasim. But as the Qawasim became bolder and started demanding tribute from ships passing their coast, this self-restraint was soon forgotten. Punitive expeditions were launched against the coastal towns, but each time the Qawasim recovered and resumed their raids. Finally in 1820 a powerful British fleet sailed from Bombay, burned or seized all the boats of the Qawasim and imposed a General Treaty of Peace on each of the ruling shaykhs of the Pirate Coast.

This Treaty still allowed the coastal tribes to fight each other, and since this disturbed the Pax Britannica which was now being imposed on the whole Gulf, a new Maritime Truce was imposed on them in 1835. This was renewed several times until it became a Treaty of Peace in Perpetuity in 1853. The Pirate Coast had become the Trucial Coast.

This Treaty only applied to the sea; the British were not interested in the land where the ruling shaykhs were free to pursue their dynastic feuds. However, in the second half of the nineteenth century Britain became concerned with challenges to its dominance in the Gulf—from the Ottoman Turks and the Persians. It was these which led the British to sign an Exclusive Treaty with the Ruler of Bahrain in 1861. But Bahrain, as an island, could be controlled by the British navy; the British were still reluctant to make any colonial-type commitment on the Arabian mainland. However, in 1892 British anxiety was increased by the activities in the Gulf of rival powers—the French and the Russians, who were gaining powerful influence in Persia. Accordingly, in 1892 Britain took the precaution of concluding agreements with each of the ruling shaykhs of the Trucial Coast which, like the one with the Ruler of Bahrain, excluded all other powers from their territory.

Despite, or perhaps because of, the treaties, the Trucial

Coast remained remote and forgotten in British eyes. Overall supervision was in the hands of political officers of the government of India, the Indian rupee was common currency on the coast (although the Maria Theresa dollar circulated among the desert traders inland), and most of the trade was in the hands of Indian merchants. The tiny population in the total area of some 30,000 square miles was about 80,000; because of their poverty and high infant mortality this remained stationary through most of the first half of the twentieth century. As elsewhere on the Arabian Coast, the people were divided between the *beduin* (or nomadic) who lived off their grazing herds, and *hadhar* (settled) who were fishermen, pearl divers, or small traders; but there was little difference in their levels of existence.

The little shaykhdoms were: Abu Dhabi, Dubai, Sharjah, Ajman, Ras al Khayhmah, and Umm al Qaywayn. Fujayrah, the seventh of the present-day Emirates, did not come into existence until 1952 when it split off from Sharjah. They all had tiny populations; some like Ajman had no more than one or two thousand. Their borders were not defined, only the small population centers mattered and the beduin wandered freely around the desert interior.

In these tiny communities the shaykhs attempted to govern as absolute rulers. But this was not easy; they had to show skill and resources. The tribes of the interior did not necessarily acknowledge their authority, but they judged the ruling shaykh by his ability to protect and support them against predatory neighbors. The rulers also had to contend—and this was the most difficult of all—with their own families. Since there was no rule of primogeniture in Arabia, the death of the ruler led to a fierce struggle for the succession among brothers, uncles, and cousins that was quite frequently bloody. The British hardly intervened until a much later date, although they did their best to encourage stability.

The consequence of this system was that the relative power and influence of the individual shaykhdoms rose and fell according to the personality of the ruler. Abu Dhabi was dominant throughout the second half of the nineteenth century, overshadowing the rival Qawasim to the north, because of the character of Shaykh Zayid ibn Khalifah (Zayid the Great) who ruled it for 55 years. The fratricidal struggle between his sons on his death undermined his achievement. Similarly, Sharjah, former center of the power of the Qawasim on the Pirate Coast and its main trading port, went into a long decline from the end of the nineteenth century, so that it fell from being the most populous of the Trucial States to one of the least significant. Its creek was allowed to silt up, and its place was taken by neighboring Dubai (population about 20,000) with its own bustling creek and thriving merchant community, the first in the area to be independent of the pearl trade. Dubai was fortunate and unique in having a ruling family that settled its differences without bloodshed.

The results of World War I swept the Turks finally out of the Gulf and removed for the time being the threat of intervention by European powers such as Germany or Russia. The Gulf was a British lake patrolled by the Royal Navy. But in the 1920s, two local powers began to exert pressure on the British position. The Wahhabi armies of Ibn Saud of Arabia, freed from his commitment to Britain by the ending of his British subsidy in 1924, would unquestionably have swallowed up the small Trucial States if it had not been for their agreements with Britain. On the other shore of the Gulf, Reza Shah, the Cossack colonel who had made himself dictator and then Shah of Iran, was asserting Iranian national independence and obliging Britain to move the focus of its authority in the Gulf across the water to Bahrain.

The Gulf had meanwhile increased in political importance to Britain for two main reasons. Always vital as the route to India, the original reason for Britain's interest, the Gulf was now seen as the course for military and civilian aircraft. The Royal Air Force made its first flights from Iraq to India in 1918 along the Persian shore, but in the 1920s it moved across the water to the Arab side where the Arab rulers were expected to be more amenable than the increasingly difficult Iranians. Kuwait and Bahrain presented no difficulties in providing airstrips and fueling stations, but the fiercely independent and suspicious Rulers of the Trucial States offered all kinds of objections. Both persuasion and pressure had to be used before the Ruler of Sharjah accepted an airport on his territory in 1932 and Imperial Airways could begin its regular flights to India. The airport rest house for passengers and crew, the first permanent British establishment on the coast, was built as a fort as protection against marauding tribesmen.

The other reason for British interest in the Lower Gulf was oil. In the 1920s this was still only a vague concern. British companies had enough oil for their needs in Iran and Iraq, and at that time only a few enthusiasts like Major Frank Holmes believed there might be some further down the Gulf. Nevertheless, in 1922 the British took the precaution of persuading the Trucial Coast rulers to sign agreements that they would grant no oil concessions except to a person appointed by the British government.

Expectations were transformed by the discovery of oil in commercial quantities in Bahrain in 1932, and oil men at once became interested in the entire eastern coast of Arabia. Concessions were swiftly granted by Saudi Arabia (1933), Kuwait (1934), and Qatar (1935). The British government was anxious that the experience in Saudi Arabia not be repeated where a purely American company—Standard Oil of California—had obtained a concession. A company was therefore formed to negotiate called Petroleum Concessions Ltd. in which Anglo-Dutch, U.S., and French companies held shares in the same proportion as in the Iraq Petroleum Company. But, as with the granting of facilities for the air route, the six rulers of the Trucial Coast were no easy target. They bargained and prevaricated to get better terms, and various forms of pressure, incuding threats to confiscate their pearling fleets on the grounds that they were still engaging in slave trade, had to be used until they gave in.

The last to succumb—in 1939—was the Ruler of Abu Dhabi, Shaykh Shakhbut. This remarkable figure has become something of a legend in the Gulf. In 1928 he succeeded in restoring stability to Abu Dhabi after twenty years of fierce family strife. He was helped by his mother, a powerful personality, who made his brothers swear to abandon the family tradition of fratricide. Shakhbut was convinced that there was oil in his territory—bubbles of oil had been seen around some of Abu Dhabi's two hundred islands—and the oil men agreed that it was the most promising of the Trucial States. This was why he drove a hard bargain for the concession. He had to wait nearly twenty years until oil was found, but then it was in enormous quantities.

Abu Dhabi's sudden change from rags to riches has been the most extraordinary of its kind. Unlike Kuwait, Bahrain, or even Qatar, it had no merchant class but only about 15,000 people clinging to existence through fishing and pearling. Qatar is similar, but Abu Dhabi has much more oil and a smaller population.

When the revenues turned into a flood, Shakhbut was quite unable to cope with them. Because his early life had been devoted to avoiding starvation and the murderous intentions of his relatives, he was naturally cautious. This explains his eccentricities, which became the subject of many popular anecdotes. He was apt to wake the manager of his only bank in the middle of the night to see his enormous balance counted out in cash. When he went to London for the Queen's coronation he took all his food with him in sacks because he was convinced he would be poisoned. Eventually, in 1966, he was quietly succeeded by his younger brother Zayid, the present Ruler, who finds the challenges of the modern age more stimulating than alarming.

But there was another side to Shakhbut—shrewd, quizzical, and humorous. Although he hoped for the discovery of oil to end his people's poverty, from the beginning he had more than an inkling of the kind of dangers that a sudden rush of wealth would bring. When it came it overwhelmed him. There is a charming portrait of him in *The Golden Bubble*, a travel book by a British writer, Roderic Owen, who spent some months in Abu Dhabi in 1955-56. When Shakhbut discovered that Owen wrote poetry, he made him temporary court poet and had him reciting his verses through a sweating Egyptian interpreter to Shakhbut's enthralled followers. Poetry is still the highest art for the beduin. Shakhbut showed a restless, inquiring mind with a tendency to ask sudden alarming questions such as: "What is the religion of Eskimos?" After his abdication, he traveled abroad for a time before returning to live in honorable retirement in Abu Dhabi.

The search for oil was suspended during World War II, as elsewhere in the Gulf, and the Trucial States remained underdeveloped and poverty stricken. Both rulers and people remained fiercely resistant to British interference in their internal affairs, having observed what had happened in Bahrain, which they regarded as a British colony. On the whole the British, who regarded the Trucial Coast as savage and inhospitable, were content to leave matters this way. Until 1939 the only representative of British interests on the Coast was an Arab, based on Sharjah, who was responsible to the British Resident in the Gulf.

It was only with the outbreak of war that the Indian government insisted on the appointment of a British Political Officer. Even then he only spent the winter months on the Coast.

It was in 1939 that another remarkable local personality appeared on the scene. This was Shaykh Rashid of Dubai who became Regent to his aging father Said until he succeeded him in 1958. Rashid was externally a traditional tribal chieftain but soon proved himself a businessman of exceptional acumen and resource, fully capable of meeting the challenges of the mid-twentieth century.

A problem that was being created for the future and for which no solution had been found was that the Trucial Coast had no fixed boundaries—either externally or internally between the shaykhdoms. Iran claimed some islands at the entrance of the Gulf which the Rulers of Sharjah and Ras al Khayhmah considered belonged to them. Ibn Saud claimed a large slice of territory on the edge of the Empty Quarter, which Shakhbut considered part of Abu Dhabi. Britain, which held responsibility for the shaykhdoms' foreign relations, held a series of desultory and fruitless talks with both Iran and Saudi Arabia. Similarly the oil companies, backed up by the farsighted Shakhbut, were pressing for the demarcation of the frontiers between the shaykhdoms. Their concessions referred vaguely to "territories of the shaykh," which were undefined.

Clearly if oil was found there could be endless disputes.

But Britain did not pursue the matter with any vigor. Its position in the region was anomalous: it had undertaken most of the responsibilities of a colonizer, but not the powers to intervene in the internal affairs of the shaykhdoms, which would have fiercely resisted them. In any case it was impossible to solve the problem through logic. It so happened that Britain had signed agreements with six shaykhs, recognizing them as independent rulers. But there were tribes or groups of tribes in the interior who considered that they should be independent, and it was difficult to argue that they should not. Why should the Ruler of Ajman, population 2,000, be independent and not the shaykh of several thousand Duru tribesmen? The matter could be postponed until oil was actually discovered. Meanwhile, there were constant border disputes. Abu Dhabi and Dubai were even at war from 1945 to 1947, although fortunately the absence of heavy weapons meant there was little loss of life. Even as late as the 1960s a British Political Agent recalled driving into the desert to meet two Rulers at a disputed boundary point, only to find them standing two hundred yards apart, each on a sand dune which he claimed was the true boundary. Neither would move away to meet the other for fear of appearing to surrender, and the agent trudged back and forth across the sand for an hour fruitlessly, finally climbing back into the Landrover and driving unsuccessfully away.

Eventually, with patience and hard work, a map was drawn up, and today it marks the official boundaries between the United Arab Emirates. But the cartographer might appear to have been deranged because each of the shaykhdoms has one or more enclaves of territory inside one of the others. This was ultimately the only way in which the boundary disputes could be solved. Even then they were not all solved. Some dozen disagreements remain to this day; as recently as 1972 Sharjah and Fujayrah were engaged in a series of violent skirmishes over a section of their borders.

In the 1950s Britain did increase its role in the internal affairs of the shaykhdoms. The Rulers were encouraged to meet regularly in a Trucial Council to discuss matters of common interest, although this produced few results. Of greater importance was the establishment in 1951 of the nucleus of a common army, with British officers. This was used to pacify the tribesmen of the interior who had become increasingly unruly. The collapse of the pearling industry on the coast had reduced the Rulers' income which they used to make payments to the tribes. The British government introduced a Trucial Coast Development Plan which included agricultural and technical training. An experimental farm was started in Ras al Khayhmah. But everything was on a very small scale. The cost of the Development Plan was £500,000. The total population of the shaykhdoms was no more than 90,000, of whom nearly one quarter went to find work in Kuwait, Qatar, or Bahrain.

Then in 1958 the event for which Shaykh Shakhbut had waited twenty years took place. Oil was discovered in vast quantities offshore; two years later another huge field was found onshore. Abu Dhabi at once became the "second Kuwait," and those who had regarded Kuwait's independence as an absurdity felt the same way, but even more strongly, about the almost uninhabited stretch of coastal desert that had suddenly become unbelievably wealthy.

As we have seen, Shaykh Shakhbut was unable to cope with the sudden shower of gold and in 1966 was peacefully deposed by his brother Zayid, who for years lived in the interior administering the Al Ayn oasis, Abu Dhabi's share of the Buraymi complex. The new Ruler at once launched into a huge development program. Within a few years the small dusty fishing village with unpaved sand tracks and a bumpy soccer field as an airfield had become a great skyscraper city with eight-lane highways and a large international airport. Schools and hospitals proliferated. In less than a decade the population increased tenfold.

Abu Dhabi was now the dominant shaykdom on the coast. The other rulers, while still hoping that oil would be discovered on their territory, looked to Shaykh Zayid for financial assistance. There was one exception—Dubai. Oil was discovered off the coast of Dubai in 1966, although in much smaller quantities than in Abu

Dhabi. The difference was that Dubai already had a dynamic merchant community as well as a Ruler in Shaykh Rashid with a genius for business. Even before the oil era Dubai port was a flourishing trading center for the region and beyond. Much of the remittances from Asian families in Britain passed through Dubai in the form of gold which was taken on by dhow to the Indian subcontinent. Dubai was said to be the second largest importer of Swiss watches in the world although no one could be sure of their final destination.

There is a natural rivalry between Abu Dhabi and Dubai which does not depend on the formidable personalities of the two Rulers. Dubai was formerly part of Abu Dhabi and split off in the 1830s. Although Abu Dhabi is stronger and got the better of the 1945-47 border war, it has to acknowledge Dubai's commercial superiority. When Abu Dhabi began to import on a large scale, it had to be through Dubai merchants. Abu Dhabi's resentment against Dubai was shared by the Qawasim ruling family of Sharjah, Dubai's other neighbor, who never accepted their loss of precedence on the Trucial Coast. Altogether there seemed little prospect of a harmonious political future for the shaykhdoms.

When in 1968, Britain announced its intention of withdrawing from all its political and military commitments in the Gulf by 1971, this at once placed the Rulers in an acute dilemma. Although they had always insisted on their own sovereignty and independence, they had to acknowledge that it was Britain that had protected them against the claims of Saudi Arabia and Iran. More recently a new threat to their shaykhdoms had developed in the left-wing guerrilla movement in southern Oman. Survival as fully independent states was hardly possible. Not even the largest had the population considered necessary to qualify for membership in the United Nations. (Neighboring Qatar was considered to have the absolute minimum.) Britain had never made more than half-hearted attempts to persuade them to unite. Admittedly this was almost impossibly difficult. For the rulers of the smaller shaykhdoms, unity meant pooling Abu Dhabi's oil revenues without any loss of their own sovereignty. Meanwhile the reas-

The United Arab Emirates

surance of the British presence enabled them to postpone facing the issue.

With the rude shock of the British announcement, the Rulers at once began to discuss with Qatar and Bahrain plans for a federation of all the Arab states of the Lower Gulf.

Britain, Saudi Arabia, and Kuwait were all encouraging, but the discussion soon stuck in the sand. Bahrain and Qatar decided the difficulties outweighed the advantages and opted for their own independence. Many experts concluded that the remaining Trucial Coast shaykhdoms would never agree.

However, by July 1971, on the eve of Britain's departure from the Gulf, six of the seven shaykhdoms had hammered out a provisional constitution for a federation which reflected the preeminence of Abu Dhabi and Dubai. There was to be a president (Zayid of Abu Dhabi), a vice-president (Rashid of Dubai), a Federal Council of all the rulers, a cabinet of 21 members, with eight ministers from Abu Dhabi and four from Dubai, including the prime minister, and a forty-member National Assembly in which Abu Dhabi and Dubai each had eight representatives.

The United Arab Emirates came into existence on December 2, 1971. The Ruler of Ras al Khayhmah at first declined to join because he was convinced that oil was about to be discovered on his territory, but he changed his mind the following February.

Even some of the most sympathetic were skeptical about the new state's chances of survival in the face of internal rivalries and external threats. The experiences of other attempts at federation in the Arab world have not been encouraging. One experienced and cynical British official remarked, "After all, the only thing the shaykhs have in common is that their ancestors signed a treaty with Britain to suppress piracy in 1820." Since there were no more than forty UAE citizens with university degrees at the time the new state was created and not a single lawyer or judge, the federal structure of government could only be created by expatriates.

There was an ominous beginning when Iran, on the eve of the UAE declaration, occupied the three small islands it claimed in the

Gulf—Abu Musa and the Greater and Lesser Tumbs. Britain had always recognized Abu Musa as belonging to Sharjah and the Tumbs to Ras al Khayhmah, but in the negotiations with Iran over British withdrawal from the Gulf, Britain accepted the Shah's claim to the islands as a *quid pro quo* for his abandoning the claim to Bahrain. The new state could do nothing against the Shah's formidable navy, and accepted the *fait accompli*.

Measured against the probabilities of disaster, the UAE has been a remarkable success. The secret lies in the use of the tension of rivalry between Abu Dhabi and Dubai, between Zayid and Rashid, for positive rather than destructive ends. Shaykh Rashid has been content to leave the conduct of the UAE's foreign policy to Shaykh Zayid while he has concentrated on making Dubai a major financial and commercial center. Through Shaykh Zayid, the UAE has gained a collective personality that has enabled the new state to play a significant role in Arab and world affairs. In 1974 he managed to settle the outstanding differences with Saudi Arabia. The twenty-year-old dispute over the Buraymi Oasis was resolved and the border demarcated; diplomatic relations could be established. As the Union of Emirates became more secure and self-confident, so the external threat subsided from radical elements aiming to overthrow the shaykhly system. Through the Abu Dhabi Fund for Arab Economic Development (ADFAED), established in 1971, and a great range of other contributions to aid programs, Abu Dhabi made the UAE one of the largest aid donors in the world, providing another good reason for its continued existence.

Progress toward integration of the Union has not been smooth and easy; there have been times when it seemed likely to disintegrate. While Shaykh Zayid has aimed to strengthen the federal government at the expense of the "states' rights" of the individual shaykhdoms, the others, especially Dubai, have resisted any diminution in sovereignty. These differences in the early days could be supported by the newspapers and the separate radio stations in each emirate. They did not hesitate to score off each other. Perhaps the greater threat to unity was that each emirate had retained its own defense force and was building it up, as it had been agreed they would be allowed to do when the UAE was formed. Abu Dhabi's defense force with its own jet squadron was six times as large as the UAE's defense force.

When Shaykh Zayid's first five-year term of office ended in 1976 he threatened to resign because of the unsettled border disputes and what he termed the lack of cooperation of the other emirates in making the federation a reality. Abu Dhabi was still virtually alone in financing the federal budget. However an extraordinary session of the federal parliament urged him to stay and he agreed. In the same year the individual emirate armies were merged into a single defense force.

The reality was that none of the rulers was prepared to see the federation disintegrate. The smaller and poorer emirates depended on federal funds for the development that was essential to preserve their identity, while even Dubai saw advantages in the federal framework provided it could continue making money as it wished.

At the same time a new generation was coming on the scene who saw themselves as UAE citizens and had reduced ties of loyalty to their own tribes or clans. Some even react impatiently when asked which of the emirates they come from. They felt that the federal government should be strengthened and that planning decisions should be carried out in all the emirates as they had not been in the past. At least some important steps have been taken, such as unifying the information media of the emirates so that their radio and television services do not criticize each other. The federal idea is fostered at the UAE's first university opened in 1977. This is on Abu Dhabi territory at Al Ayn, but the students come from all the emirates and return home on weekends. Still there are many of the younger generation of UAE citizens who feel that much more could be done to remove the boundaries between members of the Union.

In 1979 Shaykh Rashid agreed to head a new cabinet as prime minister. While no one doubted that one of his main purposes was to strengthen and maintain Dubai's position within the federation, it was also undeniably an affirmation of Dubai's belief in the future of the Union.

Can this federation survive a second decade or will some of its members secede and make a bid to go it alone? Certainly there are many hazards ahead. Although struggles for succession to the Rulers should be avoided as most of them have appointed one of their sons as their heir apparent, the mere removal from the scene through time of the powerful personalities who have dominated the UAE since its birth will create uncertainty. Yet those who said, and still say, that the members of the Union have nothing in common except the memory of their treaties with Britain are certainly wrong. They may have fought each other as rivals in the past but their struggle for survival against their harsh environment was exactly the same.

After the first euphoria of the oil rush, the people of the emirates do not need to be told that their new wealth will not last forever. The advantages of confronting an uncertain future together become daily more apparent. If the senior generation in one emirate were to think of secession they would probably be opposed by their sons.

The UAE exports about the same amount of oil as Kuwait or Libya, which in 1980 brought in an income of about $15 billion. There has been a population explosion. The 90,000 people of the 1950s have increased nearly ten times, although perhaps 75 percent of these are immigrant workers. By any measurement the per capita income is one of the highest in the world.

More than 80 percent of the oil earnings go to Abu Dhabi, and it is here that the most phenomenal transformation has taken place on the Pirate Coast. The derelict little fishing harbor has been replaced by a great deep-water port with 21 berths, handling two million tons of cargo a year. Twenty years ago there was one bank, housed in a small wooden hut. Today there are 40, about a third of them local, and no less than 32 insurance companies. Only Shaykh Shakhbut's old mud fortress palace and the British Political Agent's residence remain among the gigantic office buildings, hotels, and shopping centers to give some idea of the scale of the old town. Building is frenzied; anyone who returns after a few months' absence is likely to find new streets he does not recognize. Near the city is an industrial zone, but at Ruwais about 120 miles west along the coast there is a much larger one which is the heart of Abu Dhabi's plans for the future, with a refinery and gas, petrochemicals, fertilizers, and steel plants. Eventually this will become another city. At present the only other center of population is Al Ayn, one hundred miles east in the interior, which has developed into a flourishing town, surrounded by farms and experimental agricultural stations. A few miles along the road to Dubai there are several hundred astonishing acres of wheat defying the desert which produce enough to supply all Abu Dhabi's bread for one month a year.

In fact all Abu Dhabi reflects Shaykh Zayid's notorious passion for greenery. In the towns there are scores of acres of public parkland and green areas. For several hundred yards on either side of the Abu Dhabi-Al Ayn highway, trees have been planted to make what will soon be a great elongated forest. Other great patches of afforestation make a total of tens of thousands of acres. Shaykh Zayid endeavors to transmit his enthusiasm to the rest of the UAE. On UAE Tree Day—March 16, 1980—45,000 trees were planted or distributed throughout the country, and Zayid told a delegation from the newly-created General Secretariat of UAE Municipalities: "A tree is like a human being which needs continual care from everyone in this good land." If he sees from his car that a sapling has fallen over, Zayid is likely to get out and set it upright.

If Abu Dhabi city can be compared to a boom town of the American Middle West, Dubai is sometimes known as the Venice of the Gulf. This is not only because it grew up around the creek so that water was its main thoroughfare, but because it has the same air of commercial wisdom and experience as the great merchant republic of the Renaissance. Today it has been transformed, but it is not a new creation. The single-storied houses surmounted by their harmonious wind-towers have been replaced by air-conditioned skyscrapers, a bridge and tunnel have removed the need for the cheerful, overcrowded ferry that took passengers across the creek. The chaotic dhow-strewn wharves have been turned into an orderly waterfront, and a new deep-water port has been built outside the entrance to the creek. But the soul of Dubai is unmistakably the same.

The astonishing transformation of Dubai in recent years has largely been inspired by Shaykh Rashid. This seventy-year-old tribal leader, with no formal education, has proved to be the match of any of the great business entrepreneurs in the West. Time and again he has been willing to take risks that frightened his financial advisors, but his judgment has nearly always proved right. At first, even before the oil revenues began to flow in, he supported building a new port, airport, and other facilities to make sure that Dubai maintained its primacy as a port and entrepôt in the region. In the 1970s Rashid became more ambitious. The Dubai economy had its own dynamic to which the oil boom only added extra fuel. He decided to launch into heavy industry. Twenty miles west of Dubai on the coast the Jabal Ali industrial area has been created with its own huge port, an aluminum smelter, a liquid petroleum gas plant which began exporting to Japan in 1980, and a range of other industries either in hand or projected. Yet Shaykh Rashid's enterprise is perhaps best symbolized by the thirty-nine story International Trade Center on the outskirts of Dubai. It is proudly billed as the "tallest building in the Arab World," and five of the emirates can be seen from its roof. With its range of sophisticated services it has attracted a variety of international firms, advertising agencies, accountants, architects, etc., which set up their offices in the Center.

Inevitably there are some of Shaykh Rashid's enterprises that are not certain of success. A supertanker drydock complex, which has to face competition with the one in Bahrain, was still silent and unused eighteen months after its opening in 1979 because no company had been found to manage it. Even in this case, confident predictions of failure would be rash in view of the number of times that Shaykh Rashid has been proved right in the past, but it is undeniable that the UAE as a whole has its herd of white elephants. Competition and rivalry among the shaykhdoms has led to

---

the building of too many airports, ports, hotels, supermarkets, and apartment buildings. For those who were visiting the area a decade ago and had spent much of their time on their knees before haughty receptionists in the few hotels, it is a pleasure to be able to choose. The UAE now has over sixty luxury or first-class hotels. But most of these are only half-filled even during the winter season.

The duplication of effort is especially noticeable in Sharjah. The energetic young ruler Shaykh Sultan has carried out a number of ambitious schemes with the aim of recovering Sharjah's position on the coast which has been lost to neighboring Dubai during this century. Sharjah City in 1981, with many underused or half-finished buildings gives an impression of having outgrown its own strength.

But even here the pessimists could be wrong. At Khor Fakkan on the UAE's eastern coast which lies on the Indian Ocean and which Sharjah shares with Fujayrah, Shaykh Sultan has built a deep-water port that enables shipping to bypass the Straits of Hormuz, the narrow entrance to the Gulf. This could open new prospects for Sharjah. This coast is astonishingly beautiful and is beginning to attract tourists. The circular hotel near Khor Fakkan is slightly bizarre in appearance but overlooks an exquisite bay.

Ras al Khayhmah, the northernmost emirate, also has a highly independent-minded ruler in Shaykh Saqr. Disappointment in his hopes of a large oil strike has not stopped him from pressing on with development with the help of loans from Kuwait and elsewhere. Ras al Khayhmah has the most fertile land in this highly infertile region and its spectacular mountains, like those of Fujayrah, yield some 120 different varieties of marble.

The truth is that although there are a thousand excellent arguments why the federal government should be strengthened so that the mini-states of which it is composed complement rather than attempt to emulate each other, local pride and loyalty still act as a positive stimulus to industry and enterprise. This remains true even of younger citizens who support the idea of closer unity and even of abolishing the frontiers between the emirates entirely.

The creation of the UAE and its survival for a decade are remarkable achievements, and the best hope for the future of this federation lies in the gradual acceptance of its benefits.

17
Saudi Arabia in the 1970s

When King Ibn Saud died in 1953, his revenues from oil were about $200 million a year. This was a fabulous income compared with what he received through most of his reign although still very small in relation to his people's needs. The money was spent haphazardly, a first attempt to draw up a budget in 1947 having been a fiasco. Jiddah had received its first piped water supply; Mecca and Medina and Jiddah were linked by surfaced roads; and harbors were built at Jiddah and at Dammam on the Gulf. Riyadh was joined to the Gulf by railway at the King's request. Much of this development was carried out by Aramco and debited against future revenues. Most of the current income went on lavish gifts to members of the royal family and tribal leaders. This practice was traditional; the only difference was that the gifts were very much larger than before. The old King, who lived austerely himself, was alarmed at the effect on the morality of his people but it was too late to change the habit of a lifetime. One thing he could do which gave him the greatest pleasure. A year before he died he abolished the dues charged to Muslim pilgrims which had brought in about $30 million a year.

After his accession, King Saud and his ministers slightly increased spending on roads, schools, and hospitals, but still more was lost in wasteful extravagance. Although oil income was rising steadily, Saudi Arabia fell heavily into debt, and Aramco stopped giving advances on future revenues. It was only when King Saud handed over full powers to Prince Faisal in 1958 that any real

163

attempt was made to use Saudi Arabia's oil wealth for the benefit of the whole population. Even then all efforts had to be concentrated on restoring financial stability and the value of the shattered Saudi currency. The Saudi Arabian Monetary Agency (SAMA) was given real powers for the first time. Under its distinguished Pakistani director, Dr. Anwar Ali, SAMA's monetary stabilization program took Saudi Arabia out of the red and restored value of the riyal.

It was then that a target could be set for directing the bulk of the country's new wealth away from luxuries toward real needs. Proper budgets were introduced for the first time and the World Bank (IBRD) was asked to make a survey of the whole country. In 1961 a first attempt was made to set up a planning board advised by World Bank technicians. But this dissolved into chaos; the country still lacked a government cadre that was capable of carrying out decisions. The Ford Foundation was brought in to advise, and as a result a much-needed Administrative Reform Program was launched to modernize the entire bureaucracy which had grown haphazardly since the days when King Ibn Saud personally directed the entire administration. A new Supreme Planning Board was established in 1963 and made directly responsible to the prime minister. But it was not until 1969 that King Faisal's Central Planning Bureau, set up by the Cabinet, began the attempt to coordinate the efforts of the different ministries and establish priorities among them. The Stanford Research Institute of California was hired to strengthen the organization.

King Faisal was one of a rare breed of statesman: a conservative visionary. He had no doubts in his mind about what he wanted for Arabian society. He wanted nothing less than to transform it totally away from its dependence on natural elements and its subsistence-level living standards. He shared his father's nostalgia for the simple life and endeavored to preserve it in his personal ways. But he knew that the organization of society must become far more complex if Saudi Arabia was to attain his ambitious target of becoming as technically advanced and productive as the industrialized countries. But he was determined that as far as possible all the Saudi people, including the most conservative elements, should accept his purpose.

Always he insisted that Islam was fully compatible with material progress. On one occasion he said: "Our religion requires us to progress and advance and to bear the burden of the highest tradition and best manners. What is called progressiveness in the world today and what reformers are calling for, be it social, human, or economic progress, is all embodied in the Islamic religion and laws."

This was a theme to which he constantly returned. However, there was one major problem. There is nothing in the Islamic religion that opposes economic progress. On the contrary, the *Holy Koran* enjoins creative economic activity and hard work on every Muslim. At the same time, he must avoid ostentatious extravagance and pay his taxes for the benefit of the poor. Wealth should be equitably distributed. But what of centralized government planning? This was surely associated with socialism, and in the mid-1960s Saudi Arabia was locked in an ideological dispute with Nasser's Egypt and its Arab Socialism under which the Egyptian state had taken over all the "commanding heights" of the Egyptian economy.

In 1966 Faisal told his people: "We are going ahead with extensive planning, guided by our Islamic laws and beliefs, for the progress of the nation. We have chosen an economic system based on free enterprise because it is our conviction that it fits perfectly with our Islamic laws and suits our country by granting every opportunity to the people, giving incentives to every individual and every group to work for the common good. This does not mean leaving everything unchecked, for we will interfere when the government finds it necessary to do so, but without harming the basic principle involved and in order to correct any errors that may have occurred and secure social justice."

This clearly laid out the goal that has been maintained ever since: to turn Saudi Arabia into an advanced industrial nation with an economy that would be liberal and capitalist as far as was compatible with Islamic principles. In view of the low economic base from which the Saudi nation was starting—nearly half the population were still nomadic herdsmen in the mid-1960s—this was a breathtaking ambition. Would the Saudis take to being twentieth-century entrepreneurs? Unless they did the goal could never be fulfilled.

When Faisal first took on the challenge, the prospects were not encouraging. A few private Saudi firms had come into existence in the Eastern Province in the 1950s with support from Aramco. Their purpose was mainly to service Aramco and its workers—vehicle repair shops, trucking companies, poultry farms, etc. The construction boom in the cities had stimulated the growth of some small plants manufacturing building materials. In 1963 the Protection and Encouragement of National Industries Ordinance was introduced to encourage Saudi entrepreneurs by providing free land for their factories, the right to import machinery and raw materials customs-free, and protection against foreign imports. But the results were very meager. By the end of the 1960s some 180 small firms had been licensed, about half of them related to the building industry and the rest in food processing, clothing, and printing.

Of the eight thousand so-called manufacturing establishments at that time, 90 percent were no more than workshops employing two or three people—bakers, shoemakers, carpenters, etc. There were a few examples of vigorous private enterprise in the Hejaz. There was the Bin Ladin construction firm, founded in the 1930s to undertake the rebuilding of Mecca, the Juffali brothers, who were building electric power plants, the Alirezas, and several more. But the possibility that Saudi Arabia might become a major industrial nation was regarded as ludicrous by most of the population. Even a young man from the Ministry of Information who was supposed to impress visiting journalists with Saudi progress burst into laughter when it was announced on television that the country was to have its own steel rolling-mill. He regarded it as a myth invented by the government. As far as he was concerned, the only heavy industry in Saudi Arabia was Aramco and this would remain unchanged.

It was true that at that stage by far the greater part of oil revenues, which had risen to about $700 million, still had to be used in providing the country with the social and economic infrastructure that was still rudimentary—schools, hospitals, roads, ports, and airports. Unlike the city-states of the Gulf, Saudi Arabia is a vast country with a scattered population, so the cost and effort involved is that much greater. But Saudi Arabia did have something in common with the small Gulf states: lack of manpower. How could Saudi Arabia even consider becoming an industrial nation when there were not enough Saudis to build the new roads and ports or even to staff the civil service?

There was one institution, however, that held out a more encouraging prospect for the future. In 1962 the government had set up its own oil company, Petromin, attached to the Ministry of Petroleum and Mineral Resources as a government agency. Its main purpose was to gain a stake, however small, in the exploitation of the country's oil resources. Petromin was not successful in winning a share in oil production; it signed participation agreements with French and Italian state companies and American independents, but these were for exploration outside Aramco's concession area where oil has yet to be found. But Petromin took over all the distribution of oil products inside the Kingdom, and it branched out into other fields—refining, fertilizers, a steel rolling-mill (which was built in spite of some Saudis' skepticism). In each case Petromin was in partnership with a foreign company which set up the plant, but all the time it was gaining experience and expertise. Petromin was the nucleus of Saudi industrialization.

As Saudi Arabia's oil revenues continued to grow, its ambitions expanded with them. By 1971 they were nearly $2 billion, and in 1972, $2.7 billion. In 1969 the new Central Planning Organization produced Saudi Arabia's first Five-Year Plan for the period 1970 to 1975 with total allocations of some $9 billion. But it was very noticeable that nearly one quarter was to be spent on defense, only slightly less on education and health, and nearly 30 percent on public utilities, urban development, transport, and communications. In contrast, agriculture was to receive 3.6 percent and industry a mere 2.7 percent. Saudi Arabia was still very much at the stage of creating an infrastructure and of building up its military forces to match the country's growing financial power. In fact because Saudi Arabia was still so undeveloped it was unable to spend all its income. (Most of the former extravagance of some of the royal princes had been halted, but even this would not have absorbed the increased revenues.)

Thus in just over a decade Saudi Arabia had moved from being heavily in debt to having a large surplus. It was faced with a new problem—what to do with its excess income. But, as Dr. Anwar Ali, the Director of SAMA, pointed out in May 1973, Saudi Arabia was still a country with huge development needs and much of its population still living on the edge of poverty. Dr. Ali was concerned with restoring Saudi Arabia to financial health. He had not had time to think of the problem of surpluses.

Dr. Ali died of a heart attack in 1974, having served Saudi Arabia brilliantly for sixteen years. Before this happened, he saw Saudi Arabia's financial status transformed in a few months as oil prices quadrupled in the wake of the 1973 Middle East war. Revenues rose to just under $25 billion in 1975. The Saudi state was receiving every hour about as much as its revenues for an entire year in the 1930s.

More in hope than confidence, the government allocated just over half the revenues to development. Oil Minister Shaykh Ahmad Zaki Yamani publicly conceded that there would be $17 billion that could not be absorbed at home. (To allay fears in the United States he added that Saudi Arabia hoped to invest in special U.S. government securities and would not be buying up American industry.)

The government was able to take some immediate action to pass on the benefits to the Saudi people. All customs charges on imports were abolished, and the already very low taxes were further reduced. The prices of gasoline and electricity were cut by half. At the same time it began to distribute large sums in aid or loans. Hitherto Saudi foreign aid had been limited to its annual gifts to Egypt and Jordan following the 1967 war, outlays that were a severe strain on the budget in the late 1960s. Now the government was able to say that it would allocate 10 percent of the budget every year to foreign aid. In 1974 it contributed $50 million to the World Food Program, making it the second biggest donor after the United States.

Visitors to Saudi Arabia before 1973 had found it humming with activity. In retrospect this now looked like a period of static calm. Riyadh and Jiddah became two gigantic construction sites with cranes dominating their skylines. The second Five-Year Plan for 1975-1980 called for the spending of $142 billion, more than ten times the first plan, even allowing for the rise in prices.

It was not a question, however, of thinking up new ambitions for the country's future. The Saudi royal family and the Western-educated young technocrats who by now were playing an increasing role in government, were generally agreed on objectives. King Faisal's assassination in April 1975, although a tragic loss, did not lead to any significant change in policy. It was only a matter of accelerating the process of development.

The ultimate objective, which had already been decided in the early 1960s, was to make use of the country's enormous resources of oil and gas as the basis for a variety of other industries. This meant not only building more refineries but also a great system of gathering and processing the huge quantities of associated natural gas that are flared off at the oil fields.

Already in the early 1970s it had been decided to build a new center for this process in the oil-producing Eastern Province at Jubayl, an ancient settlement which was now a decayed fishing village on the Gulf some 100 miles northwest of Dhahran. With the great boost in revenues a further decision was taken to build another center in the west on the Red Sea coast of the Hejaz some 200 miles north of Jiddah. The site chosen here was Yanbu, the ancient port for pilgrims on their way to Medina.

The new industrial city lies twelve miles south of the town where there is deep-water access to the harbor. Huge pipelines are to bring oil and gas from the eastern oilfields over to Yanbu. Although immensely costly this has a double advantage: the west of the country would have a new focus of industrialization as well as the east, and the pipelines would provide a new outlet for Saudi oil that was not dependent on the narrow and strategically sensitive Straits of Hormuz at the entrance to the Gulf.

This huge expansion required some new organization, as Petromin could not cope with it all. In October 1975 a new Ministry of Industry and Electricity was created to take over from Petromin all responsibilities apart from the production, refining, and marketing of oil and gas, and a year later the Saudi Arabian Basic Industries Corporation (SAB), was established with a capital of 10 billion riyals (about $3 billion) which took over Petromin's role in all its non-oil enterprises such as the Saudi Arabian Fertilizer Company (SAFCO) and the Jiddah Steel Rolling Mill. SABIC, as it is now universally known, was designed to encourage foreign companies to enter into partnership with equity participation in new enterprises so that they would have a stake in success.

The towns of Jubayl and Yanbu became the centerpieces of all Saudi industrial plans for the future. This part of the plan amounted to the creation of two entirely new industrial cities on the coast of Arabia. Jubayl was to have a population of 300,000 and Yanbu 150,000. The total cost was estimated at $70 billion—a figure that was certain to be overtaken by inflation. This was greater than the cost of putting a man on the moon; it was undeniably the biggest single industrial project in history.

Such a gigantic new enterprise could clearly come to grief if it were shackled by government bureaucracy. In 1975 therefore it was decided to create a special Royal Commission for Jubayl and Yanbu under the chairmanship of Crown Prince Fahd with the power to slice through red tape. Dr. Farouk Akhdar, an energetic young technocrat, was put in charge as secretary-general with the rank of Minister. To some he probably seemed absurdly youthful to be bearing so much responsibility. He talked with enthusiasm about this opportunity of creating cities of the twenty-first century in Saudi Arabia, cities that would be planned from the beginning, that would have no slums or pollution, and, in spite of the extreme summer heat, very little disease.

Work has gone ahead on these two cities with remarkable speed. At Jubayl, before much else could be done, three years had to be spent in dumping huge quantities of sand and gravel from the desert into the treacherous *sabkhah* or salt marsh which was the site of the city. By spring of 1980, the foundations had been laid, the infrastructure of harbors, drainage, and electricity was in place, and the first permanent buildings were beginning to go up. There was already a substantial town of temporary houses for the work force of twenty thousand who were building the city; many of these will last a decade. Yanbu was at a similar stage of development and if anything slightly more advanced. A healthy rivalry was developing between the twin cities.

The building of the new cities was given priority, but when the boom began—or rather when the boom became an explosion —the country's still only partially completed infrastructure was unable to cope with the huge influx of goods. About 90 percent of Saudi imports come in by sea, and in the spring of 1976 some 100 ships were lined up at Jiddah and Dammam for as long as three months to unload their cargoes. Surcharges of 90 percent were being imposed by shipping lines. It was obvious that the $1.7 billion set aside in the second Five-Year Plan was far too little for expanding Jiddah and Dammam and building new harbors at Yanbu and Jazan on the Red Sea and Jubayl on the Gulf. Many foreign observers were convinced that the Saudis would be incapable of solving this problem for a decade. Further, many felt that all Saudi development plans were at risk.

In the autumn of 1976 Fayiz Badr, a young American-educated economist who had been Deputy Minister of Planning, was appointed head of a newly created Saudi Ports Authority. Through draconian measures he succeeded in ending the congestion with astonishing speed. By the middle of 1977, waiting time at both Jiddah and Dammam was down to nothing and the shipping surcharges had been removed, saving the country some $500 million a year.

Dr. Badr laid down the principle that Saudi ports must never be allowed to become congested again. This means constantly increasing capacity to meet the continuing surge in imports which more than doubled between 1977 and 1979 to 24.3 million tons. (The prediction in the Second Plan had been 13 million tons for 1979.) Dammam and Jiddah have now reached what is thought to be a desirable size, and it is now more a question of developing the new ports on the country's vast coastlines to serve other centers of population. Jazan is helping the growth of the impoverished southwest and the development of Yanbu has begun to bring down the price of imported goods in Medina.

If port congestion was the single most serious obstacle to Saudi development, the need to expand the airline network was almost as urgent. Here too the problems were daunting. Saudi Arabia is the size of Western Europe but has less than one-thirtieth of its population as customers for its air services. Yet in the pilgrimage season it has to cope with a massive increase of visitors. Saudia, the national airline, therefore deserves its reputation for achievement apart from its international celebrity as one of the sponsors of the Grand Prix Saudia-Williams motor racing team. It began in 1945 with three DC-3s, one of which was presented by President Roosevelt as a symbol of Saudi-American friendship. In the 1960s it was still a somewhat amateur organization that had yet to join the International Air Transport Association (IATA). Even its international flights were frequently delayed a few hours for the benefit of a notable. In 1967 Saudia joined the IATA, and by 1971 it was carrying 700,000 passengers. But it was the 1970s which saw the breakneck expansion—eight million passengers in 1979 and nine million in 1980. The country was covered by a network of twenty-two airports; within a decade Saudis, even the elderly in remote areas, have become as accustomed to taking planes as Western commuters use buses and trains. The shuttle service between Dammam, Riyadh, and Jiddah is used as casually as the one between New York and Washington. With its sixty-three jet planes in 1980, Saudia had become one of the world's ten busiest airlines.

The airports in the major cities were soon outgrown by this rapid rate of expansion. The new Jiddah International Airport covers forty square miles on a site well outside the city on the Medina Road. It has a special terminal for Muslim pilgrims which covers nearly half a square mile—reputedly the largest enclosed space in the world. The fiberglass roof resembles a giant tent. The terminal will be able to handle passengers of 20 jumbo jets at one time, transporting them directly from the planes into the ten plazas of the enclosed area, designed to resemble a modern *suq* with shops, restaurants, banks, mosques, and fountains where pilgrims can perform their ablutions. In 1974 about 170,000 pilgrims arrived by air, in 1979 nearly half a million, and by 1982 it will be 1.5 million. The new Riyadh International Airport, due to open two years later, covers 80 square miles and will ultimately serve 15 million passengers a year. The cost of both Riyadh and Jiddah Airports will approach $6 billion each.

Road building is equally vital to knit together this vast country with its widely scattered population. In 1965 there were still only fifteen hundred miles of paved roads in the country linking Riyadh with Jiddah and Dhahran and Jiddah with Mecca and Medina. By 1970 this had increased to five thousand miles and with the tremendous effort devoted to roads in the 1975-80 Second Plan it had reached thirteen thousand miles by 1980. But of even greater importance for opening up the rural areas has been the building of unpaved dirt roads of which there were fourteen thousand miles in 1980.

Only a decade ago the Saudi national and international telecommunications system was still rudimentary. While direct dialing to the Gulf states from European capitals was already possible, calls to Saudi cities could be delayed for several days. This was almost as serious an obstacle to Saudi Arabia's development as the congested ports, and was preventing Jiddah from catching up with Kuwait and Bahrain as a financial center. In December 1977 a contract was awarded to a Dutch, Swedish, and Canadian consortium to add 470,000 new lines to the existing 198,000 by 1982. In 1980 work was ahead of schedule and further expansion in the 1980-85 Plan aims to bring the number up to nearly two million or one telephone for every four inhabitants—a ratio that will be comparable to that of the advanced industrial countries and the highest in the Arab world. Even the most remote areas will be connected to the network, and car telephones, already no longer a luxury, will be regarded as commonplace.

If the statistics of Saudi development are stupefying, so are the costs. The second Five Year Plan cost some $150 billion. The third Plan, for 1980-85, is estimated to cost $235 billion. This excludes defense and foreign aid. If these are added it would reach the almost unimaginable total of $400 billion over the next five years. This in a country of perhaps six million people.

The declared purpose of the second Plan was to complete the greater part of the huge infrastructural framework which is essential before Saudi Arabia has any hope of a genuine advance towards industrialization. Until that was done, it was not possible for the economy to absorb the money that was allocated for real development. This was the situation during the first Plan for 1970-75 although revenues were only a small fraction of what they are today. By the end of the second Plan in 1980 the situation was very different. As we have seen, most of the foundations were already in place or within one or two years of completion. This was revealed in the fact that there was now no problem in spending even the enormously increased sums that were allocated for development. The Saudi system of communications could bear the huge burden imposed on it, although it required constant maintenance and expansion.

In many ways 1975-80 were years of remarkable achievement. The possibilities offered by the quadrupling of oil revenues in 1973-74 were immense, but so were the dangers. The Saudi economy was still relatively unsophisticated; its cadre of trained and experienced men remained very small. Moreover, unlike the societies of city-states of the Gulf which are so compact that problems can be seen in the round, Saudi society is scattered and relatively heterogeneous—even if this is something that is changing.

It could easily have been disastrous. At the beginning of the boom, inflation rose to a dangerous level of 50 percent, causing real hardship to the many Saudis and foreign workers who remain poor. In the cities property prices rocketed so that in 1976 three-room villas in Jiddah were being rented for $45,000 a year. This provoked the private sector into building tens of thousands of new villas. But these were for the wealthy; the state's own program to build low-cost housing fell disastrously behind schedule. Visitors to Jiddah in 1976 found the atmosphere tense and febrile; anxiety and discontent were evident.

However, the government took some determined steps to damp down the boom without abandoning any of its main objectives. By 1978 inflation was cut to 10 percent and has remained at about that level ever since. This in itself was a surprising achievement. Much was learned from the experience. Some Saudi merchants came to understand that their traditionally high profit margins could not always be maintained. But the Saudi government also became much more wary in its attitude toward foreign companies, some of which it felt had been taking advantage of the Saudi urgency for development. The Saudi view was that they had been fueling inflation by using it as a justification to charge exorbitant prices for capital goods and equipment. As Dr. Faisal Bashir, the Deputy Planning Minister, commented in 1979, "Three years ago we went through deep analysis, and we found some of the merchandise exported to Saudi Arabia had a special price that was higher than for other countries—some of which were actually bordering Saudi Arabia. This to me is unfair." He added that it had been necessary to "bloody some noses" but that since then matters had improved and such cases were rare.

The Saudi Arabians had sound grounds for satisfaction by 1980. Much of the infrastructure had been created, inflation had been brought under control, and valuable experience had been gained in dealing with foreign companies. The gloomiest of the doomsayers had been proved wrong. The major companies of the industrialized world that had been hesitating over whether to take part in the gigantic venture of creating a Saudi petrochemical industry, because they were uncertain whether it was viable or its products salable, were becoming convinced one by one. An important example was set by the Saudi Arabian Fertilizer Company (SAFCO) which, after its first disastrous years in the 1960s when it was running at only 30 percent to 40 percent capacity, confounded the prophets in the 1970s by becoming a resounding success. In 1979 it was running at full capacity and exporting 90 percent of its chief product: urea. Another powerful incentive to them was provided by the Saudi offer to supply them with a certain amount of oil—500 barrels per day—for every one million dollars they invested in Saudi petrochemicals. About 10 percent of Saudi Arabia's oil output will be committed in this way by 1985. In some quarters the use of this kind of bait was looked at askance, as if Saudi Arabia were once again using the "oil weapon," although this time to support its economic strategy rather than the political cause of the Arabs. But to Saudis it is the rational way of pursuing the overriding aim of industrialization and the transfer of technology to Saudi Arabia.

It was not only foreign companies that were finally taking an interest in Saudi industrialization. In the early 1970s the great majority of Saudis who ventured into manufacturing continued to set up the same kinds of plants as in the earlier years, making food products, soft drinks, building materials and so on, where profits were high (often over 40 percent) and there was a quick return on investment. There were a few exceptional Saudi entrepreneurs who were prepared to invest large sums for a longer term—in truck assembly plants, electric wires and cables, and aluminum products. By the end of the decade many more were coming on the scene and significantly they included some of the great Saudi merchant families. Dr. Faisal Bashir, the Deputy Planning Minister saw this as a decisive trend in 1979. "After all," he once said to a British journalist, "the history of economics taught us about your industrial revolution in the U.K., that you started as traders, and then you moved to industry mixed with trade, and then you had the pure industrialists and traders that you have now. The private sector is quite dynamic today—it is beautiful, really."

This might appear to be the natural optimism of one of Saudi Arabia's enthusiastic band of able young technocrats. The state still feels it necessary to provide all sorts of inducements to tempt Saudi investors into industry, such as loans on easy terms and cheap electric power. But it only protects the products of new industries with tariffs on imports in very exceptional cases when the new industry is considered vital. In general they have to prove that they can survive. Similarly, it is part of the philosophy of the Saudi government to sell off to Saudi citizens the government's share in any new industry as soon as it becomes profitable. This has already happened to SAFCO; after many years of difficulties the company was able to offer 10,000 of its shares to the public.

Does this mean that in the 1980s the Saudi economy will become "self-sustaining" in the sense that the initiative for economic development will come from the private sector rather than the state? Clearly this is not so. It would be a miracle if the desert kingdom had reached this stage when the first attempts to lay the foundations of a twentieth-century industrial economy had hardly begun twenty years ago. Although the private sector is playing an increasing role, the overwhelming responsibility for economic growth will belong to the state for many years to come.

There are several reasons for this. The first is the simple fact that the great majority of Saudi Arabia's huge foreign exchange earnings accrue to the state through the sale of crude oil. In 1980 these exceeded $90 billion with an additional $7 billion of income from government investments abroad. Although the income from private investments of individual Saudis is also growing at an accelerating rate, it is small by comparison.

Secondly, although remarkable progress has been made in laying down the infrastructure, there are still great tasks to be performed which can only be the responsibility of the state. In theory the third Five Year Plan for 1980-85 is concentrating more on productive investment and less on infrastructure; however, no one seriously believes that there will be much difference from the Second Plan in practice. One example of a responsibility of the state that is actually growing rather than diminishing is that of the water supply in the parched Saudi Kingdom. Not only the exploding population of the cities but the new factories in the suburbs need rapidly increasing quantities of fresh water. In Jiddah where it only rains two or three times a year, drinking water until the 1940s used to be brought from the Nile by Khedival Mail steamer. Today the city's one million people have to be supplied from the sea, and Jiddah has one of the largest desalination complexes in the world, which is constantly being expanded at enormous cost. But even this is dwarfed by the project to build a giant distillation plant at Jubayl and lay a pipeline to bring 185 million gallons a day to Riyadh and solve the capital's acute water problem once and for all. The cost will be tremendous, but there is no alternative: the ancient fossil water reserves around Riyadh are not equal to the city's steadily rising requirements.

Nevertheless, the demands of the big cities for government funds are leveling off. The vital municipal arteries are already in place and only need expansion or renewal. Jiddah's mayor is proud to point out that the city has achieved in five years what would have taken fifty years elsewhere, and he can cope with the fact that Jiddah's allocation in the Third Plan is down 37 percent from the Second Plan.

The most important reason why the government's overall responsibilities are not being reduced is that it is increasing its spending in the smaller cities and towns and the rural villages—in Abha in the south, in Tabuk in the north, and in the oases. At the end of the 1970s it was realized that there was a danger of a growing rift between the major cities and the rest of the country. It is true that in Riyadh Saudis have hospitals and clinics equal to the best in the world, but in the countryside children are dying because their mothers are too far from medical care.

If the building of the twin industrial cities of Jubayl and Yanbu remains the heart of Saudi Arabia's plans for the future, the prevention of the emergence of two nations in the kingdom, one of them affluent and the other deprived, is equally important.

18
Guest Workers

My hotel in Jiddah was typical. The receptionist was Lebanese, the hall porter was Sudanese, the room waiter was a Malaysian in the morning and a Filipino in the evening, lunch was served by an Egyptian, dinner by a Syrian, and the attendant at the swimming pool was from Bangladesh. Yemeni and Pakistani construction workers were building an extension to the hotel under a Palestinian foreman. When I came to leave, a Jordanian made up the bill. But it was a Saudi Arabian who drove me to the airport because taxi driving, like the army and police, is reserved for nationals.

In the smaller Gulf states even this does not apply. Policemen and soldiers may be Sudanese, Somalis, or Omanis. In Abu Dhabi the taxi driver was a Pathan from northern Pakistan. With a dazzling smile and eyes like sequins, he was eager to please. But he spoke no word of English or Arabic and, having recently arrived, the only landmark he knew was "Hilton Hotel" to which he wanted to take all his fares.

As soon as the oil revenues began to flow into the smaller Gulf states in the 1950s (Kuwait and Qatar) and 1960s (Abu Dhabi) their people were faced with a dilemma. Either they used their new wealth to build great twentieth-century economies or resigned themselves to becoming "rentier states," living entirely off their investments abroad.

As it was, they barely hesitated to take the first alternative. National pride virtually ruled out the second. But the decision to

179

concentrate on development—to build the schools, hospitals, roads, and housing that they had always lacked—meant resigning themselves to something that very few peoples in the world would have to contemplate: becoming a minority in their own countries. Their own tiny populations, experienced only as herdsmen, fishermen, and merchants, could not manage more than a fraction of the work that needed to be done. Only Bahrain, with its larger population and much smaller revenues, could develop gradually enough to rely mainly on its own nationals. Western technicians could be attracted in small numbers but there were a vast number of professional, skilled, and unskilled jobs to be filled.

The first wave of immigrants to Kuwait was mainly northern Arabs—Palestinians, who had lost their homes in 1948, Egyptians, and some Syrians, Lebanese, and Sudanese. They came as teachers, doctors, nurses, and administrators but also as mechanics and ordinary unskilled workers. Most of the builders on the new construction sites were illiterate and came from neighboring Iraq and Iran.

But with the northern Arabs came Indians and Pakistanis as storekeepers and clerks. The Gulf's old Indian connection was a powerful one, and the people of the subcontinent feel at home in the region. Not surprisingly, this "Indianism" grows stronger the farther eastward you go down the Gulf until it reaches its apogee in Dubai, where the first impression of an astral visitor might be that he had landed on the coast of Kerala. But even in Kuwait the 1975 census showed that more than half the tailors came from Pakistan.

When a Palestinian or Egyptian had settled successfully in Kuwait he might send for his brother or cousin to help him. The trend accelerated after the 1967 war, which created many new Palestinian refugees, and the 1970 census showed that only 47 percent of the population were Kuwaiti citizens.

From the beginning, all the Gulf oil states showed their determination not to allow their national personality to be swamped by the new immigrants. Kuwaiti citizenship has been granted only to other Arabs and even then in a very few exceptional cases for special services to the state. When Kuwait had an elected parliament in 1963 non-Kuwaiti residents could not vote even if they had been born in the country.

In theory all the non-Kuwaiti immigrants had equal right of access to the new social services. In practice things did not work out so equitably; Kuwaitis received, and sometimes demanded, preferential treatment in the hospitals and schools. In a real sense they were the only first-class members of the population. One shrewd English visitor as early as 1956 was led to wonder whether Kuwait "will always be able to afford treating its horde of foreign workers of all grades much as a *nouveau riche* might treat a new household of servants." The immigrants cannot own property, and they must have a Kuwaiti partner with a majority share in their business.

The same thing has happened and the same rules apply, with only minor differences, in the other oil city-states of the Gulf. They have been slightly more liberal in granting citizenship as they had to be, in view of their tiny populations, if they did not wish to run their own security services with mercenaries. The UAE, for example, will offer naturalization to Arabs from Qatar, Oman, and Bahrain after only three years' residence, although they have to wait another seven years for full citizenship rights. Nevertheless the proportion of noncitizens in Qatar, Abu Dhabi, and Dubai is higher than in Kuwait—at least 60 percent and perhaps 70 percent. Even in Bahrain it had risen to 35 percent in the early 1980s, as the development boom has accelerated far beyond the stately pace of the 1960s.

In all these Gulf states the influx of Asians from the Indian subcontinent has showed the sharpest increase. The need was for unskilled and semi-skilled building workers, and the Iraqis and Iranians who had earlier fulfilled these jobs were returning home as their own countries' demand for development increased. The business of recruiting workers in the cities of Pakistan, India, and Sri Lanka became highly organized. From their offices in Bombay, Lahore, or Delhi, agents were sending them over in tens of thousands on two- or three-year contracts. With this a worker can hope to save enough money to get married, perhaps buy a car or moped and start his own taxi business. Even those who are married are unable to bring their families. At the last count the population of the UAE consisted of 628,000 males and only 263,600 females.

The governments of all these little countries have tried to take stringent measures to control the flow of immigrant guest workers. They are supposed to have visas and work permits before they enter which can only be obtained when an employer, acting as sponsor, offers them a job. This system does not always work successfully. In Kuwait the non-Kuwaiti Arab population mysteriously increased by 200,000 in the year following the 1967 war, and new restrictions had to be imposed. The UAE Ministry of Labor announced in the spring of 1980 that no less than half the immigrants were illegal in the sense that they did not have the right documents. In Qatar there was a similar upheaval because it was discovered that tens of thousands of immigrants had changed their jobs without finding a new sponsor.

Superficially, Saudi Arabia does not face the same dilemma because there is no danger of six to seven million Saudis being outnumbered by immigrants. Yet the reality is much the same. From the earliest days of the development of the oil fields, skilled and unskilled workers had to be imported because there were too few Saudis available. Although the Saudi population was rapidly increasing and a steady flow was being attracted from the countryside into the towns during the 1950s and 1960s, the sudden crescendo of development in the 1970s meant a huge increase in the demand for labor and absolutely no possibility that it could be filled by Saudis. When Crown Prince Fahd in 1975 announced the gigantic plans for the new industrial cities and ports, he acknowledged that the entire work force would have to come from outside. Today, although immigrants make up no more than a quarter of the total population, they account for as much as three-quarters of the labor force.

In the early days the immigrants were similar to those in Kuwait—Egyptians, Lebanese, and Palestinians/Jordanians (although these were much fewer in proportion than in Kuwait). There were some Omanis and Yemenis—self-exiles from their countries whose rulers at that time believed in keeping them in a state of medieval stagnation. In the last decade the flow of immigrants from Yemen, a country with a larger population than Saudi Arabia, became a flood to fulfill the demand for unskilled labor. In 1980 there were thought to be at least six hundred thousand of them. As Arabian neighbors, they were given special treatment. There were virtually no restrictions on their entry, and they were given work permits on arrival without the need for a sponsor.

In about 1974 a new strain began to appear among the hosts of immigrants. They came from even further afield than the Indians —from the Far East and Southeast Asia. The first to arrive were the Koreans. Dressed in their blue denim suits, they soon became a familiar feature of Arabian cities. They were followed by others from Malaysia, Nepal, the Philippines, Taiwan, and Thailand. In 1970 they were no more than a handful; by 1975 there were 15,000 and in 1979 more than 160,000 in the Gulf oil states.

The Northern Arabs (or West Asians) tend to cling together in their private lives. There are quarters of Kuwait City, for example, that are Egyptian, Palestinian, or Lebanese. Yet in many ways they are integrated into the lives of their host countries. They share their language and culture; the great majority are Muslims and even Christian Arabs are accustomed to being part of Muslim communities. The Northern Arabs share with Kuwaitis, Saudis, or Qataris their clubs, restaurants, and places of entertainment. On the other hand the East Asians, or Orientals as they are sometimes called, lead almost entirely separate lives in their own enclaves. In the Korean work camps they eat Korean food, read Korean magazines, and watch Korean films. Occasionally they venture into the cities in small groups, but they do not mix because very few speak English, the language which—to the occasional indignation of the French—is the *lingua franca* of all the non-Arab immigrants.

They work hard and lead austere lives. They are paid in their own currency which is saved at home. It is said that their government allows young Koreans exemption from two years' military service if they work for a year on contract in Arabia. Korean companies have certainly won many contracts by putting in bids that are so low that Western companies tend to regard them as unfair.

It is easy to see why the Orientals are popular with the host governments. Because they lead separate lives and are so easily distinguishable and, because they are certain to leave at the end of their contracts, they present no political or cultural threat. Arabia will not be submerged under a tidal wave of East Asians.

The position of the immigrants from the Indian subcontinent is somewhere between that of the Northern Arabs and the Orientals. Many of them are Muslims, and they often learn to speak Arabic. Some have been settled for more than a generation. The possibility of Indians in Arabia uniting to present a real political challenge cannot quite be discounted. When the late President Bhutto visited the Gulf, local Arabs were startled to see the great crowds of Pakistanis who went to greet him at the airport.

But for several reasons the threat is not a real one. Precisely because there was a danger, the Gulf governments have favored those on short-term contracts, and the big increase in Indian immigrants in recent years has been in this kind of indentured labor. Many of them are not Muslims and are as culturally different from Arabs as the Orientals. A major source of emigration is the Indian state of Kerala where there are numerous signs of prosperity derived from the remittances of Keralan workers in the Gulf. There is little real prospect of Sri Lankan waiters, Keralan electricians, and Pathan taxi drivers uniting to demand political rights in their temporary host countries.

There is a danger in the presence of so many immigrants in the Gulf oil states which is not so easy to identify but which in the long term is more threatening. The objective of the governments of all these states, which has the support of the great majority of their citizens, is to develop a society that is as advanced on the technical level as the West or Japan without allowing their social and cultural values and traditions to be destroyed. This is a difficult aim because it involves compressing the experience of two or three centuries of the first industrialized countries into as many decades. There is no possibility whatever of achieving it if all the hard work that it involves is left to foreigners.

It would be wrong to think that the educational elite in all these countries is not fully aware of the dangers. There are several kinds of dangers here not concerned with the social effects of having foreigners to do all the disagreeable, menial jobs so much as the absolute necessity for the nationals of the Gulf states to acquire direct experience managing and controlling their changing society at all levels. This cannot be done by remote control from air-conditioned offices.

It is possible to exaggerate the problem. Kuwait was the first of the Gulf oil states to acquire sudden wealth, and there are few signs that Kuwaiti citizens are relapsing into luxurious idleness. Just as the government rejects a future for Kuwait as a "rentier state," so the average Kuwaiti, however wealthy (and the average is fairly wealthy), does not contemplate living inactively on his investments. Most of the many Kuwaitis of my acquaintance work extremely hard. Despite the surge in education in the last generation and the rapid increase in the native Kuwaiti population due to the falling death rate, there are still too few Kuwaitis to man the government service as well as run the business sector. Many have to do both. Where a real problem does exist is in attracting enough young Kuwaitis into the fields of science and engineering. The University of Kuwait complains of a lack of recruits into these faculties in contrast to the humanities. This is something that must be remedied if Kuwait is to develop and manage its own modern industries rather than leave the task to foreigners. Some strenuous efforts are being made. The Kuwait Institute for Scientific Research, an institution of key importance to the country's future, is sending training missions abroad at such a pace that 60 percent of its researchers should be Kuwaitis by 1985.

The other Gulf states, apart from Bahrain, have even smaller populations in relation to their needs. In Qatar, for example, the total labor force is minute. Of the 60,000 Qatari citizens, over half are under sixteen. Women are still excluded from most professions. This leaves a trained and educated work force of at most 5,000. In view of this it is remarkable that 30 percent of the industrial labor force is Qatari. In the oil industry it is higher. The oil company operating offshore has 631 Qataris out of a total staff of 1,478. It is even more significant that 493 of the Qataris are at the operator level, which contradicts the theory that young Qataris will not go into industry unless they can start as managers.

But it cannot be denied that some of the youth of Arabia are reluctant to dirty their hands. In Saudi Arabia, where all such problems are on a much larger scale, there is tremendous enthusiasm for university education. Every one of the six universities fills its first-year places with ease, while the prestigious University of Petroleum and Minerals at Dhahran had 1,900 applicants for 1,000 places in 1980. In addition there are 13,000 studying at universities in the United States alone. Not all stay for the full course, because the temptation is too powerful to drop out and make an easy living in the family trading business. Those who graduate can be sure of well-paid jobs in the public sector as managers, teachers, or administrators.

But most young Saudis will not make it to the university. They are most likely to seek a job that carries status such as with the national airline, Saudia. In 1980 it had 1650 applicants for 450 places. What they are most unlikely to do is to become welders, bricklayers, or electricians. In the vocational schools, which have been powerfully supported by the government, no more than 2,200 signed on in 1980. A Saudi with no qualifications at all can always drive a taxi and earn $3,000 a month. All the skilled and unskilled manual labor can be left to Egyptians, Somalis, Filipinos, and the rest.

Most Saudis in responsible positions believe that this is a problem that will be solved through a combination of natural processes and government action. As more young Saudis come on the labor market, high profits or large wages will not be so easily earned. They will have to turn to types of employment they would previously have spurned. Already there are signs of this taking place. What happened to the 1,200 applicants who did not get employment in Saudia? Even those who have graduated well from universities may not find a highly paid job automatically available in one of the professions. Inflation, although not what it was, will ensure that no one can afford to live on a fixed income.

The government can assist the process in various ways. It may make it increasingly difficult for employers to import labor and insist that foreign companies offer training programs for Saudis. At the same time it can gradually disabuse the Saudi public of its belief that it is the state's duty to hand out largesse even to those who are not in want. This cannot be done suddenly because it is a belief that is rooted in tribal society. The ruling shaykh always handed out any sudden wealth to his followers. But this was at a time when they were living on the edge of starvation. As one of the outstanding members of the Saudi government, the Planning Minister Shaykh Hisham Nazir, remarked in a newspaper interview in January 1979: "There is a belief in some circles that the fact that the Kingdom is wealthy means that each individual is entitled, without contributing to the nation's development, to a large number of free benefits in many forms."

"That is to say there is a very human tendency for people to take things for granted and to rely too much on welfare benefits, in many forms, without giving a thought to the obligations and contributions towards society that the individual is expected to make."

"Whereas the older members of our society can indeed feel entitled to a special measure of welfare benefits—as they are the ones who lived under conditions of relative poverty and hardship with little opportunity for advancement for so long—this is not true of the younger generations who have unbounded opportunities before them" (*Saudi Gazette*, January 30, 1979).

Another key member of the cabinet, the dynamic Minister of Industry and Electricity Ghazi al Gosaibi, was even sharper in tone in a speech at King Abd al Aziz University in March 1980, when he listed a series of "Saudi illusions," such as that the country has unlimited resources or that there is a "magic power of capital" which can solve all problems merely by allocating millions and setting up new bureaucratic bodies to spend them. All of these notions, he said, suffer from the belief that imported materials and expertise were a substitute for native intelligence. "We are all about to be turned into tape recorders," he said. "On one side of the cassette we repeat: 'We have no Saudi talent.' On the other we are repeating: 'Saudis don't like to work. Saudis don't like to work'" (*8 Days*, March 22, 1980).

An example of how the government can help to end the illusion of easy affluence could be observed in Riyadh in the spring of 1980. An Egyptian guest worker returning from a holiday with his family was told by the taxi driver at the airport that it would cost him 30 riyals (about nine dollars) to take him to his home. As he demurred, someone pointed to a gleaming bus, part of the brand new municipal service, which charges a standard fare of one riyal. The airport taxi drivers went into conclave and their spokesman reduced the fare to 10 riyals. But the Egyptian refused; he could take his family home by bus for 5 riyals. The easy profits of Riyadh taxi drivers, built on their monopoly and the lowest gasoline prices in the world, are no more.

Without exception the governments of the Arabian oil states have a keen interest in "nationalizing" (that is Saudizing, Qatarizing, Kuwaitizing, etc.) their societies as rapidly as possible. They are doing so by exhortation as well as regulation, and they can easily touch a chord in their people.

Every time a local national takes over a position of responsibility—a new Kuwaiti company manager, a Saudi hospital director, or a Qatari head of a university faculty—it is a source of national pride. But these same governments are aware that for a very long time to come this "nationalization" can be no more than partial. Foreigners will have to retain many of the responsibilities at all levels and can only gradually be replaced. The alternative would be to slash back all their ambitious plans for development, and this they have no intention of doing.

(a) *Northern Arabs*

An Egyptian journalist, one of the best known in the Arab world, was once talking to me of the flooding into Arabia and the

Gulf of those we call Northern Arabs—Syrians, Lebanese, Palestinians, Egyptians, and, perhaps surprisingly, the Sudanese. He said that in the past the movement had been in the opposite direction—north and westward to the great Arab/Muslim cities of Baghdad, Damascus, Aleppo, and Cairo. Now it was merely a question of the tide flowing back. It was a manifestation of the natural and easy mobility within the Arab world.

The Northern Arab migrants include many unskilled laborers but also some of the intelligentsia, like my Egyptian friend who now spends most of his time in the Gulf.

The cynical view, which is held by some Westerners but is not unknown among Arabs, is that the northerners have only mercenary intentions, that they despise the people of Arabia as uncivilized nomads who resent and dislike them in return. This view holds that the Southern Arabs will exploit the northerners as long as they need them—using the power of their wealth to patronize and humiliate them whenever possible—and then get rid of them as soon as it is convenient.

There is an element of truth to this view. Certainly there are cases of friction and resentment between Northern and Southern Arabs. Yet as a general proposition it is grossly misleading. The real cause for astonishment is the extent to which the different representatives of the allegedly divisive and disputatious Arab nations have succeeded in working together. In my experience many more Palestinians, Egyptians, and Lebanese speak well of their Saudi or Kuwaiti employers or partners than criticize the treatment they receive from them, while the latter are quite ready to admit without resentment that they need the skills and experience of their northern cousins. The many intellectuals from the north—writers, lawyers, economists, and scientists—who are invited to visit the Arab oil states where they lecture and are interviewed on television, are treated with high respect. Despite Oscar Wilde's cynical observation about ''the barrier of a common language'' with reference to the English and the Americans, the shared Arab cultural and religious background (which is shared by Arab Christians as well as Muslims) creates a natural bond which is not immediately obvious only because it is taken for granted.

One of the reasons that the outsider often receives an impression of total disharmony among the Arabs is their own use of an exaggerated language when talking of each other. This is especially true of the northerners. (A Kuwaiti who has become an international figure explained to me his theory that the Arabs of Arabia are "Anglo-Saxon"—that is hard-headed and logical— while the Northern Arabs are "Mediterranean"—that is, emotional and rhetorical. I was not entirely convinced, having always understood that the English are illogical in contrast to the Cartesian calculators across the Channel. But it is true that the Arabians are more matter-of-fact and less given to high-flown language than their northern cousins.)

Thus you will hear that Egyptians are either obsequious or arrogant (and sometimes both), that Palestinians are self-serving and ambitious, and that Sudanese are drunken and feckless. As for the Lebanese. . . Yet none of this seems to make much difference to the personal relations between these groups. A Lebanese engineer who has made a highly successful career as a contractor in one of the Gulf states assured me that all his Palestinian colleagues were corrupt. Without exception they hired out their women to rich local businessmen. (He did admit that some Lebanese might do the same but this was unusual.) No Palestinian, he said, ever came into his house.

Later I discovered this was quite untrue. Not only did he have the most amicable relations with his Palestinian colleagues but they were constant visitors to his home. Natural human warmth usually triumphs among the Arabs.

However, just as Arabia's dependence on the skills of the Northern Arabs will be harmful in the long run if it inhibits the Southern Arabs from developing their own abilities, so the exodus from the northern states—the drain of both brains and hands— will damage their own economies. A report by the International Labor Organization in August 1980 pointed out some of the dangers: while the remittances sent back by these workers is helping the economies of these northern states and has become a crucial element in their balance of payments, it may be more harmful that they now lack the manpower for their own development. The ludicrous situation has arisen that Pakistani agricultural workers have to be imported to till the fields in the Jordan Valley while Sudan, which it is hoped will become the "breadbasket of the Arab world" with the help of Arab investment, has to bring in labor from its African neighbors. On the other hand, a common market for employment within the Arab world is an ideal to which most Arabs subscribe, and for each country to put up barriers against migration would do more harm than good.

19

Oil: Power and Responsibility

*I*n the summer of 1979, at the height of the Iranian crisis, a Western newspaper cartoon showed an immense, gloating Arab shaykh plucking the feathers one by one from a cowed and miserable American eagle.

The message, which was repeated in countless similar newspaper cartoons and headlines, was clear. The "oil shaykhs" were callously using the overwhelming power of their monopoly to squeeze the suffering Westerners. Other drawings showed them laughing as they chalked up the price of gasoline in front of a line of enraged but helpless motorists.

There are several comments that could be made on these cartoons. The "oil shaykhs," with their huge bellies contrasting oddly with cadaverous semitic features, are invariably labeled OPEC in spite of the fact that the Arabian oil producers account for only one third of OPEC's total production. Also the most important of them—Saudi Arabia—has taken a lead in trying to steady the rise in oil prices to consumers. But the great significance of these Western attitudes is not that they are often based on misconceptions, but that they represent a major change in power relationships. The governments of the oil-exporting countries are now regarded as major independent factors in world affairs by all the industrialized nations, including the United States.

This is only a recent phenomenon. Throughout the first half of this century the views of the governments of the oil-producing countries counted for very little in world councils.

193

In the Middle East, oil was first discovered in Iran in 1908. The Qajar Shahs, the weak and corrupt rulers of Iran, had in their desperation for money given British interests an exclusive mineral concession for the entire Persian Empire, except for the five northern provinces which were a Russian sphere of influence. These British interests formed themselves into the Anglo-Persian Oil Company (later the Anglo-Iranian Oil Company). The British government, having decided to adopt oil instead of coal for the navy in the years before World War I, bought a controlling share in APOC. Winston Churchill, First Lord of the Admiralty at the outbreak of World War I, was to remark later that this "brought us a prize from fairyland far beyond our brightest hopes." The profits from the original investment of £2.2 million paid for the biggest fleet in the world in the three years that led up to the war. Lord Curzon, the Foreign Secretary, remarked after the war that the "Allies floated to victory on a sea of oil." The Iranian government was due to receive a small sum as its share of the profits, but even this was not always forthcoming because it was unable to protect the oil company's operations from marauding Bakhtiari tribesmen, and the company refused to pay.

In the aftermath of World War I Iran remained partitioned into Russian and British spheres of influence. But in 1921 Colonel Reza Khan seized power and four years later was proclaimed Shah. Here was a new type of twentieth-century national leader who attempted to assert his country's independence of the great powers. His demand for better terms from APOC involved a long dispute. He canceled the concession, which was then renegotiated so that Iran received a royalty on every barrel of oil produced and a 20 percent share of the company's dividends. The new concession brought peace with the oil company for twenty years. Reza Shah pursued his efforts to modernize the country through strong central government with some success. But he remained heavily dependent on the oil royalties and his real independence was strictly limited. During World War II Iran was occupied by Russian and British troops, and Reza Shah, regarded as too pro-German, was forced to abdicate in favor of his son Muhammad.

Iraq, or Mesopotamia as it was then called, was the next place after Iran in which oil was discovered in the Middle East. In fact the existence of Mesopotamian oil had been known for many years. Seepages in the north were sold by the donkeyload to fuel the lamps of the Ottoman Empire. Before World War I the Turkish Sultan sold the concession to a consortium of German, Dutch, and British interests who together formed the Turkish Petoleum Company.

When Turkey was defeated in World War I and the British occupied Iraq, they expropriated the German 25 percent share in the TPC which then went to France as part of a secret agreement whereby France, in return for abandoning any claims to Palestine, was given a free hand in Syria and Lebanon and a share in Iraq's oil. This was a great prize as Iraq was widely believed to be floating on a sea of oil.

The mandate system established by the League of Nations after the war prolonged British control over Iraq. In fact the Hashemite Kingdom of Iraq was a British creation. Prince Faisal, the military leader of the Arab revolt against the Turks who had been ejected from Syria by the French, was placed on a throne in Baghdad. The Anglo-Iraqi Treaty of 1922, which King Faisal and his cabinet were obliged to accept, guaranteed British interests and predominance in Iraq.

Nevertheless, the forces of Iraqi Arab nationalism soon found expression in this newly-established state. A parliament elected in 1925 was fiercely critical of many aspects of the 1922 Treaty and only ratified it under extreme pressure. But seven months before this, King Faisal and his cabinet had been persuaded to ratify the new concession of TPC, or the Iraq Petroleum Company as it now became. The Finance Minister fought hard to protect Iraq's interests but the struggle was unequal. However, one feature of the oil convention was attractive to all Iraqi nationalists. This stipulated that when shares in IPC were offered to the public Iraqi nationals should be given preference for at least 20 percent of the issue. The fact that no such shares were ever offered, on the ground that the company was private and not public, led the Iraqis to feel that they had been hoodwinked.

In the 1920s American oil companies succeeded in making their first entrance into the Middle East through Iraq. They had strong backing from Washington, which accused Britain of quietly seeking to control all the oil resources of Mesopotamia and argued that the Versailles Treaty agreement guaranteed an "open door" for the commerce of all nations in the former enemy territories. Eventually, by reaching a private agreement with the British owners of IPC, Standard Oil of New Jersey and Socony Vacuum (later Mobil Oil) jointly obtained an equal share with the British, the Anglo-Dutch, and French companies.

The Iraqi government had almost no say in this matter. But the entry of American oil companies onto the Middle East scene was highly significant for all the states of the area, for it marked the end of the British monopoly. When the future oil states of Arabia (Saudi Arabia, Kuwait, Bahrain, and the Trucial States) came to grant exploration concessions, they were able to some extent to play the Americans off against the British, and where the British believed that their exclusive treaties with the Gulf shaykhdoms covered oil concessions, the United States was ready to support American companies on the "open door" principle.

This does not mean that the power of the major international oil companies did not remain overwhelming in relation to the Middle East governments. These were Esso (now Exxon), Shell, Anglo-Iranian (later BP), Gulf, Texaco, Mobil, and Socal (later Chevron), immortally named the Seven Sisters by Enrico Mattei, the buccaneering head of the Italian state oil organization.

This power was amply demonstrated in the Iranian oil crisis of 1951-54. Over the years Iranian nationalists—which meant the great majority of the Iranian people—had come to regard the Anglo-Iranian Oil Company as an instrument of British imperialism. For them it was a state within a state—a crippling limitation on Iran's sovereignty and independence. Under the leadership of the elderly radical politician Dr. Muhammad Mosaddegh, Iran nationalized AIOC in April 1951 amid great public enthusiasm. The action also electrified public opinion in the Arab states.

But Dr. Mosaddegh had ill-prepared his move. The AIOC, having secured the promise of its six sisters that they would not try to take its place, merely ensured, with the backing of the British government, that Iran could not sell its nationalized oil. A Panamanian tanker that dared to take on oil at Abadan was forced into Aden by RAF planes and had its cargo impounded. It made no difference that the International Court of Justice ruled in Iran's favor or that the UN Security Council refused to act. Faced with economic disaster and rising discontent, Dr. Mosaddegh turned to extreme action. He briefly succeeded in seizing full powers for himself and in August 1953 the young Shah fled abroad, only to return a few days later after a coup planned by the United States and Great Britain had secured Mosaddegh's overthrow. A year later the dispute was settled by an agreement in which Iranian oil operations were taken over by a consortium in which AIOC (the former APOC, or British Petroleum as it now became) had a 40 percent share and the rest was shared among its sisters (including the French state company which is often regarded as the eighth sister). Iran retained some face-saving advantages. In theory the act of nationalization was not reversed; the consortium was acting on behalf of the National Iranian Oil Company established by Mosaddegh. But the reality was that the sisters had recovered control.

While they were boycotting Iranian oil, the oil companies had stepped up production in rival producing countries such as Iraq, Kuwait, and Saudi Arabia. At the time the governments of these states were content to be earning increased revenues at Iran's expense, but it was not many years before they came to regret it and to see where the common interests of all the oil-producing countries lay. To the mass of the people in all these countries Dr. Mosaddegh remained, and remains, a hero. His action might have been hasty and ill-judged. With his pajamas and his habit of constantly bursting into tears, he was more than slightly ludicrous. But he had tried to strike a blow against the overwhelming power of the industrialized Western world.

The governments of the oil states had learned the lesson that hasty and premature nationalization would be disastrous. But this did not mean that they were resigned to their relationship with the oil companies. Their position had improved sharply in 1950 with the introduction of the so-called fifty-fifty profit-sharing principle between host governments and companies. This had first been successfully demanded by the Venezuelan government. King Ibn Saud had then wanted to know why he should not have a similar share. With the Saudi Finance Minister Shaikh Abdullah Sulaiman, Aramco negotiated a formula which lasted for the next ten years and was widely adopted by the other Mideast oil states.

This new arrangement was highly satisfactory to the oil companies, especially the U.S. companies. The 50 percent share of the profits on the sale of crude oil was paid in the form of income tax to the host government, and under U.S. tax laws this could be set off against the companies' tax liability to the U.S. government. In other words, the extra $50 million that Saudi Arabia received from Aramco in 1951 under the fifty-fifty formula was paid for by the U.S. Treasury and not the company. At the same time the sense of cooperation between the companies and the host governments created by the fifty-fifty slogan greatly increased the companies' sense of security. They could hope that they would no longer be regarded as an independent "state within a state" because they were working with the government. They could also claim that they were giving the host governments financial security by relieving them of all the costly risks involved in searching for oil in other areas. The profits shared were only on the sale of oil that had already been discovered.

For a time this formula seemed to satisfy the oil-producing countries. It is at least possible that it could have averted the Iranian oil crisis if it had been introduced in 1950. However, the oil-producing countries were not satisfied for long as they came to realize that the new arrangement was not a partnership in any real sense. All the important decisions about the rate at which their vital but exhaustible natural resource was being extracted and the price for which it was sold were still in the hands of the powerful international oil companies.

Until the fifty-fifty formula was introduced, the oil companies had never bothered to consider what their "profits" were on the sale of crude oil. Nearly all the crude went straight to their own refineries, and very little was sold on the open market. In other words, for the oil companies the extraction of the oil was only part of its long progress from under the ground to the gasoline pump. However, they now had to establish a theoretical price for crude oil as a basis for calculating the profits that were to be divided with the host country, and they did this by declaring a so-called "posted price" for the sale of crude oil in the Middle East. Posted prices were established according to a complex basing-point system centered on the Gulf of Mexico; they were not at all the result of impersonal market forces. The result was that the production of crude oil in the Middle East, where costs were much lower than in the Western hemisphere because the oil was so much more accessible, became immensely attractive to the international oil companies. There was the additional incentive of the tax dodge—known as the "golden gimmick"—which had first been agreed to by the U.S. government for Aramco in Saudi Arabia and was then adopted by other oil companies and their governments. This was a tremendous inducement to American oil companies to invest in the Middle East rather than at home.

The upshot was a huge increase in the production of Middle East oil during the 1950s. Output tripled during the decade. For a time, things ran smoothly as the revenues of the oil-producing countries were rapidly increasing along with the profits of the oil companies. Among the Arabs there were some who felt that they should make use of oil as an instrument of political power. This was when the phrase "the oil weapon" first began to be heard. President Nasser of Egypt wrote in *The Philosophy of the Revolution* in 1954 that: "Petroleum is the vital nerve of civilization, without which all its means cannot possibly exist." Two years later his daring nationalization of the Suez Canal Company made him a popular hero in the Arab world. But unlike Dr. Mosaddegh, he did not have to contend directly with the oil companies and he was able to exploit the divisions in the West over how to deal with him. Above all, Egypt was not an important oil-producing country, and despite Nasser's high prestige he had no means of making the oil states such as Iraq and Saudi Arabia employ the oil weapon to further Arab national causes—something they knew at that stage they were quite unequipped to do.

There were a few voices of radical nationalism to be heard among the representatives of the Arab oil states. One of these belonged to Abdullah Tariki, the fiery young Saudi director-general of petroleum and mineral resources. He accused the oil companies, by their arbitrary and discriminatory pricing of Middle East oil, of having gained nearly $5.5 billion, half of which should have gone to the Middle East producing countries. The oil company experts were able without difficulty to discount his statistical calculations. But, as Tariki well knew, he was making a political point: that the oil companies were unilaterally deciding how much revenue they were paying the host governments. This meant that in effect they were determining these countries' national incomes. In 1962 Tariki was replaced by the sophisticated Shaykh Ahmad Zaki Yamani who expresses himself much more cautiously and diplomatically, although he would yield nothing to Tariki in patriotism. In 1960, however, Tariki was expressing a deeply felt national sentiment.

The governments of the oil-producing states, with rising needs for revenues, were constantly urging the companies either to increase production or prices or both. This the companies were unable to do. For a while the emerging surplus, that is the increasing availability of oil at prices below those posted by the companies, was concealed by various fortuitous events such as the Anglo-Iranian crisis which removed Iranian oil from the market for nearly four years, the Korean War, and the Suez crisis of 1956 which closed the Suez Canal and the Iraqi oil pipeline across Syria. As soon as the effects of the Suez crisis wore off, the pressure on the prices of crude oil and petroleum products intensified. But the oil companies were still paying their oil revenues to Middle East governments on the basis of the artificially posted prices. Accordingly, in February 1959 they announced a cut in the posted price which automatically reduced the oil revenues of the main Middle East producers by about 10 percent. But the market did not stabilize, and in August 1960 they made a further cut.

The oil-producing countries were at last provoked into joining together to try to protect their interests. Their revenues, on which they depended for all their development plans, had been slashed without their having had any say in the matter. Venezuela took the lead in forming the Organization of Petroleum-Exporting Countries —OPEC. Iran, Iraq, Kuwait, and Saudi Arabia were its other founding members.

This "cartel to confront the cartel," as it was called at the time, is probably now the best-known association in the world. Its meetings are major international events. But initially OPEC was not nearly as powerful as it is today. Many people, including most oil company officials, were skeptical about its ability to hold together. It did have some success in preventing further cuts in posted prices, although it was unable to restore them to their pre-1959 position. It also managed to oblige the oil companies to stop treating their royalties per ton of oil as part of their nominal 50 percent share of "profits" and in this way increased their revenues even when the world price of oil was falling. But on the vital question of holding back output in order to raise prices—the normal function associated with a cartel—the OPEC countries were quite unable to agree. The "prorationing" of oil, which would mean that OPEC would collectively agree on a level of output for each of its members, was still quite beyond OPEC's capacity. Saudi Arabia was not interested, and the Shah of Iran was still determined that his country should recover its position as the foremost Middle East oil producer, which it had lost in 1951. Moreover, in the 1960s other states such as Algeria, Libya, Nigeria, and Abu Dhabi joined the ranks of major producers, and they all wanted to increase their output. The world of output of crude oil, having tripled in the 1950s, tripled again in the 1960s.

None of the Arab oil states was considering nationalizing the oil companies at this stage. The lesson of Iran had been learned and the power of the companies was still overwhelming, although the dominance of the Seven Sisters among them had diminished with the advent of new "independent" companies in the new oil areas of Algeria and Libya. (The closure of the Suez Canal in the 1967 Arab-Israeli war gave them a big comparative advantage over the Gulf states east of Suez.) But if these Arab governments shrank from nationalization—and at least for the Saudi and Kuwaiti governments this would have been contrary to their principles—they all wanted to participate in the industry. As their development accelerated after World War II they were all producing an increasing number of skilled administrators and technicians of their own. Some of these were oil experts on a level with those in the West, and inevitably they wanted to play a greater part in the exploitation of their own great natural resource. National pride demanded that they should want to reduce the role of foreigners in running their economic affairs. This was the spirit behind the UN General Assembly resolution of November 25, 1966, on a country's right of permanent sovereignty over the development of its natural resources. At its sixteenth conference in July 1968, OPEC followed this up with a "Declaratory Statement of Petroleum Policy" which said that the best way for OPEC members to ensure that their oil resources were used for their benefit was for them to be "in a position to undertake for themselves directly the exploitation of their hydrocarbon resources, so that they may exercise their freedom of choice in the utilization of hydrocarbon resources in the most favorable conditions."

The obvious method the oil states could use to start achieving this objective without nationalization was to insist that the oil companies relinquish the parts of their concession areas that they had been unable to exploit. Concessions granted after the war all had timetables for relinquishment written into the agreement, and the companies with the old pre-war concessions, which were usually so vast as to cover most of the country, were persuaded to do the same. All the major oil-producing countries—Iraq, Iran, Kuwait, and Saudi Arabia—had set up their own national oil companies, and they gave preference to foreign companies that would enter into joint ventures with the national companies when new concessions were granted in the relinquished areas. The Japanese and the Italians were the first to go into such ventures. Both were bitterly resentful that they had consistently been excluded from the Seven Sisters' magic circle. All the national oil companies gained invaluable experience in all stages of the oil industry, from drilling to refining and marketing oil at home and abroad. Saudi Arabia's Petromin took the lead in pushing joint ventures and succeeded in obtaining more and more favorable terms. But in every case the essential core of the oil industry in each country remained under the control of the oil companies. They naturally refused to give up their concessions in the major oil fields, and no really big discoveries were made in the relinquished areas. When in 1961 Iraq's radical dictator Abd al Karim Qasim unilaterally expropriated 99.5 percent of the IPC's concession area, instead of the 90 percent which IPC had been ready to give up, the oil company responded by cutting back output in all Iraq's major fields under its control, with disastrous consequences for the Iraqi economy. The Anglo-Dutch, American, and French companies which owned IPC were not unhappy to be able to teach Iraq a lesson, and they had plenty of oil elsewhere.

The oil states had one other way of obtaining a larger share in the management of the industry. They could ask to participate in the equity of the major companies operating on their territory. Here they met a blank refusal. The Iraqis felt especially embittered about this because they believed that they had been promised a 20 percent share in IPC when the concession was granted in 1925. The other major companies were equally adamant. Shaykh Ahmad Zaki Yamani's request for Petromin's participation in Aramco's oil production was politely refused. Suggestions that the oil states should have an equity share in downstream operations—such as refining and marketing in Western Europe—were rather more sharply rejected.

OPEC survived the 1960s, confounding the many skeptics, and its members gained some valuable experience in running the oil industry. But the basic relationship between the oil companies and the host governments had hardly changed. The prevailing attitude toward OPEC among oil company officials was that it would not amount to very much.

Very few people foresaw the astonishing transformation of this relationship in the years between 1970 and 1974. This was the period of the "Oil Revolution" as it has been called. The basic reason was something that had developed without the world's being fully aware it was happening—a secondary industrial revolution in the West based on abundant Middle East oil. The Western industrialized countries and, to a lesser extent, Japan had come to take cheap energy for granted. It was remarkably inexpensive. Saudi oil, for example, actually fell in price from $2.18 a barrel in 1947 to $1.80 in 1970. This was at a time when other prices were rising so that the fall in real terms was more like 50 percent. At the beginning of this period the United States first became a net importer of oil; by 1970 it was becoming heavily dependent on oil from the Middle East (although, as I discovered during a six-month visit to the United States in the winter of 1970-71, very few Americans were aware of this or what it meant). At the same time there was worldwide inflation (except in oil prices) and currency instability, especially of the U.S. dollar.

The long glut in world supplies was coming to an end and the oil states were quick to take advantage. The first to do so was Libya, where the new regime of the young Colonel Qaddafy had just replaced the monarchy. Through tough and uncompromising bargaining the Libyans secured new profit-sharing terms which shattered the arrangements of the past two decades. Led by Saudi Arabia and Iran, the other OPEC members soon obtained even better terms. The companies agreed to make provision for the effect on oil revenues of inflation and currency devaluation. It was more important that for the first time the companies agreed to "recognize" OPEC as a negotiating body. This was because they feared the effect of continual "leapfrogging"—that is, the Gulf producers and the Mediterranean producers competing with each other to obtain better terms. The "cartel to confront the cartel" was now a reality.

The two sides gathered in Tehran in February 1971 for a confrontation that was historic because for the first time the cards seemed evenly stacked on both sides of the table. In return for an increase in prices which, although tiny by later standards, the oil companies declared was ruinous, the OPEC negotiators agreed to stabilize prices for five years.

In 1972 Iraq's Baathist regime which had taken power in 1968, having failed to settle the differences with IPC, issued an ultimatum demanding increased output and royalties and a 20 percent participation in the company's assets. When the ultimatum expired, Iraq nationalized IPC. This was not a repeat of the Iranian crisis in 1951. The other Arab oil producers helped Iraq instead of exploiting its difficulties. A year later IPC came to terms with a settlement. It was therefore much less of a surprise than it might have been that the oil companies agreed in 1972 to the oil states' long-standing demand, which they had so fiercely resisted, of equity participation in the companies which produced oil. In December 1972 Saudi Arabia acquired a 25 percent stake in Aramco's assets.

There was now an irreversible trend toward a new structure of the oil industry. The governments of the host countries were taking over from the companies the crucial power of deciding the level of prices of crude oil. Then in 1973 an event took place which greatly accelerated the process—the October Arab-Israeli war. But the trend would have continued anyway; the war merely speeded it up in a way which jolted the world out of its complacency and created an atmosphere of crisis.

The October War actually broke out while the OPEC ministers were meeting the oil company representatives in Vienna to discuss a revision of the Tehran agreement. The gap between the two sides was large. OPEC was asking for the doubling of the posted price to $6 a barrel. The companies proposed a 15 percent increase. As they were meeting, news of the war and the aid that the United States was pouring into Israel hardened the attitude of the five Arab delegations (Saudi Arabia, Kuwait, Iraq, Abu Dhabi, and Qatar). The companies asked for time to consult with their main customers, the governments of the industrialized countries, but the OPEC delegates refused, and flew home to announce an increase in price to $5.12 a barrel. This was an even greater milestone than the Tehran Agreement of 1971. The oil-producing countries unilaterally decided on a price increase.

Events now moved swiftly. The Arab oil cutback in production and embargo of countries supporting Israel, led by Saudi Arabia, exacerbated the world oil shortage. In December, OPEC decided on another doubling in price to $11.65 a barrel. This time it was the Shah of Iran who took the lead. He had not taken part in the Arab oil embargo—in fact Iran supplied oil to Israel—but he was prepared to make use of this tremendous new power in OPEC's hands. It was no longer even a "cartel confronting a cartel." The oil-producing countries had become the only cartel in the business.

However, it is a cartel with a difference. Its decisions are not only financial and economic; they are also strongly political in their implications. They affect the economic condition of the noncommunist world and hence the balance of power between East and West. Equally, they influence the relationship between North and South—that is, between the industrialized world and the Third World or lesser developed countries. The OPEC countries are therefore in a unique position because, although they are indisputably members of the Third World in their level of development, they have the kind of power and responsibility that is normally attributed to the advanced industrial countries.

Of the thirteen members of OPEC, the three big producers of Arabia—Saudi Arabia, Kuwait, and the UAE—have the greatest responsibility of all. Their huge surpluses of revenues over their immediate requirements have given them assets of "petrodollars" which can affect the entire world monetary system. Finally, it is Saudi Arabia which stands alone on a pinnacle of responsibility. As Faisal al Hegelan, Saudi Arabia's Ambassador to the United States, pointed out in a speech on July 9, 1980, his country has "one fourth of the planet's proven oil reserves and a third of all the oil in the world internationally available."

Speaking in London in September 1974, that is a few months

Oil: Power and Responsibility

after the Oil Revolution had taken place, Shaykh Yamani summarized what had happened. For years, he said, the world had been either unaware of or unconcerned about the anomalies in the structure of the oil industry. "One of the most serious of those anomalies was probably the lack of any form of direct contact between the producers and the consumers, for which both, in addition to the oil companies, were to blame. The major industrial consumers, assured of the availability of cheap abundant energy, were complacent; the oil companies were happy with the excessive profits they made; the producers, due to a combination of market conditions and an inability to assert their rights, were acquiescent."

Yamani said the time had come for an "objective dialogue" between the producers and consumers of oil. He showed no animosity toward the oil companies, but pointed out that their role had now irretrievably changed. Since the origins of the oil industry, this role had been as a link between the producers and consumers, extracting the oil and then refining and marketing it. Now that the principle of participation had been accepted there had been "a shift in the control of oil exploitation and trade away from the oil companies to the producing countries' governments. Those governments retain now almost entirely the decision-making powers for price determination, production levels in their countries, future expansion of oil facilities, and, to a greater extent, the destination of oil exports. Consequently the role so successfully played by the oil companies as bridge and buffer between the exporting and consuming countries has diminished, giving rise to the need for filling the vacuum thus created by a new two-party relationship between the two groups of countries. The role being played by the oil companies now is properly that of a purchaser, refiner, and provider of technology."

Kuwait was the first of the Arabian states to follow Iraq by taking over 100 percent participation in its own oil industry. Abu Dhabi has preferred to take only a majority interest in the foreign operating companies. In 1974 Saudi Arabia increased its share from 25 percent to 60 percent but announced its intention of raising this to 100 percent. Negotiations for this were still dragging on after four years because the Saudis did not regard it as being of major importance. The principle of national control of the industry was well established. Negotiations were fully completed by September 1980.

How well do the governments of these Arabian oil states feel they are discharging the enormous responsibilities that they have partly undertaken of their own free will and have partly had thrust upon them? The question is of some importance in any Western study of these countries in view of the barrage of criticism they sustain in the Western media. They have difficulty in finding the right means of responding.

The first and salient point, to which a representative of any of these governments is likely to turn in conversation with a Westerner, is that they have two kinds of responsibility, and these are often in conflict—toward the world at large and toward their own people. Perhaps it is so obvious that few Westerners bother to think of the implications, but the stark reality for the oil-producing countries is that oil is a finite, exhaustible resource. The hydrocarbons that took hundreds of millions of years to develop from the remains of aquatic plants and animals will be used up in a century. For the people of Arabia it is almost their only source of natural wealth apart from the fish around their shores and other minerals which may yet be discovered.

It is true that these countries took time to absorb the fact that nemesis was so close at hand—perhaps within the lifetime of their own grandchildren. In the early, carefree days when huge new oil fields were being discovered each year on the coasts of Arabia, there were few who bothered to think that their people might go from rags to riches and back to rags again in two generations. Moreover, the oil was being sold so cheaply that the only way to increase revenues was to sell more and more. But this has not been true for some time. They are all deeply conscious of the fact that, in the striking phrase of a Qatari oil expert: "A barrel sold is a barrel lost." By this he meant that the oil and gas are being taken out of the ground to feed the hungry machines of the

West far more rapidly than the oil states would accept if they thought only of their own interests. What they were being asked to do can be compared to a landowner's selling off some incomparable and irreplaceable piece of property in order to buy some dubious shares.

The Kuwaitis were the first to take action by putting a ceiling on their annual output of two million barrels per day which would sustain production for at least 90 years instead of the 40-50 years that was forecast at one time. But, as always, it is Saudi Arabia that bears much the heaviest responsibility. It is the only "swing producer" among the OPEC states—that is, the only one with the capacity to make a huge enough increase or cutback in production to affect the world market single-handedly. Saudi Arabia alone can influence the state of the world's economy.

Since 1974 Saudi Arabia has consistently used this power, or threatened to use it, in order to try to moderate the price increases imposed by OPEC. At times it was even prepared to break up the organization. It had to contend with a hawkish group in OPEC led by Iran, Iraq, and Algeria (until the Shah of Iran changed his attitude in the last year before he was overthrown) that argued on a basis of national interest that the price of oil should at least keep pace with inflation in the price of the manufactured goods of the industrialized countries.

When I saw Shaykh Yamani in February 1979, Saudi Arabia was producing oil at the rate of about eight million barrels per day. He had no doubt that this was much more than the country needed to take out of the ground to provide the revenues it required. Saudi Arabia would continue to do this in order to satisfy the international demand for oil, although there was a limit beyond which it would not go. "What we are doing is against our national interest," he said. (A distinguished Arab intellectual remarked of this that it must be the first case of a senior minister admitting that what his government was doing was against the nation's interest without risk of impeachment.) A year later, as followers of Ayatollah Khomeini cut back Iran's production by more than half, Saudi Arabia increased its own output to 9.5 million barrels a day.

This was at a time when its own planners estimated that an output of 6.8 million barrels a day would earn more than enough revenues to finance all Saudi economic development and defense requirements. In other words, Saudi Arabia was selling off its oil at a rate that would shorten the life of its reserves by one third more than was necessary.

It would be absurd to suggest that Saudi Arabia does this out of altruism toward the industrialized countries of the world. The interests of all the Arabian states are bound up with those of the West. For Saudi Arabia especially, with its unrelenting anti-communist convictions and special ties with the United States, neutrality between the West and the Eastern bloc countries is inconceivable. The collapse of the dollar, let alone that of the entire international monetary system, would spell disaster for the Saudis.

Leaders of the Arabian oil states would acknowledge that they have a vital interest in the economic health of the noncommunist industrialized countries. And this is why they resent being represented by the West as enemies of its prosperity. Criticism ranges from the weighty denunciation of governments to the crude abuse of some of the media. An example of the former was contained in the communiqué of the Venice summit of seven leading industrialized nations (the United States, West Germany, Great Britain, Canada, Japan, France, and Italy) in June 1980, which asserted that the "successive increases" in the price of oil "bearing no relation to market conditions" have "produced the reality of even higher inflation" and the threat of unemployment and recession in the industrialized countries. The communiqué also threw the blame for the troubles of the Third World on the oil producers, saying that higher oil prices "have undermined and in some cases virtually destroyed" prospects for growth in the developing countries.

The attitude of the media is represented by the cartoons of "oil shaykhs" delighting in the troubles of the Western motorists. But there is another tendency, which is to exult in and exaggerate any discovery of a new source of oil (such as Mexico—the "new

Saudi Arabia''), of any alternative to oil as a form of energy, or of some new method of saving in the use of oil. In these cases the ''oil shaykhs'' are shown to be shaking with rage and jealousy. (''How to Make a Shaykh Shake'' was the advertisement for a new fuel-saving model of a European car in 1979.)

To these attacks the oil states have several replies. In the first place no economic expert has been able to prove whether increasing oil prices cause inflation and financial instability or the reverse, but there is at least a strong argument for saying that the waves of inflation that have afflicted the Western world in the last twenty years—first in the late 1960s and then in the late 1970s—actually preceded the big rises in oil prices. Moreover, even the most hostile critics of the oil states have to admit that a doubling in oil prices does not add to the inflation of the industrialized countries by more than two percent, whereas their inflation rates are mostly in double figures. Another point of which the Western public is either unaware or forgetful is that of the price of a gallon of gasoline or fuel oil, perhaps 30 percent goes to the oil companies, another 30 percent to the oil states, while the remaining 40 percent goes to the governments of the industrialized countries in the form of taxes. Again it is at least possible that these governments add more to their own inflation through these taxes than is caused by the increase in oil prices.

The suggestion that the ''oil shaykhs'' are in a state of neurotic anxiety about the possibility that the industrialized countries will find an alternative to their oil is ironic in that they have made it clear that they would welcome this. Shaykh Yamani especially has been urging repeatedly and emphatically for several years the need for the West to do more research into other types of fuel. Whatever new sources of energy are discovered, or even if the industrialized countries were to revert to using coal on a large scale, oil will not lose its value either as a form of energy or as raw material for the petrochemicals industry. As we have seen, the oil states would much prefer to keep more of it underground. Therefore for them it is wholly desirable that the increase in the price of oil encourage the search for alternative sources of energy and of new oil fields in the new areas. (It is quite probable that the Mexican discoveries would not have been made if the price of oil had remained at its very low pre-1973 level.)

If the typical newspaper cartoon of the "oil shaykh" shows him happily squeezing the West, it also represents him as callously indifferent to the suffering and poverty of the Third World countries. (Says one oil shaykh to another in one particularly offensive example: "As my contribution to World Hunger Year, I am only allowing my wives to dine at the Ritz once a week.")

An attempt is even being made to pass off responsibility onto the oil states for the great division in the world between the wealthy North and poverty-stricken South.

Not surprisingly the "oil shaykhs" have strong feelings about being portrayed in this way. They insist that by any normal criteria they are not part of the affluent North but are among the developing countries of the Third World. (The national income of even the poorest of the industrialized nations attending the Venice summit meeting, Italy, is greater than that of all the OPEC countries.) While it cannot be denied that the increase in oil prices has added to the difficulties of the other developing countries, this is certainly not the cause of the great division in the world between the richer and poorer nations. In crudely oversimplified terms, the latter suffer because they are exporting raw materials which are underpriced in terms of the increasingly expensive manufactured goods that they have to import from the industrialized countries. The raw material exported by the oil states is nonrenewable, and the Arabian oil exporters have virtually no alternative sources of income. This point has to be made with wearisome repetition as long as those who caricature the "oil shaykhs" fail to grasp its significance.

If the Arabian oil states have built up large financial surpluses since 1974 it is precisely because their economies are not sufficiently developed to absorb their revenues. Industrialized countries, such as Britain or Norway, have no such problem of coping with oil revenues. The Arab oil states' objective is to end this situation as soon as possible, which is why they all have ambitious industrialization plans. Already the almost hysterical predictions about the size of these surpluses that were being made in the West have had to be scaled down. It now appears that they are likely to disappear altogether in a few years in view of the enormous cost of their development plans.

In the meantime the Arab oil states have done much to distribute their wealth among less fortunate people of the Third World. In 1973, when the meteoric rise in oil prices made them temporarily much richer, their combined aid was $1.3 billion. Since 1975 it has been running at more than $5 billion a year. Kuwait, the first with a surplus, pioneered with the Kuwait Fund for Arab Economic Development, founded in 1961. Others followed, such as the Arab Fund for Economic and Social Development (1968), the Abu Dhabi Fund for Arab Economic Development (1971), the Arab Bank for Economic Development in Africa (1973), the Saudi Development Fund (1974), and the Jiddah-based Islamic Development Bank (1977).

The huge aid program that this represents is still open to criticism in certain Third World countries. The great bulk of the aid goes to Arab and Muslim countries (although the Kuwait Fund, for example, has extended its activities to non-Arab countries since 1974). Non-Muslim black African countries, in particular, feel that the Arab states have not helped them as much as they promised at the Arab African meeting in Cairo in 1977, which was held to discuss their problems. The Arab donors prefer to tie their aid to specific projects in the countries to which they are lending money, but invariably the governments of these countries want help for their overall balance of payments, their most pressing problem.

It could be pointed out that it is not unknown for Western countries to favor their friends and allies when handing out aid. But by any criteria the Arab oil states' efforts to distribute some of their wealth are substantial. Kuwait and the UAE are giving more than 10 percent of their GNP, and Saudi Arabia, more than 5 percent. This compares with the 0.31 percent of GNP provided by all the industrialized countries of the OECD since 1975 which has never approached even the 0.7 percent recommended by the UN in

World Development Year, or the 1 percent called for more recently by the Brandt Commission.

The first communiqué of the Venice summit meeting in June 1980 contained the following paragraph: "The democratic industrialized countries cannot alone carry the responsibility of aid and other different contributions to developing countries: it must be equitably shared by the oil-exporting countries and the industrialized Communist countries." When this is related to the aid statistics, the oil states may be forgiven for finding it sanctimonious and highly misleading.

Another current fantasy is that of oil-rich Arabs flushed with ambitions of world domination. Arab finance, whether government or private, has been used to buy property or shares in banks, industries, and commercial companies in Western Europe, North America, and the Third World. But the targets have been modest and very often even these efforts have failed because of Western resistance. Suggestions that the oil states either could or would take over the major multinational companies are exaggerations. Similarly, the idea that they could somehow seize control of the international monetary system is fantastic. Certainly they are concerned with the health of their foreign investments and have acquired considerable sophistication in handling them. The Arab financier may be formidable, but his expertise tells him the limits to the power and durability of Arab finance. The decline in the value of the dollar is a cause of anxiety, and some financial shaykhs would favor its replacement by a basket of major currencies as a means of international payment in the oil industry, although the Saudis at least believe there is no real alternative to the dollar. When I suggested to the Saudi Finance Minister, Shaykh Muhammad Aba al Khail that the Saudi rival might become an international reserve currency he rejected the idea as absurd.

The oil states can claim that, having at last succeeded in winning control over their own oil industries, they are shouldering their enormous responsibility with caution and restraint. But it is a double responsibility: toward their own people and the world at large, and the two do not always coincide.

Oil: Power and Responsibility

20
The Challenge of Change

The young Saudi multi-millionaire businessman was optimistic. We were discussing the chances of his people and society surviving the shattering pace of material changes they were undergoing without the loss of their identity and the destruction of their traditions. "If we were to evolve in exactly the same way that the West evolved," he said, "then there would be a danger, but if we evolve in our own special way I don't think there will be a problem. Take the Japanese as an example. They have changed in a hundred years from a feudal and agricultural society into one of the most powerful industrial societies without a fundamental break in their traditions. If they can do it—and other societies have also done it—why can't Islam?"

I noticed that he said "Islam" rather than "the Arabs" or "Saudi Arabia." Like nearly all his fellow countrymen, he sees himself and his society as representing Islam, and it is by Islamic standards that he thinks they should be judged. Because he is infinitely proud of his faith and confident that it represents the final revelation of God's truth to mankind, he believes—as he must believe—that Islamic society can cope with such a thing as twentieth-century technology. Unlike Christianity, Islam, through the *Holy Koran* and the *Hadith* and the *Shariah* which is derived from them, prescribes how society on this earth should be organized and administered. There is no question of leaving things to be sorted out in the next world.

Even the quietly confident young Saudi had to admit that the

215

scale and pace of change in the Arabian Peninsula is awesome. Less than fifty years ago Bertram Thomas, the British Arabist and explorer who was the first Westerner to cross the Empty Quarter, could write: "The mode of human life...is tribal and nomadic, a life economically precarious, politically unstable, but socially fixed and unalterable...The prosperity of the tribe is measured by the number and condition of its camels. The sources of wealth are good pastures and the manly prowess of its members...physical fitness, brute strength, and an aggressive character are the qualities which Nature demands and rewards."

The grandchildren of these people today are attempting to manage an economic enterprise on the scale of the opening up of Siberia or the Amazon basin. If they are not to be overwhelmed they have to be able to understand and control it themselves.

Some, although by no means all of the Western visitors to Arabia who were rare until thirty years ago, idealized the society they encountered. Upper-class Englishmen were prominent among them. The late-Victorian romantic poet Wilfrid Scawen Blunt wrote after a visit to central Arabia in 1878: "In Nejd alone of all the countries of the world I have visited, either East or West, the three great blessings of which we in Europe make our boast, though we do not in truth possess them, are a living reality: 'Liberty, Equality, Brotherhood,' names only even in France, where they are written up on every wall, but here practically enjoyed by every free man. Here was a community living as our idealists have dreamed, without taxes, without police, without conscription, without compulsion of any kind, whose only law was public opinion, and whose only order a principle of honour. Here, too, was a people poor yet contented, and, according to their few wants, living in abundance, who to all questions I asked of them (and in how many lands had I not put the same in vain) had answered one invariably. 'Thank God, we are not as the other nations are. Here we have our own government. Here we are satisfied.' "

Blunt would have been appalled to see Arabia today. Eighty years after him Wilfred Thesiger, an Englishman in a similar mold and the last of the great Arabian travelers, was writing: "Today the desert where I travelled is scarred with the tracks of lorries and littered with discarded junk imported from Europe and America. But this material desecration is unimportant compared with the demoralization which has resulted among the Bedu themselves. While I was with them they had no thought of a world other than their own. They were not ignorant savages; on the contrary, they were the lineal heirs of a very ancient civilization, who found the framework of their society the personal freedom and self-discipline for which they craved. Now they are being driven out of the desert into towns where the qualities which once gave them mastery are no longer sufficient...Now it is not death but degradation which faces them."

Most of the people of Arabia would find this much too pessimistic. Life in the Peninsula has never been purely nomadic but a fertile synthesis between the bedu and the *hadhar*, that is the settled life of the oases towns and villages and the centers of population on the coast. Most important of all, Islam—contrary to a widespread misunderstanding in the West—did not originate in the desert but in the towns, when it transcended the ancient tribal laws and traditions of Arabia. This did not mean that the desert values and customs died out, but only that they were incorporated into the framework of Islam and the Holy *Shariah*. It was the bedu warriors who formed the spearhead of Islam when it exploded from the Arabian Peninsula. Their qualities of courage, independence, and self-reliance—those which Blunt and Thesiger so admired—were invaluable. But they have always required the higher discipline of Islam to prevent them from reverting entirely to their ancient ways. (As we have seen, Blunt remarked of the Najdis in 1878 that they were a people "whose only law was public opinion, and whose only order a principle of honour." He was suggesting that they were governed by tribal law rather than the *Shariah*.) It was the purpose of the original Wahhabi reformer to restore this discipline. A century later King Ibn Saud faced the same problem with the bedu but he went one stage further. In addition to restoring them to the pure faith in One God, he attempted, with some success, to settle them on the land.

This productive synthesis between the *hadhar* and the bedu is also a feature of the city-states on the coasts of Arabia—Kuwait, Qatar, and the UAE. Although the real nomadic life has now almost disappeared in all of them, the people retain close contact with the desert. Shaykh Shakhbut, the former Ruler of Abu Dhabi, laughingly described himself to me as a "half-bedu." The idea of rest and relaxation for many is to retire to a tent pitched on a sand dune or in a lonely wadi some miles outside the city.

Seen in an historical perspective, the outlook for Arabian society at the end of the twentieth century is much less bleak. Islam in the past has provided the framework for highly sophisticated economic systems. Throughout the Middle Ages the Muslim states and empires were more materially advanced than those of the Christian West. The first crusaders were startled to find that the Saracens had a much more advanced civilization than their own. It was only from the sixteenth century, with the opening of the routes to India and China which by-passed the Muslim world, and later when the Industrial Revolution came to northern Europe, that the economy and technology of the Christian states surged ahead of what was then the Ottoman Empire. Arabia, with its lack of natural resources, was the poorest part of the Muslim world. But Muslims do not have to believe that there is anything in Islam as such which prevents them from catching up. Hidebound conservatism and fear of change is another matter, but this is something that is found in any traditional civilization.

The Arabian bedu who are attracted to the cities do not have to face the certain degradation that was foreseen by Wilfred Thesiger. In fact many of them seem to be making the transition with the greatest ease. Their self-reliance and competitiveness bred in the desert serves them well. One of the brightest young ministers in the Saudi government is pure beduin. He likes to recount that when he received word that he had been awarded his doctorate from a prestigious American university, it took him three months to find his father who was roaming the desert to find pasture for his flocks. When I was on a recent visit to Riyadh, the papers carried the story of a fifteen-year-old beduin youth who had been hauled in by the police because he was working fifteen hours a day driving a six-wheel Mercedes truck, which he had altered to suit his small frame, bringing in loads of sand from the desert for the booming construction sites in the capital. The police dealt leniently with this example of vigorous private enterprise. But what was most interesting was that he was handing over without question his entire earnings of about six thousand dollars a month to his father. This example of family unity and respect for parents is still characteristic of Arabia.

(a) *Thawbs and Suits*

While the forces of tradition and religious conservatism are immensely powerful throughout Arabia, nothing can remain untouched by the tornado of modernization. But it is the determination of the people and their rulers to hold on to as much as they can of their tradition. This prevents the loss of identity that leads to the kind of enraged counterreaction which has been observed in Iran.

Nothing symbolizes this retention of identity more strongly than Arabian dress. A Palestinian who holds a high position in the Qatari government service remarked to me on its importance for national self-confidence. "Alas," he said, "we northern Arabs have long since abandoned our national dress—at least in the cities—to adopt Western clothes. In this respect we have accepted permanent colonization."

Men's clothes vary little throughout northern and eastern Arabia, although in Oman and the Yemens they are somewhat different. The basic garment is the ankle-length shirt fastened up to the neck—the *thawb* (pronounced "thobe,") or *dishdashah* in Kuwait. Beneath it is loose underwear (which in the bitter Najd winter may be "long johns"). Above the *thawb* is a cloak of brown, black, or white wool, with gold braided edges which is the *bisht* (or *aba* in the Hejaz). But it is the headdress which is most characteristic. A small skull-cap, the *taqiyah* which usually cannot be seen, is covered by a white or colored (often red check in Saudi Arabia) *ghutrah* headcloth (the *kaffiyeh* of Syria or Jordan) which is held in place by a black or white wool ring called the *agal*. This last was a camel hobble which the beduin used to keep on their heads when they were traveling, but it has now lost its original usage. The *ghutrah* and *agal* are harmonious and elegant. A young Arabian will arrange them with great care. He feels exposed without them and often keeps his head covered in the home. On his feet he usually wears a simple open leather sandal.

Women also wear a *thawb* but when they leave the house, if they are over the age of puberty, they envelop themselves in the black *abayah* cloak which passes over the head: unlike the men's *bisht* it is often made of silk. Saudi women wear in addition a black translucent veil over the face, while in Qatar or the UAE they may put on the peaked black canvas mask or *burqu* which covers the face except for the mouth and eyes. However, the *burqu* is worn less and less by younger women—especially in the cities. The traditional women's dresses of Arabia were magnificent examples of silver and gold brocade embroidery or *takhwir*. Sadly, but inevitably, the art of hand embroidery is giving way to the machine. There is only one lady left in Bahrain to make the wedding dresses for which the island used to be famous, and the art will probably die with her. However, the splendid gold jewelery worn by Arabian women—necklaces, bracelets, anklets, rings, earrings, and head ornaments will survive longer as the craft is still thriving.

The wealthier women of Arabia are now likely to wear European dress in the height of fashion underneath their *abayahs*. Normally these will only be seen by their husbands or other women.

Some young educated women in Kuwait, Bahrain, and to a lesser extent in Qatar and the UAE have abandoned the veil and the *abayah* entirely. In the universities in the Gulf, however, there is a new phenomenon. Some of the women teachers and women students have adopted the *hijab*, the head-scarf which covers the hair but not the face. This is not peculiar to Arabia; it is now common among young women at Egyptian universities. The wearing of the *hijab* is something that is decided upon by the women themselves as a demonstration of their Islamic feeling rather than something imposed upon them by a male-dominated society. The women say that it is the *hijab* that is required for feminine modesty by the *Koran* and that the veiling of the face was a later accretion to Islam from Iran or Turkey. One highly emancipated Kuwaiti lady on the staff of the university clearly regarded it as a step backward for her countrywomen. But it is likely to become more widespread in the Gulf states.

Arabian dress is wonderfully adapted to the environment. Westerners have generally assumed that it is the whiteness of the robe, reflecting rather than absorbing the heat, which keeps the occupant cool. But this does not explain why desert dwellers in other parts of the Middle East and North Africa wear black. Experiments by some American scientists have shown that the real secret is the "chimney" effect of the *thawb* which draws in air at the bottom and cools the occupant of the robe by convection.

King Ibn Saud used to insist that Western visitors put on Arab dress when they came to see him in Riyadh, but it was said that very few of them looked at ease. I have always felt that it was unwise for non-Arabs to wear Arab clothes as a general practice. One thinks of the misguided *memsahibs* of British India who put on *saris*. Even Lawrence of Arabia looks as if he were about to leave for a fancy dress ball in his photographs. Yet, as a Saudi friend recently pointed out politely, many men from Arabia wear suits and ties when they visit the West—and no one is surprised. Why shouldn't we return the compliment? The trouble is that very few Westerners have the facial characteristics—the bone-structure, moustache and beard—to harmonize with Arab dress. It is for this reason that Egyptians and Palestinians are equally unsuccessful if they try to merge into the background in *thawb* and *ghutrah*. One large, pale, and beardless British acquaintance complained that when he first tried Arab dress he looked in the mirror and saw a "dissolute nun."

The flowing and spotless robes of Arabia are of course unsuited to the factory and machine shop. While some young Arabs have not hesitated to put on coveralls during their working hours, there are others who are reluctant. This is a real obstacle to industrialization and especially to the development of an artisan class in Arabia. A *thawb* is not ideal for a plumber or plasterer. No doubt attitudes will change through economic pressures, but there is no likelihood of Arabian dress being abandoned except where it is absolutely necessary for practical reasons. It will remain a vital element in the Arabian personality.

(b) *Tents to Apartments*

If there has been no revolution in what the people of Arabia wear, there has been in where they live. Little more than a generation ago the houses of the settled population of central and eastern Arabia were all built on much the same principle. Of one story—or two at most—they were centered around a *majlis* or men's reception room which had facilities for the preparation of the traditional welcome of coffee or tea. The size and complexity of the *harim* or family living quarters depended on the wealth of the household. Furnishing and decoration were simple and austere except for plasterwork on the walls and the heavy carved and studded wooden doors. In the Najd these were painted with brilliant arabesques in strong primary colors. On his first visit to Riyadh in 1923, the Lebanese-American Ameen Rihani was thrilled by this antidote to Wahhabi puritanism. In the Hejaz, where Ottoman/Egyptian influence endured for some time, there were a number of elaborate buildings in the Turkish style.

In the Gulf states a variety of ingenious wind towers and ventilators (of a kind that were first used by the ancient Egyptians of the Old Kingdom) were used to deflect the cooling breezes down to circulate through the living quarters.

In thirty years virtually all this architecture has disappeared from the towns to be replaced by modern apartment blocks and private villas for the wealthier residents. The little that survives marks a belated attempt to conserve a heritage—two or three palaces on the Kuwait seafront, a few fine Turkish-style villas in Jiddah and Taif, some wind-tower dwellings in Dubai and Bahrain, where one has been admirably converted into a restaurant. In the Najd the old ruined Saudi capital of Diriyah is being preserved and partially restored as a historical monument.

It is only in the mountainous Asir of the southwest and in Najran, even further south towards the Yemeni border, that a traditional building style survives. In Asir the houses are tall with stables on the ground floor and upper storeys that have grown as the family expands. But elsewhere in Saudi Arabia and the Gulf the headlong rebuilding of the towns has produced an uneasy farrago of styles. Some of the new residential housing estates are admirable, thoughtfully adapted to the environment. Others are much less successful as they appear unrelated to the land on which they stand. Many of the villas of the new rich are unimaginably hideous--heavily ornamented with clashing colors. Yet the time has already come when a new generation of architects and town planners in Arabia is trying to develop a new idiom of Arabian architecture which will be Arab/Islamic in flavor but in a way that is functional rather than superficial. It will be some time, however, before these architects can wean their wealthier clients away from the "oil-shaykh baroque" style of furnishing and decorating their houses.

The new homes of the people of Arabian towns and cities have changed their lifestyle. First is the simple fact that they now live in an almost entirely air-conditioned environment. Homes, vehicles, schools, and offices are all insulated against the fierce Arabian climate.

I suggested to a middle-aged Qatari acquaintance who had known great poverty in his youth that he must be delighted that, with all the new medical facilities available, his seven children should be much healthier than his own generation had been. He said that sadly this was not true. His sons and daughters had built up no resistance to changes of climate and caught diseases much more easily. Also he felt that he had kept much healthier on the rice, fish, and dates than his children on the ice cream, sweets, and sugary soft drinks which he as an indulgent father was unable to refuse them. His wife would probably not have held the same views because the dangers of childbirth and the rate of infant mortality have been dramatically reduced.

But obesity and the diseases that are associated with a high standard of living are already a serious problem in Arabia, as a glance around a beach club in any Gulf state will tell you. One of the few serious drawbacks of the *thawb* is that it conceals a swelling waistline so effectively for so long. On the other hand, an increasing number of young people are taking to open-air sports on water and land. Thirty years ago only fishermen or foreigners swam in the Gulf; today the beach clubs are crowded with the local population. After the initial conservative opposition to young men wearing shorts had been overcome, soccer has become a passion throughout Arabia. A few lonely joggers can even be observed in the relative cool of the Arabian evenings, although they are still mostly expatriates. There are signs that the old Arab proverb which associated plumpness with prosperity and success is no longer true. Bahrain, as in many social matters, leads the way. A survey by a Bahrain newspaper among leading business-men showed that, on the contrary, a fat man would be regarded as lazy and a thin man as likely to be energetic and successful.

The change in one generation from extreme poverty to rela-tive ease and comfort for most of the people of Arabia has already had a marked physical effect. As I observed some years ago in a Kuwaiti kindergarten, the plump, doe-eyed children seemed to belong to a race different from that of the lean and bony parents who came in to collect them. But it is the changes in social rela-tionships that are being brought about by the revolution in the environment which are of far greater importance.

A Westerner arriving in Arabia for the first time would prob-ably find it difficult to believe that there had been any dramatic and revolutionary changes over the past generation. He would find a strongly patriarchal system, with women—especially in Saudi Arabia—both segregated and secluded. He would be assured by those in authority that family life was still the basis of society and that young people still held it in the utmost respect. He would also be told that there is no Western-type movement of radical dissent among youth, no desire to overthrow tradition or reject the Islamic way of life. Women's liberation does not exist in Arabia because for females to organize a revolt of this kind would mean that they were spurning their religion and that is unthinkable for them.

There is much truth in this. Respect for the family remains immensely powerful. There has been no "Dethronement of the Father," to borrow the phrase coined by a distinguished Arab sociologist to describe what is happening in the northern Arab states. Yet the situation is both more complex and less rigid than this implies. Things are changing both profoundly and continuously. One important reason for this is that the new affluence and employment opportunities are breaking up the old system of extended families and replacing them with the smaller nuclear families. A generation ago it was still normal for several generations of the family to live in a single household. Today it is increasingly likely that a young Kuwaiti or urban Saudi will set up in his own apartment or house as soon as he gets married. (Many young Saudis who go abroad for their higher education are married before they return.) It is the young father and not the grandfather who is the head of the household, however much respect he retains for the patriarch. In fact we might talk of the "Dethronement of the Grandfather" in Arabia and the consequences are just as profound.

(c) *The Shriveling Veil*

Another force for change is the change in the status of women. This might seem paradoxical when Saudi women lead such restricted lives. They are forbidden to drive a car, take a taxi alone, or leave the country unless escorted by a male member of their family. In the summer of 1980 a new decision was made that they should no longer go abroad for their higher education. Yet I have no hesitation in saying that the single most revolutionary element in Arabia is the universal acceptance of the principle of female education. The fact that much of its effect remains potential rather than actual does not make it any less important.

Thirty or forty years ago the most emancipated women in Arabia were the beduin. Seclusion was impossible in the desert, and they shared the lives of their menfolk, looking after the flocks and even supporting them in battle. Unveiled beduin women could be seen holding hands with their husbands in the oasis *suqs*.

Schools were rare enough for boys; they were practically nonexistent for girls. Only Bahrain had the rudimentary beginnings of female education. Women were confined to studying the Koran, and some became fine Koranic scholars.

An important witness is Shaykh Hafiz Wahba, an Egyptian who was a close and trusted advisor of King Ibn Saud in the early days of the Kingdom and then for over thirty years the Saudi envoy in London. His memoirs *Arabian Days* provides one of the very rare inside accounts by an Arab. Although the book was published in 1964 he was clearly describing an earlier period when he wrote: "On the whole the position of women in Najd is better than in Kuwait and Bahrain, where so abject has their position become that if the word 'woman' is mentioned in conversation the speaker usually feels it incumbent on him to excuse himself as if he had mentioned some inferior kind of animal; in fact some men even go so far as to apologize after mentioning their mothers, but this custom is gradually dying out and the younger generation of educated men seldom do it."

Even in the 1960s this was no longer true, but in 1980 Kuwaiti and Bahraini women are holding their own with men in a variety of professions. Teaching is the most common, but there are women in all the other social services and government departments and in radio and television. Kuwait has a woman under secretary for education, several female diplomats, and an acting dean of the law school. Kuwait University is a pioneer in Arabia in being co-educational in some of its classes. If Shaykh Hafiz were still alive he would have been astonished to have joined me in attending a brilliant lecture to a mixed class of boys and girls on Kuwait's relations with Britain and the Ottoman Turks by a Kuwaiti lady professor—a masterful bluestocking who was also totally feminine.

Perhaps more surprising than all this is the extent to which Kuwaiti and Bahraini young women appear on the stage and in television. A ravishingly beautiful Kuwaiti woman leads a company that performs satirical sketches on such subjects as drunkenness, government bureaucracy, and Kuwaiti men who marry foreigners.

At the end of the sketch she comes before the curtain to discuss it with the audience.

Qatar and the UAE are only a short way behind Bahrain and Kuwait, if at all. In Qatar University the first professors with Ph.D.s are women, and women play at least as important a role as men in television. In the UAE Shaykh Zayid is an enthusiast for promoting the status of women. He has strong support from his wife Shaykhah Fatimah, and indeed the role of some of the women in all the ruling families of the Gulf states has been crucial, especially in overcoming the doubts of the more conservative families about allowing their daughters to take up employment.

The need for women to be educated—the key to emancipation—was not accepted without a struggle anywhere in Arabia. It was easier in the small city states once it achieved the support of the Ruler. The battle was most prolonged in Saudi Arabia because there the House of Saud, despite its prestige, was confronted by the countervailing power of the conservative *ulama*, the religious authorities. In 1960, King Faisal's Queen Iffat founded the first modern school for girls in the Kingdom, Dar al-Hanan, in Jiddah. King Faisal lent his support to a great national drive for female education. But it was not always easy. As recently as 1962 the citizens of Buraydah, the second city of Najd after Riyadh, objected to the foundation of their first girls' school on the ground that it would teach their women loose and wicked ways. King Faisal allowed the matter to rest for two years and then decided they had had long enough to think about it and must have their girls' school. Five hundred Buraydah citizens came to Riyadh to protest. Faisal told them that if they could quote one phrase from the Koran which said girls should not be educated he would bow to their wishes. They failed; Buraydah had its girls' school and no thunderbolt fell from heaven.

Although the number of Saudi girls in school is still only about half that of Saudi boys (whereas in the Gulf states they are nearly equal) the girls are rapidly catching up. With a few exceptions, such as Kuwait University, teaching in Arabia is segregated. In Saudi Arabia female students may hear lectures from male professors over closed circuit television; religion is taught by blind shaykhs. The rector of one Gulf university explained to me that there is nothing in Islam that forbids coeducation. The *ulama* in early Islam taught men and women together. It is just that they find segregation produces better results.

This could well be true, at least as far as the young women are concerned. In every university in Arabia I have visited—which is nearly all of them—I was told that the female students work harder and achieve more. This can partly be explained by the fact that more of the brighter male students are studying abroad. But it is also because the young men have so many more distractions. For the women learning is the outlet to the wider world. In one Gulf university the splendid new library was empty except for two or three male students. "Boys and girls use the library on alternate days," explained the Iraqi lady librarian. "Come tomorrow and you will find it crowded."

In the Gulf states the barriers to women's employment are breaking down but the opportunities remain limited. Saudi women are confined to teaching and to the treatment of women in the medical profession—that is, to jobs in which they will have no contact with men. Unfortunately, one of the most likely professions for women—nursing—is held in low esteem in Arabia because it is associated with servants' work and it inevitably involves close contact with them. But it is the job of office secretary that is most suspect in the eyes of conservative Saudis. The Western image of the secretary who succeeds because she makes herself attractive to the boss has a powerful influence. I have often been told that in the West advertisements for secretaries stress qualities other than professional efficiency. On the other hand, there are many young Saudis who feel that these fears are exaggerated. But while the conservative resistance to change is powerful, the pressure in favor of it is mounting in two ways. In the first place it seems absurd to Saudi Arabia's eager young technocrats that in a country with a desperate shortage of skilled manpower, half the population should be kept unemployed. Both the minister of planning and the secretary-general of the Royal Commission for Jubayl and Yanbu have said that the extension of some types of employment of women is inevitable. In the second place the rapidly growing body of educated Saudi women—some of them now highly qualified—form their own natural pressure group. Although they do not breed female revolutionaries, it is quite wrong to regard them all as docile and compliant. Saudi teenage schoolgirls will openly scorn the idea that they will be wearing the veil at all times outside their homes.

The debate about the position of women in Arabia carries on continuously in private conversation and in the press, but always within an Islamic context. Some women who join the discussion tend to argue, with much justification, that their status in Arabia has nothing to do with Islam but with male chauvinist attitudes that have been institutionalized over the centuries. Women's lot was greatly improved in the time of the Prophet. The killing of baby girls was stopped; women's legal and property rights in marriage, divorce, and inheritance were all established. Polygamy became a privilege, hedged around with qualifications, such as that each wife should be given absolute equality of treatment. Contrary to a widespread Western belief, it was not required, or even recommended, for male Muslims. At a time when life was short—especially for men—and the unmarried women needed to be cared for, it was socially desirable. Today it is very rare, largely for economic reasons, and Muslim women do not regard it as a serious threat to their status. Certainly the *Koran* establishes the man as the head of the household, but this is because of his role and responsibility as the principal breadwinner, something that is widely accepted in nearly all Western societies. Muslim women regard the suggestion that women should enjoy absolute equality of function and responsibility with men as absurd. It is only in the eyes of God and their duties toward Him that they are equal. On the other hand, wherever the rights of Muslim women established by the *Koran* and the *Shariah* have not been overlaid by laws and customs devised by men, they have often excelled those of women in the West. It was only with the Married Women's Property Act of 1882 that an Englishwoman acquired control of her own property after marriage; the Muslim woman has always had that right. Equal pay for equal work for men and women is taken for granted in Arabia—a principle that has still not been established in some Western countries. The arrangements for women who are working in the Gulf states or Saudi Arabia to choose their leave of absence for childbirth would be regarded as favorable to women by any standards. The segregation of the sexes has not prevented the women of Arabia from using their property rights to pursue vigorous business careers through male agents. The introduction of special banks for females in Saudi Arabia has been a huge success, and Saudi women are scrambling to take the training courses that are offered in banking practice.

There are questions that may occur to the newly-arrived Western visitor to Arabia. How happy are Western women with their political rights and social freedoms? The Arabian view of relations between the sexes in the West is excessively lurid if it is based solely on films and television. But the better informed can point to the statistics of school-age pregnancies and the spectacular increase in divorce rates. In Arabia, on the other hand, divorce is becoming less common. If women's liberation movements in the West demand that women should not be treated as sex objects, is this not precisely what Muslim society maintains? On the other hand, Islam, unlike Christian puritans, has never denied the sexual nature of women or insisted that sexual relations should be confined to procreation.

It is not my intention to suggest that there is anything ideal about the situation of women in Saudi Arabia. Certainly many Arab women from the northern Arab states find it intolerable. "Saudi Arabia is no place for a woman," they are apt to say. In many ways their position is more difficult than that of Western women in the country. The latter accept from the start that they are outsiders; within the limits of the rules of Saudi society they can make their own separate lives. Northern Arab women, whether they like it or not, are part of the system.

As I have suggested, the attitudes of Saudi males range from the extreme conservatives, who are mostly, but by no means exclusively, the elderly, to those who would favor very rapid movement. The great majority seem to want and expect change but want it to come gradually. This is the approach favored by the regime although the continuing power and influence of the ultra-conservatives means that sudden steps toward further puritanical restrictions are sometimes taken—such as a ban on mixed bathing in hotel swimming pools, pictures of females in the newspapers, or male hairdressers for women. The religious police, the *mutawwiun*, still have power to invade government ministries to see whether they are employing female secretaries, and they can be seen in the *suqs*, wielding their staffs, reproaching women for immodest dress (although I have observed one roundly denounced by a sharp-tongued Saudi lady for exceeding his authority).

In my view the trend, despite the pauses and reversals, is inexorably toward greater freedom and opportunities for women in Arabia. Nothing can stop Saudi Arabia following in the same direction as the Gulf states. In the office of a young but senior Saudi television director I was watching an episode of a popular Saudi soap opera which concerns a rural family who come to live in the big city. I asked innocently whether the actresses were Saudi women. "No, they are Kuwaitis and Bahrainis," he replied. "Our women would not want to upset their families by going on the stage." But I could tell he was not convinced he would receive this assurance if he asked a Saudi girl for her opinion. In Qatar, the position, as in many other social matters, is somewhere between that of Saudi Arabia on the one hand and Kuwait and Bahrain on the other. Qatar's outstanding young playwright and producer, Abdu Rahman al Manai, told me that his leading lady had just asked that none of his plays should be shown on television for the time being. She was about to get married, at the age of thirty, and did not want to spoil her chances with her future husband, although it is hard to believe he was unaware of her career on the stage.

Even in Saudi Arabia there has been a certain relaxation in the stages that lead up to marriage. In the early 1960s it was still rare for a husband to see his bride before the wedding. Now it is possible for them to meet in the house of relatives. The telephone also penetrates the *harim*. Even if the young couple do not meet before their marriage they may know each other quite well from countless telephone conversations. Much therefore depends on the social milieu; liberalization has advanced further among the more affluent and better educated. But future husbands of all social spheres face one problem—the payment of the *mahr* or bride-price. Under Islamic law this is paid directly to the bride, and in former times she used it to buy gold or silver as a form of economic security in case she was divorced or widowed. Before the days of oil wealth the sum was small but it took many years of hard toil for the bridegroom to save. Today the bride price has soared so that even a Riyadh taxi driver will have to find $10,000 or more. Part of the money now goes to the bride's father to help pay for the wedding and household furnishing. The UAE government has tried to limit the *mahr* to $3,000 but with little success.

An admirable booklet entitled "Successful Transition into Saudi Arabia," published by the Saudi national airline for the benefit of Americans working in the country advises that a dinner invitation to a Western married male from a Saudi colleague presents a range of possibilities.

- His wife may not be invited at all.
- She may be expected to go and be taken directly to the women's quarters.
- She may be included at dinner, but the Saudi wife may not appear.
- The Saudi wife may be included.
- If so she may or may not be veiled in the presence of a man outside her immediate family.

Overwhelming evidence suggests a trend is toward the latter alternatives. Saudi women are gradually but inevitably sharing more of their husbands' social lives. Obviously the tendency is stronger the higher the level of education of the wife, and this is why the foundation of the first public Saudi girls' schools in the 1950s and 1960s was an act of social revolution. The trend could reach unexpected dimensions. In more than one Gulf state I heard of women who preferred to remain unmarried because none of the suitable young men suggested by their families was sufficiently educated. The senior citizens of Buraydah who told King Faisal they did not want a girls' school might feel that their fears were justified—but hardly in the way they imagined.

At Dhahran Airport I fell into conversation with a young Saudi business representative who talked nostalgically about his long annual holidays in Thailand, the Philippines, and Bali. "But I am getting married soon," he said, "and then I shall be able to settle down and stay at home." "But supposing your wife wants to travel?" I suggested. He looked astonished; the thought had not occurred to him. I felt sure that it had occurred to his future wife.

(d) *The Call to Prayer*

One of the sights of which Londoners are still justifiably proud is that of an evening newspaper stall that has been left unattended by the seller while he enjoys a cup of tea. He trusts people to leave their coins when they take a newspaper.

Westerners visiting the gold and jewelery *suqs* in Riyadh and Jiddah for the first time are likely to be very much more impressed by the piles of precious stones and metals that have been left unguarded by the stall keepers for similar reason. They might be covered with a cloth, but this is to stop bank notes from blowing away in the breeze.

The visitor's next thought is likely to be that this amazing sense of security must be due to the harsh penalties for crime. Most Westerners have heard that the strict Islamic *Shariah* prescribes the amputation of the thief's hand. But further inquiry and reflection would show that this provides only a very partial explanation. In the first place, if the thief has stolen out of hunger or real need he is let off. He must have acted from simple greed for that penalty to be applicable. Moreover, if he has taken government property he is not guilty of theft because he was stealing from himself.

This provision, which is so surprising to foreigners, underlines a vital difference between Islamic and Western societies. The Islamic *Shariah* cannot be compared with Western secular law, which is based on Roman law. The *Shariah*, which is the essence of Islamic society, is not secular but an ethical system. Crimes against the laws of this system are not crimes against the state but against the will of God. This is why stealing is held in such abhorrence and this—not the penalty of hand-chopping—is the really effective sanction against it. The feat of this penalty, which is rarely imposed, would hardly be enough to dissuade the thief when stealing is so easy.

No Westerner therefore need feel guilty about enjoying a high sense of personal security in Arabia. The extreme rarity of rape, mugging, or simple hooliganism does not depend on a brutal police and savage punishments. For the Western woman, especially, the result is paradoxical. Her life is highly restricted by local laws and customs, and yet she can enjoy an unusual sense of liberty in being able to walk a city street without fear of being molested or having her handbag snatched from her arm.

In the same way the penalty of public flogging imposed for certain offenses, which has such a medieval sound for Westerners, is intended to humiliate the wrongdoer rather than inflict pain. The man who administers the punishment is supposed to hold a *Koran* under his arm so that he can only give a modest swing to the whip. The death penalty for adultery under Islamic law (as opposed to tribal law, which is supposed to be transcended by the *Shariah* but still survives on occasion) can only be applied if there are four male witnesses to the act of sexual penetration. This condition is so rarely fulfilled that the moral sanction is much more important than the penalty, which has not been imposed under the *Shariah* more than a few dozen times in the whole Muslim world over the past two centuries.

A differing attitude toward the law is only one, although one of the most important, cause of the myriad misunderstandings between Islam and the West. The roots lie deep in history—in the five centuries of war between the World of Islam and Christendom during the Middle Ages and Renaissance, in the anti-colonial struggle of the past century against overwhelmingly powerful Western empires, and now the fight against Zionism which Muslims regard as the last phase in the struggle. Because anti-Islamic prejudice is so deep-rooted in the West it is often subconscious and therefore difficult to eradicate. Day after day the Western media publish absurdities about Islam. "Serious" newspapers will write that Muslim women are not supposed to have souls or are not allowed to make the pilgrimage to Mecca, or that Islam has a close affinity to communism.

I am not suggesting that the fault is all on one side. Muslims in general show little appreciation or understanding of what is good in other societies. As with other religions, the more pious and ardent they are, the less sympathy they are likely to show. This is especially true of those parts of Arabia in which there has been no indigenous population of non-Muslims—Christians or Jews—for many centuries. It is also true that, while the Western media tend to draw a harsh and unappealing picture of Islam, Muslims often do the same themselves. Muslim spokesmen seem to emphasize the restrictions and prohibitions in Islam rather than its positive commands to acts of nobility and kindness. One is rarely reminded that God's principal attribute is compassion. In one of the Gulf states I was watching a popular weekly television program in which a venerable religious shaykh was answering viewers' questions. Since this was Islam, the questions covered all aspects of life and not only those which a secular society would regard as related to religion. One of them concerned extravagance and display by wealthy Muslims. The shaykh launched into a splendidly wise and humorous homily on moderation and modesty in Islam. He said that good Muslims could enjoy the senses God had given them but it was disgusting that they should overeat or spend luxuriously when they were surrounded by poverty and hunger. But then his face darkened and he devoted the last ten minutes of his lengthy reply to the wickedness of certain young men who were wearing gold chains around their necks. This was wrong on all counts. It was a Western habit and effeminate. (The Wahhabis forbid men to wear precious metals or silk but not perfume. King Ibn Saud was especially fond of it.) Somehow the sense of proportion the shaykh had been proclaiming so eloquently had been lost.

Repeatedly one hears it said that some ''good Muslims'' drink, gamble, and break the fast of Ramadan either in the privacy of their homes or as soon as they can travel abroad. Another common accusation is that Islam's strict prohibition of the payment of interest is got around by devices such as the banks' service charges.

Hypocrisy exists in all societies to some degree, and each one tends to specialize in one form or another. The Christian countries have shown some fine examples from the courts of the Renaissance Popes to Victorian London, where the purity of upper-class marriages was maintained with the help of 100,000 prostitutes. The British, in particular, have to remember that many foreigners still regard hypocrisy as one of their national characteristics, but no Westerners can feel entirely complacent. The prudish Hollywood movies of the 1940s and 1950s hardly reflected the reality of American society.

The question is whether modern Muslim society is self-deceiving. In one sense the question is misconceived because it is based on a false analogy with other religions, especially Christianity. Westerners have become accustomed to the idea of the secular state which is alien to Islam. Millions of them have had no connection with the church since they were baptized or married, and it is perfectly possible for one to declare himself an agnostic or atheist (even if, out of convenience or habit, most would continue to accept the label of Christian). This would be almost inconceivable for a Muslim in Arabia. He might gamble and drink and fail to say his prayers when he is abroad, but it would not occur to him to say that he was no longer a Muslim because that would amount to denying his own identity. It is not necessary to be a ''good Muslim'' in the sense of obeying all its laws, to be proud of belonging to the *ummah* or the Brotherhood of Islam, because Islam is not only a faith but a way of life and a civilization.

You cannot forget the presence of Islam for long in an Arabian city. If you are not within sight or earshot of a mosque, which is unlikely, you will hear the call to prayer on a thousand radios or television sets. The saying of prayers is much more than a mere formality, which, at least in Saudi Arabia, is required by the religious police. During my stay in Qatar, I had four different government drivers who came from various parts of Arabia, and each of them arranged to attend prayers at the appointed hours provided it did not interfere with their work. It seemed apparent that this regular declaration of faith in an act of communal worship made a difference in their lives. Their dignity and courtesy, which is normal in Arabia, derived from an inner certainty of belief.

The feeling of brotherhood, which is of the essence of Islam, is greatly enhanced when a Muslim makes the Pilgrimage to Mecca. I have been told by many people in Arabia, including some of the most skeptical and worldy, that it has transformed their lives. Its importance may be compared with that of the pilgrimage to the Holy Land of medieval Christians, although a much greater proportion of Muslims in Arabia can make the journey at least once in their lives.

Nevertheless, it would be quite wrong to suggest that the Muslims of Arabia are all satisfied with the present state of their society. Saudi Arabians do not believe, for example, that they have achieved an ideal Islamic state. You may hear quite radical views on this subject from apparently conservative pillars of society. An ex-minister, who is head of one of the famous Saudi merchant dynasties, said sharply that of course his country did not have a true Islamic government. It was only Islamic ''in patches.'' He added that while reports in the Western media of widespread corruption in high places in Saudi Arabia were exaggerated, it undoubtedly existed and it was quite wrong that a few poor men should be punished for theft according to Islamic law while a few of the powerful who had embezzled millions should get off scot-free. Another prominent Saudi, a former newspaper editor who now devotes himself to his many business interests, makes a related point. He says that while the Saudis, and the Arabs in general, have a right to resent the biased way in which their image is presented in the West, the Arabs' own information media carried much of the blame. There was no investigative journalism in

Arabia and the local media presented an idealized picture. Until this was remedied, the public would accept the Western image of their society.

Those who criticize present-day society from an Islamic viewpoint (which means the great majority, because Westernizing secularists are a tiny minority) are apparently united because they all agree on one thing: that the true Islamic faith provides an answer for all human needs. But in fact they include a wide range of views on how a genuinely Islamic society can be achieved in the twentieth century. There are the "fundamentalists" who in their most extreme form would hold that it is simply a matter of returning to the way of life at the time of the Prophet and the first Caliphs and rejecting any influences that can be detected as coming from infidel sources. They are equally opposed to capitalism, communism, industrialization, and parliamentary democracy. Some of their kind were among the young zealots who caused such havoc when they seized the Great Mosque in Mecca in 1979 to make their protest.

There is another type of reformer who regards this fundamentalism as simplistic and ultimately disastrous. They would agree that Muslims should reject all forms of "Westernization" where they conflict with Islam but believe that they both can and should demonstrate the capacity of Muslims to match the achievements of the West and surpass them, as they did in earlier centuries. They are not "modernizers" in the usual sense because they believe that the *Holy Koran* provides a satisfactory blueprint for human society at all times. But they are "reinterpreters" of Islam by necessity as they have to find formulas by which Islamic principles can be applied in the twentieth century in such matters as education, scientific research, government administration, or financial and economic organization. This process of legal reformulation or the reinterpretation of the basic principles of Islam is called *ijtihad*. It was one of the means by which the Islamic *Shariah* was developed. Hitherto it has been widely assumed that the "Gate of *Ijtihad*" was closed some three centuries after the death of the Prophet. There was to be no further reinterpretation of the *Koran* and the *Sunnah*. Now those who wish to see the Islamic world match the material and technical achievements of the West are concerned with prying the "Gate of *Ijtihad*" open again.

In the early days of the Kingdom of Saudi Arabia, the great majority of the powerful religious shaykhs—the *ulama*—held pure fundamentalist beliefs that were opposed to any form of *ijtihad*. Shaykh Hafiz Wahba, who was made director of education by King Ibn Saud, tells how in 1930 he was sent to meet a delegation of Najdi *ulama* who were protesting against the inclusion of drawing, foreign languages, and geography in the school curriculum on the ground that drawing is akin to painting which is unquestionably prohibited, foreign languages "because they are a means of learning the religious opinions of unbelievers and their ungodly sciences," and geography because "it presupposes the assertion that the earth is round, and reaffirms the astronomical theories of the stars and planets held by the Greek philosophers which were opposed by our learned men in the past."

When he reported back to King Ibn Saud, Shaykh Hafiz had little difficulty in showing that the *ulama*'s objections had no historical or religious foundation. He pointed out, for example, that many of the Companions of the Prophet spoke the languages of the surrounding countries. King Ibn Saud overruled the *ulama* and since then such ultra-conservative views, which today are held by only a minority of the shaykhs, have not been allowed to interfere with education.

One field which engages the special interest of the reformers is banking. It provides a good example of their outlook.

(e) *An Islamic Economy?*

Westerners tend to assume that Islamic banking is a contradiction in terms in the modern age, because no rational and efficient system could be devised without the use of interest payments which are prohibited by Islam. However, the Muslim reformers say that, on the contrary, a system in complete conformity with the *Shariah* not only can be perfectly effective in the twentieth century, it can be even more equitable than other systems. In an Islamic bank, the payment of interest on bank loans by borrowers is replaced by a system of partnership in which the bank and the client share the profit or the loss in proportions which are previously agreed upon. All the usual criteria would be employed by the bank to decide whether the purpose for which the loan was to be used was viable, but under this system the risk would be equitably shared by the bank and its client. Interest is not paid by the banks on savings deposits but, the Islamic bankers argue, most savings are not made for the sake of the income they earn but for some specific purpose such as marriage, or the purchase of a house or car. The Islamic bank has a much closer relationship with its customers than in other systems; it is concerned with their welfare, and it helps them when they are in difficulties such as widowhood or sickness.

An Association of Islamic Banks has been created with its headquarters in Jiddah. Its chairman is Prince Muhammad al Faisal, an American-educated son of the late King Faisal who is active in promoting the idea of Islamic banking throughout the Muslim world and in countries with large Muslim communities. There are now Islamic banks in Egypt, Sudan, the Gulf states, and further afield. But curiously enough there are none in Saudi Arabia—except for the Islamic Development Bank which is purely an instrument for channeling foreign aid. The reason is that the Saudi government feels that if one Islamic bank were established in the Kingdom, all the existing banks in which foreign banks play an important role would have to be converted to the same system and that this is not practical at the present time.

This is just one example of the compromises that Saudi Arabia and the Gulf states have to make in their efforts to develop rapidly in a world that is dominated technically and economically by non-Islamic systems. One of the viewers' questions which the famous television shaykh is constantly being asked in one form or another is why the Arab oil states are so dependent on infidel institutions.

One of the most common queries is: "Why do we invest in Western organizations that are helping our enemy Israel?" In his

The Challenge of Change

answer the shaykh is severely practical. We must look at the world as it is, he says. Partly through our own fault we have not yet reached the point of establishing our own international institutions. We are not in a position to replace the dollar with an Islamic Dinar as a world currency. But the shaykh left no doubt that he hoped this day would come.

No one in authority in Saudi Arabia or the Gulf states will admit that the *Shariah* is not completely self-sufficient as a legal system. In practice it has to be supplemented by a whole series of legal codes governing company law and commercial relations with the outside world. These are codes constantly being revised and extended to meet new needs such as, for example, the Offshore Banking Units in Bahrain. The governments of these states can only claim that none of this legislation conflicts with the basic principles of Islamic law. Sometimes, however, there are ambiguities and confusion. If you drive a car in Saudi Arabia, for example, you may take out insurance if you wish but this is not compulsory because some of the religious authorities hold strongly that to take thought for the future in this way would be trespassing on the domain of the Almighty. Modern traffic legislation is not easy to derive from the *Shariah*.

Nevertheless, there is a much wider area of contemporary social and economic relations that can be regulated according to basic Islamic principles with less difficulty than most Westerners realize. Islam has something clear to say on matters of social justice—the laws governing labor relations, the rights of landlords and tenants, and the distribution of wealth. All is derived from the principle that man is the trustee of all the earth's resources which belong to God.

When I first came to the Middle East I recall being astonished by a Lebanese Muslim scholar who suggested that there was no reason why the classical Islamic system of taxation should not replace the usual contemporary taxes on income and expenditure. It seemed to me inconceivable that something could apply equally to medieval Arabia and a modern industrial state. In fact there is no reason why it should not. The Islamic *zakat* is a 2-1/2 percent tax on all your wealth that remains after you have deducted your expenses for the year. It is not "progressive," in the Western sense, because it is not graded in proportion to a man's wealth, but it is a tax on capital as well as income. In Saudi Arabia a wealthy man used to pay his *zakat* directly to the poor, starting with his own relatives and friends. Today there is an arrangement whereby everyone is supposed to pay half his *zakat* to the government and the other half is left to him to distribute directly.

The *Koran* makes it clear that the payment of *zakat* is a duty and not a favor. But it has a second objective on a higher plane, which is to give pleasure to God, and the great majority of the wealthy in Saudi Arabia pay the tax very precisely. In addition many of them pay *sadaqat* or voluntary alms. The *Koran* makes it clear that there is no shame for the poor to accept charity, and the Prophet himself said: "The one who gives out of wealth is no better than the one who takes out of need." But *sadaqat* is more beneficial to the giver than to the receiver because the giver is rewarded in this world and the Hereafter while the receiver only satisfies his hunger. The Caliph Umar said: "The prescribed prayer will take you half way to the house of the Lord, and fasting will bring you to the house of the Lord, but *sadaqat* will admit you inside the house."

Can a system which depends much more on a citizen's desire to obey the will of God than the law of the land create an equitable and just society? Can it provide incentives for hard work and the creation of wealth while eliminating the wide disparities between rich and poor which lead to social upheaval? Western capitalists and communists are equally skeptical, but good Muslims have no doubt that it can, provided it is honestly and wholeheartedly applied. They deny that the celebrated "fatalism" which is supposed to be a characteristic of Islam is an insurmountable obstacle to material progress. On the contrary, they say, God enjoins Muslims to work hard and make full use of the things of the earth. A Muslim should try to produce more than he consumes so that he can give the rest to the poor. Above all, the argument which any visitor to Arabia will hear repeatedly is that the communist and the capitalist worlds are in crisis and their people dissatisfied. The possibility that an Islamic order could provide an alternative at least deserves attention.

(f) *"East is East..."*

In the spring of 1980 relations between the West and the Arabian oil states were passing through an unusually difficult phase. Many Arabs were convinced that there was an orchestrated campaign in the Western media to denigrate them and their religion. One of the brightest and most engaging young ministers in the Gulf states said to me: "What was it your poet Kipling wrote? 'Oh, East is East, and West is West, and never the twain shall meet.' Perhaps it really is true."

Taken literally, this is certainly nonsense. In the Middle Ages the Arab-Muslim empires were the true link between East and West. They inherited and helped to preserve much that was finest in Hellenic civilization for the benefit of Western Europe. Even when Christendom and the World of Islam were constantly at war, as in Spain or Palestine, their two civilizations were intermingling, largely to the advantage of the Christians. It is true that there followed a long period of Western ascendancy in which the World of Islam tended to retreat within itself, but the links were never broken. Finally in the nineteenth century the West invaded and seized control of much of the Muslim-Arab world. The two civilizations clashed again but no one could say they were not meeting.

The two centuries of Western ascendancy in power caused a new intermingling of cultures. It was not only in the Arab-Muslim countries that came under direct Western control, such as former French North Africa, that a new elite became familiar with Western languages and ideas. In all except the most remote and isolated areas, such as the mountains of Yemen and Oman, the Arabs had little hesitation in learning from the West whatever would help the development of their own society. In the 1980s there are tens of thousands of young people from the Arabian Peninsula receiving some higher education in the West, and their numbers increase each year. A substantial governing and business class is emerging which seems to shuttle easily between the capitals of Europe,

America, and Arabia. Even for those who never travel outside Arabia there are large communities of foreigners, many of them Westerners, from whom they cannot be entirely isolated. My Gulf minister friend is a living disproof of the truth of his quotation. Unlike Ronald Reagan, who ascribed it to Mark Twain when he used it in a speech, he knew the name of the author.

But perhaps this is to miss the point of what the minister was trying to say. Granted that the two cultures and civilizations have met and intermingled in the past, could they, in spite of superficial appearances, be moving further apart today? As the Muslim world, led by the Arab oil states, asserts its new power and self-confidence it might try to detach itself from all dependence on the West. As soon as their universities reach a sufficiently high standard they might try to dispense with foreign education by keeping all their students at home. There are some influential voices making this demand. Is the outraged rejection of all forms of Westernization which has characterized the Iranian Revolution only a foretaste of what will happen on the other side of the Gulf?

I do not believe this is likely. Revolutions are never as total as they sometimes appear, and the one in Iran is no exception. When the dust and smoke have disappeared it will be seen that the Iranian people have not cut all their ties with the West. It is even less probable in Arabia, where it has never looked as if an enforced and over-hasty Westernization were threatening the people's sense of identity.

The conflicting influences of two cultures do create tensions among the people of Arabia, and it is the youth who are most affected. (A university lecturer friend told me that one of his brightest students always carried with him two tape recorders: one had tapes of the *Koran* and the other of the Beatles.) It might be expected that those who travel regularly to the West would suffer from schizophrenia, so great is the contrast between the mores of the two societies. Some do undergo a moral collapse under the strain, but the real cause for surprise is how few of them do. On a journey from Dhahran to Riyadh I fell into conversation with a Najdi in his early twenties who was returning home from a trip to Europe which he had clearly enjoyed. I discovered that his father was a stern Wahhabi. No music was allowed in his home; there was television but it was only switched on for religious programs or the news. Although a regular smoker, the young man would not dream of smoking in front of his father. As I accompanied him along the road from the airport he remarked that he was only really happy when he returned home to Riyadh. There was no doubting his sincerity.

All young people in Arabia have to suppress their taste for Western habits for the sake of their parents to some degree, although this young man's case was exceptional. The authorities also have to compromise, and nowhere is this more apparent than in the television services. In the 1950s the transistor radio was an immensely powerful feature of political change, carrying Cairo's Voice of the Arabs into the most remote mountains of Arabia. (I recall a Yemeni herdsman with a radio hitched over the horn of his leading ram.) In the 1970s and 1980s it is television that promotes social change and inevitably introduces foreign values into every Arabian household.

As might be expected, Saudi Arabia, which still has no public cinemas, was the most hesitant about permitting television. The government opened its first station in 1966 against powerful and even violent conservative opposition. It began very gingerly. Foreign films were a problem because all love scenes between the sexes had to be cut out. Even Mickey and Minnie Mouse were forbidden to embrace. This led to a heavy concentration on all-male American war films until the German Embassy understandably complained about Germans always being represented as the villains.

Saudi television has evolved since then, but a careful balance still has to be maintained between the wishes of the conservatives who would prefer to see nothing that is not positively Islamic on the screen to the majority of the younger generation who would like to expand the boundaries. The senior government official responsible for television told me of the difficulties of making programs which were both observant of Saudi values and entertaining. But he said he found it stimulating, and "We ask God to help."

What all the Arabian television services are attempting, with the Kuwaitis at the forefront, is to adapt Western types of programs to an Arab/Islamic idiom. For news and current affairs and sports this is fairly straightforward; entertainment and culture are much more difficult. But Arab situation comedies, historical dramas, soap operas, dance, and cultural magazine programs are now being produced—although I have yet to see an Arabian talk show. The results are of varying quality. While the Kuwaiti operettas are imaginative and highly entertaining, someone had the mistaken idea of producing Kuwait's answer to Shirley Temple, an unnaturally self-possessed seven-year-old who sings at immense length, wandering through sunlit gardens.

The response from the public to the amalgam of Western and Arab programs is not always obvious. In one of the Gulf states, my driver was delighted with a new daily radio program of local music—pearl fishers' and beduin songs and instruments peculiar to his part of the Gulf. Clearly they were close to his heart. But when I asked him what television programs he liked, he said he had no taste for Arabic films (mainly Egyptian and full of *hubb*—love). He preferred wrestling—which is not in the Arab tradition—and films of action—especially westerns. But then he called them "American bedu films" which may explain his taste for them.

In looking at the Muslim world the most disastrous mistake that can be made by Westerners, whether governments or individuals, is to equate "Westernization" with "progress" in all matters. A recent British television documentary on the situation in Turkey showed shots of the main highway into Ankara with some elderly farm-carts ambling toward the city. "Kemal Atatürk attempted to take his country away from its Islamic past into the modern world," said the commentator. "As you can see, he was not entirely successful."

This is not only offensive but absurd. There is no doubt whatever that the great majority of the people of the Arabian oil states want Westernization if it means acquiring Western technology and know-how to develop economically and to eliminate poverty. But it cannot be assumed that any of the inevitable social changes that accompany this development are for the better. This includes the one which seems most obviously an improvement to Westerners: the changing status of women. No one could possibly begrudge the women of Arabia any increase in their liberties. But it is not a simple matter of expanding their freedom of choice. The traditional extended family, for example, provided a community of sisters, cousins, and aunts who shared the housework and the care of the children. Today the extended family is speedily being destroyed under the pressure of progress and replaced by the Western type of nuclear family. If the wife is educated and has a job she will need to have a servant to look after the home because there will be no relatives to help. She will have to fight the male chauvinism of her husband alone, and it is doubtful whether the real balance of power in the family has shifted in her favor.

21

Toward the Year 2000

Anyone who is rash enough to claim some special knowledge of the Middle East will find himself being asked to make predictions. Will there be another Arab-Israeli war this year? Will the regime in X country survive, and if so for how long?

The wise, if uncourageous, course is to give replies which are so heavily qualified that they cannot be disproved. This applies to even such apparently straightforward questions as "How long before the oil runs out?" Yet certain "experts" are always ready to make very precise predictions. In the early 1970s they said that King Faisal would never use the oil weapon. In the spring of 1980 a report was circulated widely in the Western media "based on intelligence sources" that gave a precise date for the fall of the Saudi monarchy.

Such calculations are all based on the same error. They presuppose a quite extraordinary—and, for an outsider, certainly unattainable—knowledge of the feelings and aspirations of the people of the region and the way they will find expression. Such predictions assume that we know how they see their own self-interest to an extent to which no Western political commentator would dare speculate about his own people. That these calculations are inevitably proved wrong does not lead to any greater modesty but to even rasher assumptions based on analogy. Thus when the supposedly rock-like regime of the Shah of Iran, based on the overwhelming power of his police and armed forces, was swept aside by Islamic revivalism, some people at once assumed that the rulers of the neighboring Arab oil states, with much less military power, would be overthrown by the same forces. This is how even the exact month of the demise of the Saudi regime was predicted. The only comfort for Westerners is that East European commentators, with their Marxist analysis of Middle Eastern society, seem to fall into even greater errors.

All that can be done is to suggest the kind of factors that are shaping and will shape the actions of the people of the states with which we are concerned. It is hoped that they have all been indicated in earlier pages but they may be worth summarizing.

At the risk of ignoring my own warning, I would suggest there is one assumption that can be made about the aspirations of the people of this region. They would like to see an increase in the power and influence of the Islamic nations within the international community. They regard this as a wholly desirable reversal of the trend of the last five hundred years. They are aware that, through their possession of more than half the world's known oil resources, a large share of the responsibility falls upon them, but since these resources are finite and being depleted they know that they must translate them into self-sustaining economic power—and to some extent into military power—with all the risks that this implies. The minority who would prefer not to undertake this responsibility but to keep Arabia isolated as far as possible from the forces of the twentieth century, is small and rapidly dwindling. Nevertheless, the adventurous, if inevitable, decision that has been made by the majority does involve a series of dilemmas that are related to the real world. Most of these can be summed up in the need to find a balance between traditional values, without which Islam would be meaningless, and the exigencies of the twentieth century. In every case it is the Kingdom of Saudi Arabia that carries the main responsibility for resolving these dilemmas. But the city-states of the Gulf, precisely because of their size, can be more daring and experimental. By their example, they may help Saudi Arabia to solve its problems.

The first and most obvious of the tradition versus modernization dilemmas relates to the system of government. Given that none of the regimes in this area can afford to remain static but must develop, what are their chances of remaining stable?

Here the future of Saudi Arabia is crucial. A sudden change of regime in one of the Arabian Gulf states would be threatening but not necessarily fatal to the rest. If the Saudi monarchy were over-turned, the others could hardly survive.

The Saudi royal family has certain invaluable assets. The Kingdom, unlike most other past and present Middle Eastern monarchies, owes its existence to the efforts of its founder, King Ibn Saud, and not to the wishes of the great powers. Then, despite its traditional mold, it has proved both flexible and adaptable. A lively sense of self-preservation has enabled it to survive crises that would have destroyed many other houses: such as the oust-ing of King Saud or the defection to the country's enemies of some senior princes who later returned to the fold. In general, indi-vidual members of the family are fully prepared to subordinate their ambitions to the interests of the whole. Thus Prince Muham-mad, the elder brother of King Khalid, has never challenged his being passed over for the succession while he retains the honored place in the family that is due to him as the eldest surviving descendant of Ibn Saud. There are known to be important differ-ences of outlook among the senior princes. Crown Prince Fahd and Prince Sultan, the defense minister, incline toward close cooperation with the West, especially the United States, in spite of obvious differences, while Prince Abdullah, commander of the National Guard, favors giving priority to Saudi Arabia's interests in Arab/Islamic causes and in the conservation of the country's oil resources. But it is a difference of emphasis and not a funda-mental clash of ideology. All have strong personalities but have subordinated them to the general consensus.

The many royal princes in this fecund family are scattered throughout this huge country in key positions. In the summer of 1980 some new young princes were appointed to provincial governorships. The royal family is so numerous that only those who show real ability need be chosen. Some are being trained as senior active members of the armed forces, and since most Third

World revolutions emanate from the military this could well prove crucial.

It has often been observed that a revolution to overthrow the monarchy in Saudi Arabia would be no easy walkover as it was in Egypt, Iraq, or Libya. Apart from the omnipresent royal family, the widely scattered centers of population would form a difficult obstacle. Even if the putschists seized control of one province, loyalists would have time to rally their forces elsewhere.

Yet it can also be argued that these two factors—the numerous princes and the huge, underpopulated territory—are also sources of vulnerability to the regime. The fact that the sources of power are so demonstrably in the hands of the Saudi family, however much the non-royal "technocrat" ministers and officials are increasing their share in decision making, means that they must bear the responsibility for any popular discontent. The dispersed centers of population may create difficulties for potential revolutionaries but they are also hard to protect against outside attack. In particular, the great center of the oil industry in the Eastern Province is a sitting target. And Saudi Arabia's lack of manpower makes it a slow and difficult task to build up effective defense forces.

The Saudi regime has been in no haste to develop political institutions through which popular feelings could be expressed. It was felt there was no advantage in unsettling a system which has proved itself to be flexible and durable through dangerous and difficult times. But the loss of King Faisal's exceptional charisma as a focus for national unity and the sharp jolt of the seizure of the Great Mosque in Mecca in 1979 have caused some second thoughts. In January 1980 Prince Fahd announced that 200 Articles of Basic Statutes of Government would be issued and a Majlis al Shura or Consultative Council would be appointed. A committee headed by Prince Nayif, the minister of the interior, was set up for this purpose.

Saudis watch with interest the evolution of the political system in Kuwait. In August 1980 the Ruler of Kuwait decreed that Kuwait's parliamentary system would be restored in February

1981, four years after it was suspended because the ruling family and the cabinet claimed that it was making government impossible. Elections for a 50-member National Assembly were duly held in February. The Kuwaiti Crown Prince and Prime Minister has said that he personally favors the granting of votes to Kuwaiti women and this could well happen in time for the next elections. It seemed quite probable that Bahrain would follow Kuwait's example by restoring its own suspended parliamentary system and that the UAE would introduce an elective system into its legislature. The senior members of the Saudi royal family, on the other hand, continue to favor a system of selection rather than election for any parliamentary body. Shortly after the death of King Faisal, when the formation of a Consultative Council was already being proposed, Crown Prince Fahd told an Egyptian journalist he was against elections "because we all know the results of elections in the world at large . . . . I do not think such elections reflect true public opinion."

There is no sign at present of any strong demand for elected institutions even among Saudi Arabia's expanding educated elite. This could change, especially if elected parliaments become permanently established in the Gulf states. What is certain is that the Saudi royal family will not remain rigid and isolated from public opinion.

The seizure by religious zealots of the Great Mosque in Mecca in November 1979 was a severe shock for the regime. That it happened at all and took such trouble to bring to an end showed grave weaknesses in the country's internal security. But it gave an exaggerated view to the outside world of the extent of dissidence inside the Kingdom.

The threat presented by the Ayatollah Khomeini's Islamic republican precepts was a greater, if more distant, danger. It is an error to suppose that the Khomeini revolution appealed only to the Ayatollah's fellow-Shiite Muslims in Arabia and not to the Sunni majority. As a triumph of the spirit of Islam over great material and military power it was an inspiration for many of them, and the Saudi government blundered in expressing support for the Shah until the time of his overthrow. Iran's switch from the Shah's *de facto* alliance with Israel to enthusiastic support for the PLO was strongly approved in Arabia.

However, the Iranian threat to the Arab regimes on the other side of the Gulf has declined since 1979. The new Iranian regime began to reassert Iranian Shiite nationalism rather than Islamic brotherhood. Although Iran's main quarrel was with Iraq, and most Arabs in the Gulf privately acknowledge that Iraq has been provocative, they would take its side if obliged. Of greater importance has been the deterioration of the situation inside Iran. Very few of Khomeini's Arab sympathizers feel that his Islamic ideals are being successfully translated into practice. Also the concept of clerical government is alien to Sunni Arabs.

There is one sector that Saudi Arabia has no hesitation about modernizing—the military. Defense expenditure was already staggering before it received an extra stimulus with the upheaval in Iran and the Soviet invasion in Afghanistan. It accounts for about one-third of the national budget and gives Saudi Arabia by far the highest per capita defense expenditure in the world—about $2,000 per head, compared with $520 in the United States, $243 in Syria, and $54 in Egypt. It is even more startling that military spending works out to more than $230,000 a year for each of the 44,000 members of the regular armed forces and the 26,000 in the paramilitary forces (which includes the National Guard).

Because a substantial modern army is being built up with unprecedented speed, the spending on infrastructure is enormous. Huge "military cities" are being built: the King Khalid Military City in the northeast near the Iraqi border, another at Tabuk in the northwest near Israel, and a third at Khamis Mushayt, near the Yemeni border. The King Khalid, which is the largest, will have cost over $10 billion by the time it is completed in the late 1980s. These are much more than military bases; their purpose is to serve as vast vocational training centers, capable of turning out young Saudis who can contribute to all sections of society. When it is completed, the King Khalid Military City will have a population of 70,000, of whom 30,000 will be on active duty. This is equivalent to two-thirds of the present total armed forces, but by then these are planned to have increased to 300,000.

There must be doubts about such a target and about Saudi Arabia's overall ambition to become a formidable Middle Eastern military power before the end of the decade. Saudi wealth can buy the most sophisticated and efficient military equipment, but the lack of manpower remains the principal problem. The beduin warrior tradition is a potent force for recruitment to the National Guard, whose principal task is to protect the royal family and guard the cities. But few young Saudis are at present prepared to volunteer for the rigors of life in a military training camp as long as easier alternatives are available. Army salaries are high but there are other equally well-paid opportunities.

Prince Sultan, the minister of defense, favors the introduction of conscription, and this has been adopted by the government as a long-term aim. It is seen as contributing to the development of the nation and, in the words of one cabinet minister, "fostering a sense of Saudi citizenship." The potential social consequences would be tremendous and involve a calculated risk for the royal family. The ultra-loyal National Guard would hardly be effective as a counterweight for a regular army which had been quadrupled in size, and the chances of the armed forces—confident in their key modernizing role in the state—developing their own political ambitions would be increased. Nevertheless, it is a risk that most members of the Saudi family are prepared to take for the sake of the overriding aim that Saudi Arabia be able to undertake responsibility for its own security and for a share of that of the region.

This it is not capable of doing at present. Despite the rapid progress in recent years, especially in air defenses, Saudi Arabia does not yet have the military capability to defend its own vast borders and scattered centers of population, let alone to help maintain the security of the Gulf and Red Sea regions. The Saudis resented the overweening ambitions of the former Shah of Iran but were tolerant of the Pax Iraniana he aspired to impose on the Gulf because there was no acceptable alternative. As it is, Saudi Arabia's own expanding military machine is still heavily dependent on foreigners—on Korean, Pakistani, and Taiwanese technicians and Yemeni laborers, on French radar and tank experts, on the British Aerospace Corporation for airforce training, and above all on American technicians and servicemen. Americans in fact still form the technological backbone of the Saudi armed forces.

This is the reality that underlies Saudi Arabia's chief political dilemma, which also confronts all the Arab Gulf states to some degree. This is the problem of reconciling their *de facto* alliance with the United States, as the principal power that can counteract the threat of Soviet and communist expansion, with opposition to the United States' sponsorship of Israel.

This dilemma cannot be avoided; it intrudes continually on all matters of policy. A report of the American Enterprise Institute in 1979 suggested that the United States "should draw even closer to Saudi Arabia in its defense relations than it is now, and Riyadh should be considered less in regard to the Arab-Israeli conflict and more as a major power in the Gulf." This may be sound advice for the United States government. It takes little account of the feelings of the Saudis. Even if an American administration can overcome opposition from Congress to strengthening the military alliance with Saudi Arabia, which is always doubtful, Riyadh will continue to give at least equal weight to the Arab-Israeli conflict as to the security of the Gulf.

Any belief that the Arab-Israeli problem can somehow be bypassed or ignored in dealings with the Arab oil states is an illusion. Even if their leaders' concern was merely cynical, which it is not, they would have to take account of the feelings of their own people. These may be primarily religious—a conviction that Palestine, and especially Jerusalem, should be governed by Islam as God's final revelation to mankind. Or they may be political—a belief that Palestine is Arab and that their fellow Arabs, the Palestinians, should be allowed to return to their homes. Almost certainly the two emotions are merged in any individual.

Sometimes outsiders, on hearing some dismissive or hostile remark about Palestinians from an inhabitant of the Gulf or Arabia, are seduced into thinking that he regards the Palestine question as unimportant. In fact this is rather less true than the deduction that an Anglo-Saxon criticism of the behavior in exile of Charles de Gaulle and his Free Frenchmen meant that British and Americans cared nothing about the Fall of France in 1940. The loss of Palestine has left a scar somewhere on every Arab.

When Saudi leaders say, as they frequently do, that Saudi Arabia has pursued moderate policies to no avail, they mean something specific: that Saudi Arabia, in return for its consistent efforts within OPEC to moderate oil price increases for the benefit of the Western economy and its self-denial of any move toward the Soviet Union to balance American power, expects the United States to put real pressure on Israel to withdraw from the occupied territories including East Jerusalem. This has not been done. The Saudis do not believe the United States lacks the means but the political will. Washington expresses formal disapproval of Israel's annexation of East Jerusalem and establishment of new settlements in the occupied territories; Israel pursues these policies that would be impossible without American aid.

The dilemma in Saudi-U.S. relations was never more apparent than in the wake of the Soviet invasion of Afghanistan. Saudi spokesmen deplored what they felt to be the inadequacy of the Western response to the communist threat. Shaykh Yamani, the oil minister, has since developed in a number of speeches and newspaper interviews his considered but alarming view that the invasion is part of a strategy that will lead the Soviets through Baluchistan in Iran and Pakistan to the shores of the Gulf. He reasons that the Soviet Union will cease to become a net exporter of oil in the 1980s and may even become a net importer for a time. Thus it will be deprived both of its levers of economic control over its Eastern European satellites, which depended on oil power, and invaluable hard-currency earnings which it cannot afford to lose. In a speech at King Abdal Aziz University in Jiddah on April 16, 1980, Shaykh Yamani asked the question: "What is the U.S.S.R. to do? All it can do is to take control of one of the Arab Gulf states—the nearest oil-producing area—and make it a satellite whose economy is tied to the Soviet economy, on which the Russians can impose their exports while taking from it what they want on payment terms suitable to them."

After his lecture Shaykh Yamani was asked, in view of his concentration on Soviet intervention in the area, what he thought about American intervention in the Gulf. His reply was significant. "Until recently the Gulf was an area of Western influence and the U.S., as the leader of the West, had no need to conduct maneuvers there. But the situation has begun to change lately as a result of the strained relations between Iran—a major Gulf state—and the U.S. *However, the U.S. does not wish to intervene militarily against the will of the people of the area, who in turn do not want such intervention.* [My italics] Hence America's military maneuvers fall outside the area, and it has no need of political maneuvers because the area falls outside the sphere of Soviet influence."

Shaykh Yamani's clearly stated belief that American military intervention in the Gulf would be opposed by the people of the area is shared by all the governments of the Gulf states. This is in spite of the fact that they also accept his assessment of the Soviet threat, if not always in such stark terms. They know that any land-based American military presence would be so unpopular that it would destroy the stability of their regimes. Thus although they all had considerable sympathy with the American dilemma over the hostages in Iran, they hastened to deny any collaboration with the attempt to rescue them.

While all the Gulf states accept, as they must, that their security is a vital interest of the West, they will not voluntarily agree to any direct American share in its protection as long as the Palestine problem remains unresolved.

What the West can do is to help the Gulf states build up their own defense forces. There is little danger of their increased military strength developing into the kind of megalomania that helped to destroy the Shah.

One of the most encouraging portents is the steadily increasing cooperation between the Gulf states. This covers all spheres and not only the military. It also involves Iraq which is something the West finds difficult to understand. How can this militant Baathist regime, with its long record of hostility toward the West, collaborate with the conservative and fundamentally pro-Western governments in Arabia? Do they not fear that Iraq is trying to subvert them?

Certainly the Iraqi delegates, in their Western suits, look the odd men out at the increasingly frequent Gulf regional conferences. Their manner, temperament, and approach all seem different, emphasizing the "barrier of the common language." But in practical terms this is less important than that Iraq has become an enthusiastic convert to cooperation with the other Arabian Gulf states. Its formidable President Saddam Hussein has dealt ruthlessly with his own communists and cooled toward the Soviet Union. He denounced the Soviet invasion of Afghanistan and since then has consistently emphasized the virtues of nonalignment and the need to keep both superpowers out of the Gulf region. While Iraq has hardly abated its criticisms of the West, it has not hesitated to award most of its foreign contracts to non-communist firms, many of them American. In 1980 something resembling an axis developed between Iraq and Saudi Arabia, and after the outbreak of war between Iraq and Iran, Saudi Arabia provided Iraq with substantial aid. However, there were signs of a rift in the summer of 1981. In May, the heads of state of six Arab Gulf states—Saudi Arabia, Kuwait, Bahrain, Qatar, the UAE and Oman met in Abu Dhabi to found a Gulf Co-ordination Council to provide the organizational framework for their regional unity. The exclusion of Iraq while it was at war with Iran might have seemed logical but Iraq did not see it in this light. Iraq's President Saddam Hussein expressed his bitter disapproval and laid much of the blame on Saudi Arabia. He made it clear that Iraq would expect to belong to any future Gulf confederation.

With good reason there is widespread skepticism about attempts to translate the ideal of Arab unity into action. But those who feel that the kind of instant merger of two or three Arab states which is proposed from time to time is doomed to failure usually believe that real progress can be made with a step-by-step approach. This means starting in the easier fields—such as communications, trade, protection of the environment, education, and cultural exchange—and from there moving to economic planning and foreign policy while leaving to the last the most difficult of all—the merger of political institutions.

This is very much what the Arabian Gulf states have been doing for the past four years, quietly and unobtrusively but at an accelerating pace. In any of their cities, at any time of the year except the high summer, there is certain to be a regional Gulf conference taking place—urban planning, labor relations, vocational training, language teaching, historical archives, tourism, air pollution, or television. Sometimes a sharp editorial in the local press asks whether these perennial gatherings achieve anything. The answer is that they do, if not always as much as the resolutions passed at the end of each conference would suggest. No one who has recently moved around the area can have failed to see the shape of a union of Arabian Gulf States emerging.

A Gulf "Common Market," a Gulf Monetary Fund, followed by a common Gulf currency are all goals that could be attained within the next decade. But the heart of the problem, as everyone realizes, is the coordination of development policy—especially industrial and manpower planning. If the Gulf states cannot prevent the duplication of their efforts to industrialize, all their other moves toward unity will be of little avail.

In 1979 the planning ministers of seven Gulf countries met in Riyadh to lay the foundations for eventual economic unity. Since then they have been meeting regularly. There are still many skeptics who do not believe that, when it comes to the point, any of the individual states will be prepared to abandon any of its favorite projects because a rival one in the Gulf region is more advanced. They can point to the huge dry dock and repair yard in Dubai that duplicates the one in Bahrain. The Gulf Organization for Industrial Consultancies (GOIC) which is based in Doha where it is presided over by an impressive, brooding Saudi, is intended to draft plans to prevent such duplication. So far, say the critics, GOIC has made many excellent proposals, but none has been adopted.

This is no longer true. Saudi Arabia has abandoned its plans for an aluminum plant in Jubayl in favor of the Bahrain aluminum rolling mill in which it has a twenty percent share. Saudi Arabia, Kuwait, and Bahrain have moved a long way toward creating a joint petrochemicals industry. Private businessmen are encouraged to set up joint ventures and invest in other Arab Gulf countries and are doing so on a wide scale. It might be added that the Arab shareholders in Petra Capital Corporation, the first Arab investment bank to open in the United States, are from Kuwait, Saudi Arabia, Dubai, and Bahrain.

22
Conclusion

Any attempt to chart the course of the Arab oil states to the end of this century would be absurdly rash. Since they have long since abandoned any idea of isolating themselves from the rest of the world, their destiny is far from being entirely in their own hands. They are all profoundly affected by events in the rest of the Arab and Muslim worlds. In countries where the personalities of the rulers count for so much, chance or an assassin's bullet can alter their political complexion overnight.

Yet certain trends seem to me unlikely to be reversed whatever happens because their aspirations will not change. Their efforts to catch up with the West in material terms and to translate the fabulous divine windfall of their oil resources into self-sustaining economic growth will continue. This will require a further tremendous effort to acquire and absorb the technology and know-how of the industrialized countries. They will all try to moderate and control the inevitable social changes this will bring. And, in order to avoid the kind of upheaval which has affected Iran, they will try to reconcile these changes as far as possible with their own traditions. Revolutionary Marxists will have no patience with their aims or methods, but those who believe that attempts at instantaneous change in human society are always disastrous will sympathize with their approach. Their achievements over the past generation have not been unremarkable. Both rulers and people made many errors of judgment, especially when the wealth was new, but they have usually learned from mistakes and rectified them. Above all they have not allowed their dependence on more powerful countries to sap their own willpower.

Continuing determination will be required. The initial euphoria created by the flow of oil revenues in the 1950s did not last long. Even the sudden acceleration in their rise in value in the 1970s only underlined that the oil reserves were being depleted. Individual "oil shaykhs" may behave as if the sources of their wealth were permanent, but governments and people as a whole have a lively awareness that this is not so. There is no mistaking their will to prolong the life of the oil as long as possible to give time to develop alternative sources of wealth. Collaboration among the Arab oil states is essential if this is to succeed, which is why they are most likely to continue moving closer together.

There are two trends which are especially encouraging; they are related to each other but still only in their infancy. One is a growing interest in conservation, not only of oil resources, but also in the preservation and improvement of the environment. A few years ago this was hardly mentioned. Now there is a clear determination that neither the waters of the Gulf nor its shores should be allowed to become as polluted as the Mediterranean. The shaykhs of Arabia were once famous for hunting the Peninsula's rare wildlife to extinction. They greeted the arrival of the motor car with delight, as it enabled them to chase and kill the animals more effectively. Today the trend is against the hunter. As one example, the delicately beautiful Arabian oryx, which had practically disappeared, is being bred and preserved on farms in Qatar.

The second trend is toward an interest in what has been called the "greening of Arabia." The prospects do not appear immediately encouraging. Shaykh Zayid of Abu Dhabi has a passion for forestation, and Shaykh Khalifah of Qatar has a dream of making his country self-sufficient in food production. But this might be, as many still believe, a waste of resources. Will the carefully nurtured shrubs and crops merely crumble into the sand when the oil income used to irrigate them so expensively declines?

On my first visit to Saudi Arabia in 1966 one of the most

impressive personalities I encountered was a younger son of King Faisal, Prince Muhammad, who at that time was in charge of the Kingdom's water projects. He was concentrating at that time on the purchase of desalination plants to release natural underground supplies for agriculture, but he was looking forward to a time when a cheap method of desalination would be discovered so that Saudi Arabia's potential would be limitless. "We look forward to the time when we shall be helping to supply India with food," he said.

Clearly a visionary. Prince Muhammad is now president of the Association of Islamic Banks, but he is also interested in a scheme to tow a giant iceberg from the Antarctic to the Red Sea as a means of helping to solve the water problems of the Hejaz.

Many people refuse to take such ideas seriously or to believe that even with the current advances in methods of water conservation, the use of distilled seawater for agriculture could ever be economic. I am not convinced. "Never" is a word that should not be used in matters of scientific discovery any more than in politics. If the Arab oil states devote an increasing share of their resources to the transformation of the desert as they surely will, there will be even more startling changes in Arabia in the next century.

The people and governments of Arabia are fully aware that their internal problems and the task of securing their future cannot be tackled in isolation. They are surrounded by dangers which are the greater because of the region's importance to the rest of the world. The Soviet thrust into Afghanistan could be extended to the warm waters of the Gulf, the Iraq-Iran conflict could involve them against their will, and the constant challenge of the Islamic revolutionaries in Iran could upset their best laid plans.

However, there are many signs that these external dangers, like those of the declining oil reserves, are creating their own response. Just as the governments of the Arabian states know that they cannot ultimately rely on outsiders to answer the problem of their depleting oil reserves, so they are aware that the prime responsibility for protecting their societies rests with themselves. They know that if they have to be conservatives in the preservation of their own values they have also to be radicals in their responses to a changing world.

The leaders of Arabia have been given very little time to learn to act as international statesmen, but they have not rejected the challenge. Within the region, they are evolving a common policy to preserve Arabia's integrity and independence. On a world level, they are attempting to develop a grouping of Islamic nations which would speak with one voice in world affairs. In this the Kingdom of Saudi Arabia has played the leading role and bears the major responsibility. Although the people of Arabia represent only a small proportion of the World of Islam they are bound to play a crucial part in any Islamic movement.

Saudi efforts to establish this new Islamic grouping, which began with King Faisal in the early 1960s, entered a new phase with the summit meeting of thirty-eight Muslim nations which was held at Mecca and Taif in January 1981. In spite of the differences which inevitably affected any such large gathering of states, the event clearly marked the emergence of an authentic Islamic world movement at government level. This was underlined by the practical decision, first proposed by Saudi Arabia's Crown Prince Fahd, to establish a new $3 billion Islamic World Development Program Support Fund as an instrument for cementing Islamic solidarity and promoting Islamic consciousness.

There are some in the West who regard this development of an Islamic bloc of nations as a threat. The affair of the American hostages in Iran did nothing to increase Western sympathy for Islam. But the Islamic nations see their solidarity and mutual cooperation essentially as a means of strengthening their internal stablility. In his opening message to the summit King Khalid referred to the "blessed awakening" which he said had restored to every Muslim a feeling of pride in his faith and heritage. He declared: "Though this awakening may have expressed itself in different political and social manifestations from society to society, its basic content lies in the condemnation of imported ideas and exported ideologies, and in the firm conviction that the problems affecting the Islamic countries can be ended by Islamic solutions inspired by the true *Shariah* and responding to the needs of the age." He added: "This awakening is not directed against any other person or bloc; it has erupted to put an end to the backwardness which ruled the Islamic world for long centuries and made it victim to intellectual, economic, and military invasion . . . . Our allegiance should not be to an Eastern bloc or a Western bloc, but only to God and His Messenger, and after that, to the Muslim masses everywhere on earth. The security of the Islamic nation will not be achieved by joining a military alliance or sheltering under the wing of a big power. It springs from faith in God and in oneself and from the solidarity born of a profound Islamic brotherhood which outlives transitory temporal interests."

There can be no doubt that these eloquent words express the true feelings of the vast majority of the people of Arabia.

Index

268

269

270

271

Saqqaf, Omar (Saudi Arabia), 97
Saqr, Shaykh (Ras al Khayhmah), 161
Saud, Viceroy; Prince; King (Najd), xiii,
  59, 61, 75, 78, 81, 82, 83, 85-88, 251
Saudi Arabia
  aid to, 68, 69, 90
  economics in, 65-70, 75-80, 85-99,
    163, 164, 166-178, 187-188, 207,
    208, 254
  education in, 67, 70, 186, 227, 228,
    232, 239
  foreign aid from, 79, 85, 94, 95, 168,
    169
  foreign policy in, 67, 68, 70-73, 75-77,
    79-83, 85-100, 101-104, 251
  foreign workers in, 78, 182, 186, 188-
    191
  government in, 75-78, 85-87, 88-89,
    101, 252, 253
  military development, 254-256
  modernization of, 65, 77, 78, 79, 86-
    87, 88, 89, 163-168, 169-178
  natural gas in, 169, 170
  oil in, 66-70, 75-77, 96, 97, 98, 99, 102,
    149, 167-170, 204, 205, 207, 208,
    209-210
  religion and progress, xiii, 165, 166
  unification of Hejaz and Najd, 61, 62
  vs. Egypt, 81, 82, 87, 88, 89, 90, 91,
    92, 103, 165
  and Yemen civil war, 61, 87, 88, 89, 90
Saudi Arabian Basic Industries Corpo-
  ration (SABIC), 170
Saudi Arabian Fertilizer Company
  (SAFCO), 170, 176, 177
Saudi Arabian Monetary Agency (SAMA),
  77, 80, 85, 164, 168
Saudi Development Fund, 213
Saudia airlines, 172, 186
sayyid, definition of, 16
Seven Golden Odes: see Muallaqat
Scylax, 9
Shah of Iran: see Muhammad, Shah; Reza
  Khan, Shah; Qajar Shahs; for earlier
  times see Shah of Persia
Shah of Persia, 32
Shakbut, Shaykh (Abu Dhabi), 149, 150,
  151, 153, 218
Shakespear, (Captain) W.H.I., 41, 42, 67
Shariah (Islamic law and ethics), 21, 22,
  23, 57, 58, 86, 217, 233, 234, 238, 239,
  241, 267
Sharifs, 30, 31, 40
Sharjah: see United Arab Emirates
shaykh, definition of, 16

Shell Oil Company, 136
Shiite Muslims, 23, 24, 120, 128, 274
Six-Day War, 92
slaves, 62, 89
Socony Vacuum, 67, 196
  See also Mobil Oil.
South Arabia, 33, 36, 87, 93
  See also People's Democratic Re-
  public of Yemen.
Soviet Union, influence of, 57, 58, 79, 80,
  86, 91, 95, 101, 102, 257, 258
spiritual leader: see Imam
Standard Oil of California (Socal), 66,
  122, 149
  See also Bahrain Petroleum Com-
  pany.
Standard Oil of New Jersey, 67, 196
Stark, Freya, 108
Strabo, 9, 11
Straits of Hormuz, ix, xi, xii, 32, 161, 170
Suez Canal, 39, 80, 95
Suez Canal Company, 80, 199
Sulaiman, (Shaykh) Abdullah (Saudi
  Arabia), 58, 65, 198
Sultan, Prince (Saudi Arabia), 251, 255
Sultan Shaykh (Sharjah), 161
Sunnah, 21, 239
Sunni Muslims, 23, 24, 36, 126, 128
Syria
  and Baghdad Pact, 79
  and France, 47, 195
  Lebanese civil war, 102
  October War, 97
  Ottoman Empire, 31, 39
  Six-Day War, 92
  union with Egypt, 82, 87
  and U.S., 98

Talal, Emir; Prince (Saudi Arabia), 86
Tariki, Abdullah (Saudi Arabia), 96, 200
taxation
  of individuals, 19, 241, 242
  of oil companies, 76, 77, 198
television, 143, 245-246
(Al) Thani clan (Qatar), 133, 134
Thani, (Shaykh) Ahmad al (Qatar), 136,
  137
Thani, (Shaykh) Khalifah al (Qatar), 15,
  133, 136, 137, 264
Thesiger, Wilfred, 216, 217, 218
Thomas, Bertram, 216
Trans-Arabian Pipe Line Company
  (Tapline), 70, 75
Transjordan, 49, 58
Treaty of Jiddah, 58

273

274